THE
CRAMPTON LOCOMOTIVE

Thomas Russell Crampton

THE

CRAMPTON LOCOMOTIVE

by

M. SHARMAN

ISBN 0 9509067 0 0

Designed by Speed Publications, 5 Lewis Close, Risinghurst, Oxford

Phototypesetting by Gem Publishing Company (Oxon) Ltd, Brightwell, Wallingford, Oxfordshire

Printed by S & S Press, Ashville Trading Estate, Abingdon, Oxfordshire

Published by M. Sharman, 10 Swindon Road, Cricklade, Swindon, England

Bibliography

The writings of the following were consulted for this book:

Alfred Rosling Bennet
E. W. Twining
G.A. Sekon
C. Hamilton-Ellis
E. L. Ahrons
Emil Reuter
F. Gaiser
K. E. Maedel
P. C. Dewhurst
Model and Allied Publications
E. F. Carter

Acknowledgements

Drawings and photographs from:

The Engineer
The Model Engineer
The Locomotive Magazine
The Locomotive
Model Railways
Model Railway News
Speed Publications
L. Ward
D. Allenden
P. L. Towers
Museon di Rodo
Die Crampton Locomotive
C. J. Freezer
Beasdale Collection
and Author's Collection

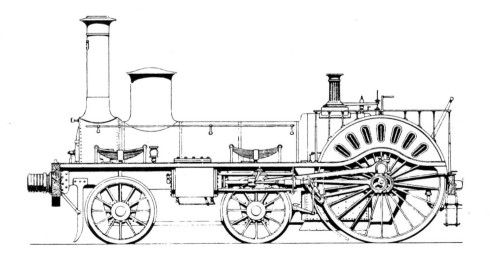

Contents

Thomas Russell Crampton

Thomas Russell Crampton was, by all accounts a very kindly man and much the family man.

He was born into an age of 'great pride in workmanship' in Broadstairs in the County of Kent on the 6th of August 1816. It was also an age when one either had comfortable means or had to work very hard indeed to maintain a living wage, resulting usually in little or no schooling at all for the children. In this respect he was fortunate in starting his scholastic life at a small private school on the south coast.

Thus armed, he started his engineering training in May 1831 with John Hague, an engineer in Cable Street London, where he worked and studied until 1839. He now made possibly the best move available to him in joining the elder Marc Brunel as an assistant on the staff of the Great Western Railway. Here, he worked under the young Daniel Gooch (later to be Sir Daniel) taking part in the design of the 'Firefly Class' locomotives, some of the first built at Swindon. This period of his life gained for him a healthy respect for the concept of the large boiler, driving a really worth while pair of driving wheels, which we know from the Great Western histories to have been in the seven to nine foot range! Unfortunately, or fortunately, depending on your own views of the Crampton Locomotive, the cult of the low centre of gravity was also in vogue at the time, and this took very firm root, as the rest of the book bears evidence.

In 1844 Thomas left the Great Western to work with Messrs Rennie until 1848, when his inventive juices were stimulated to the point where he set up in private practice. During this time he submitted many patents of his now famous style of locomotive which in France, at least, became a household name. One must keep in mind when viewing the work of Thomas and his contemporaries (from this distance in time) that railway engineering was still very much in its infancy. All the terms that we take for granted today—pressure energy, kinetic energy, centrifugal force, centre of gravity, pressure drops and velocity and so on were still being evolved the only way they knew, in the hard world of experience, and every new machine built was to some extent experimental. So, although 'unusual' by today's standards, Crampton's patent was based mostly on a six-wheel layout, with large driving wheels at the rear for speed and stability, and a large boiler for those days, which, due to its low centre of gravity, had to be oval in section to fit between the wheels. The first of his

engines to be adopted and built were the two engines for the Belgian Railways, *Liége* and *Namur*. Several hundreds of locomotives saw service in many countries of Europe, two even finding their way to Egypt. One end product of his continental success was the award of many honours. He was made an Officer of the Legion of Honour in 1855 by the Emperor Napoleon III, and from Prussia, the Order of the Red Eagle. In 1848 his designs were adopted by the Compagnie du Nord, and for the next forty years these locomotive designs headed the light expresses of Northern and Eastern France.

In Britain there were only some forty-two Cramptons in use, and these are listed in Chapter Two **The Crampton in Britain**. He played his part in the battle of the gauges which raged for many years (and is *still* raging!!). One result of which was the magnificent eight-wheel engine *Liverpool*, one of the London and North Western Company's answers to the Broad Gauge.

His engineering interest and inventiveness did not stop at railway locomotives. In 1851 he laid, under great difficulties, the first practicable submarine cable between Dover and Calais raising £10,000 of the capital required in only the seven weeks left before the concession expired. Some of the many other projects, railway and otherwise, that he was associated with, were: The Berlin Water Works with Sir Charles Fox; The Ottoman Railway from Smyrna to Aidin; The Varna and Rustchuck Railway; The East Kent Railway from Strood to Dover; The Hurn Bay and Faversham Railway; The Sevenoaks Railway to Swanley, which later became absorbed into the larger London Chatham and Dover Railway and which still owed him money at his death. The involvement into the world of iron and steel resulted in him designing in 1872 a furnace for burning powdered fuel. It was a high temperature iron 'puddling' furnace which was unfortunately far too advanced for the materials available at the time for furnace linings. He also designed brick-making machinery, cast iron forts, and tunnel-boring machinery, which he hoped would enable him one day to build a long dreamed-of tunnel under the English Channel.

In Britain he was elected in 1846 into the Institute of Civil Engineers and later became an associate member of council and transferred to the Roll of Members in 1854, becoming vice president.

He is still remembered in his native Broadstairs in which he maintained an active interest all his life, presenting the church with its clock, and starting the town gas works for which he provided a large part of the capital for its construction.

In his family life he was twice married and left six sons and one daughter who became Lady Rumbold, wife of her Victorian Majesty's ambassador at the Hague. His second marriage was to the daughter of the Rev. Werge of Somersauld, Derby.

Not many of his locomotives have escaped the scrap yard to the present day. The French have the fine example of *Le Continent*, and the Germans a beautiful replica of *Die Pfalz* at the Nürnberg Museum. In Britain we have kept nothing!! In the land of invention, where these delightful machines were born, we have seen fit to scrap the lot, though there is a very marked Cramptonian air about the *Fire Queen* with its cylinder position and jack-shaft drive in lieu of a centre axle. It would seem that until we too are rich enough to build a replica of *London* or *Liverpool*, we shall have to be content with our replicas in model form, many of which have been built over the years in gauges from 5″ live steam, down to 4mm scale electric.

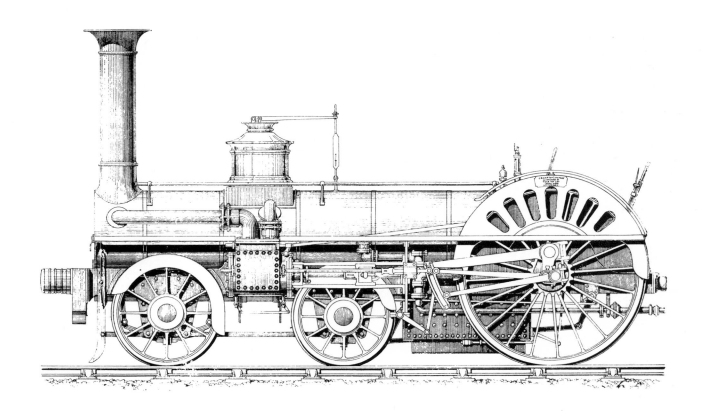

Introduction

This book is a little unusual in that, although on a subject definitely historical, it has been written not by an 'eminent historian' but by myself, a practical railway modeller, with some fine drawings and assistance from another modeller and prolific writer Dennis Allenden. We started the book together many years ago when, after a short time, Dennis had a heart attack and died. The work was shelved until the early 1980s when I came across a lot more information and decided to extend the original concept to cover all 'Cramptons' large and small! We were neither of us 'steam' engineers, so will not attempt to analyse relative boiler designs other than to discuss their attributes in relation to models, in fact my own servicing career has been with the internal combustion and gas turbine field.

Dennis Allenden spent most of his time commuting around America in aeroplanes for an American company, with occasional visits to France and the United Kingdom where, through our mutual interest, we met and the book idea explored. The next few years found me sending all kinds of information over the Atlantic to be re-drawn and re-written (I had acquired a copy of **Die Crampton Locomotive**), while Dennis found the information on the American and the other 'odd ball' Cramptons in the States. During this time he also managed those entertaining articles for *Model Railways* of the late 1960s and '70s, one of which has been reproduced for the final chapter.

Those of you who were Dennis Allenden devotees of long standing, can hardly fail to notice the difference in style of our two writings, his work has deliberately been left unedited so contrasts with my own leaning to the precis type of presentation.

I started Railway modelling while serving my twenty-three years with the Royal Air Force, so between periods of hectic activity I have long peaceful stretches of time for modelling, when most of my Cramptons were built. I left the Air Force in 1974 for self-employment in the Model Railway world to find that time for purely pleasure modelling or writing was a scarce commodity, but I got there in the end as I hope the book will prove.

Many articles have appeared over the last hundred years or so on the works of Thomas Russell, and it is from these that the material has been gleaned, taking note of some of the differeing accounts (and some *do* differ) that were found in books, maga-zines, and museums, sifting the reports and drawings, and presenting what I must stress are my own opinions on the evidence available. I have had to do it this way as those of us who actually knew Thomas are getting a little scarce!! A fact which, combined with the loss of the Tulk and Ley records in a fire some years back at Whitehaven, has made a lot of the information almost impossible to verify.

The drawings which have been redrawn have been copied, for the most part, from documents of credible authenticity, usually makers or company working drawings, with details added from photographs. Except in one or two cases there is no conjectural detail, if we were not sure we have left it out, which accounts for the varying amount of detail in the different drawings. When a tender is shown, Dennis has drawn one that could have credibly been used by that locomotive, if there was no information on the original. We have done this with the model builder in mind as there is no point in building an incomplete model—even if all the old draughtsmen used to draw them that way! The Russian Crampton is the one case where we have added something without direct photographic evidence, and for that one we have taken an accurate French builder's drawing and photograph as a starting point, and simply added what we know to have been standard Russian features and fittings of that period.

Most of the photographs available are of French and German origin because the Crampton locomotives lasted longer on the continent thus resulting in more photographic records being taken. Sadly, due to the locomotive's lack of adhesion, most of the British ones were retired before they could be photographed at all, so you will find I have had to resort to photographs of models. To save boring the non-modelling reader, I have confined the models to the two last chapters, one on 4mm scale, and one on 7mm. The main drawings have been completed in 7mm scale as I believe it is easier to build from a larger drawing with a scale. The secondary drawings are in 4mm to save space but, with modern reproduction techniques, can be easily resized for buil-ding in 7mm. I would also point out that many drawings and photographs are not to a high standard of clarity but, as I have previously stated, they are the only records available and so have been included to complete the story.

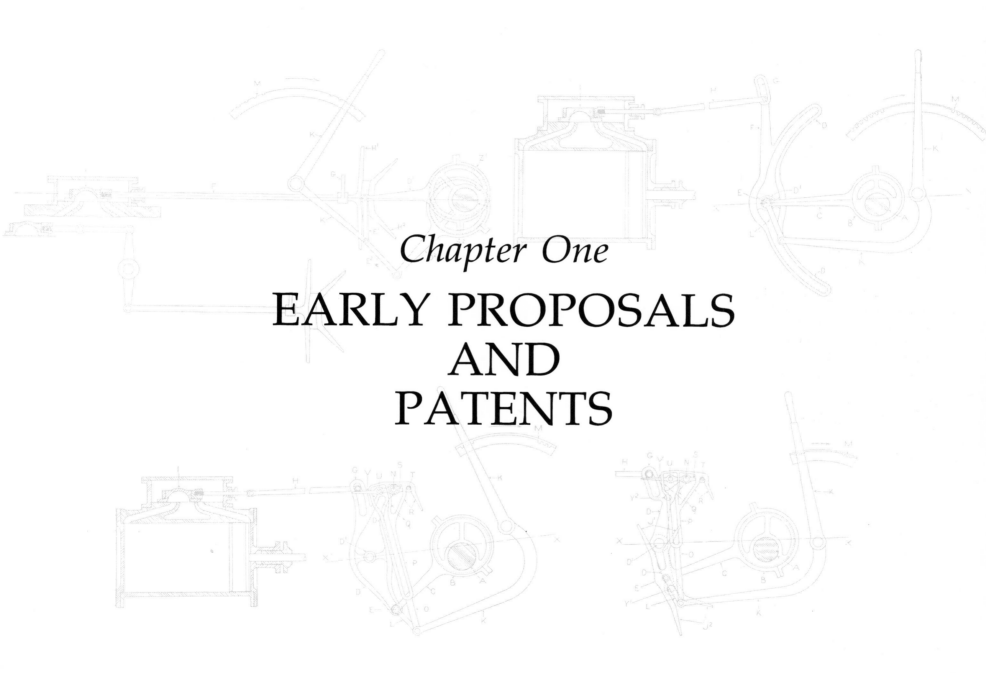

Chapter One

EARLY PROPOSALS
AND
PATENTS

Featured in this opening chapter are a range of drawings taken from the very many 'improvements' lodged by Crampton with the Patent Office during the early period of his engineering life as his ideas evolved. Few of them were actually built, but as one studies them and the reasons for their various features one can follow the gradual development to the Classic Cramptons that we, the followers of the breed, recognise today. There is plenty of scope here for the modeller who would like to model the 'exotic', and, just think, you can design your own liveries with the most outrageous results!

I have only discussed the patents relating to railways and not *all* of these. For example the ones on 'ways of achieving the control of variable expansion of steam in the cylinders' are not included. I felt that this depth of theoretical discussion would fill many pages and detract from the overall story about the man and his machines that I wanted to portray. For those of you who *do* wish to delve deeper without actually visiting the Patents Office, the story is very well told in the *Locomotive Magazine* starting in October 15th 1942. These articles include all the actual patent number references.

In this chapter I have picked out the patents most relevant to the locomotive story as it unfolded and, where possible, have related them to locomotives that were actually built.

Figure 1 shows the basic concept of a boiler slung as low as possible between the frames to keep the weight and therefore centre of gravity as low as possible, and using the large drivers for speed. Please remember that at this time it was widely thought that the human body could not stand speeds as high as 25-30 mph and that it would fall apart. Also any locomotive built as high as these were going to be constructed would certainly fall over going round the bends if the boiler weight were to be above the frames! You will notice the old haystack firebox and that the driving wheels are still in the centre. We will see how a similar system to this was used on Trevithic's *Cornwall*, later in *figure 10*.

Figure 2 shows the arrival of the Crampton locomotive proper, *i.e.* the large driving wheels behind the firebox rather than in front, and *figure 3* shows there were some doubts about how the remainder of the weight should be carried with, I suspect, a hint that broken crank axles were expected to be quite common. He also wished to dampen down the fears of the interested parties who would be putting up the money for any new engineering ventures.

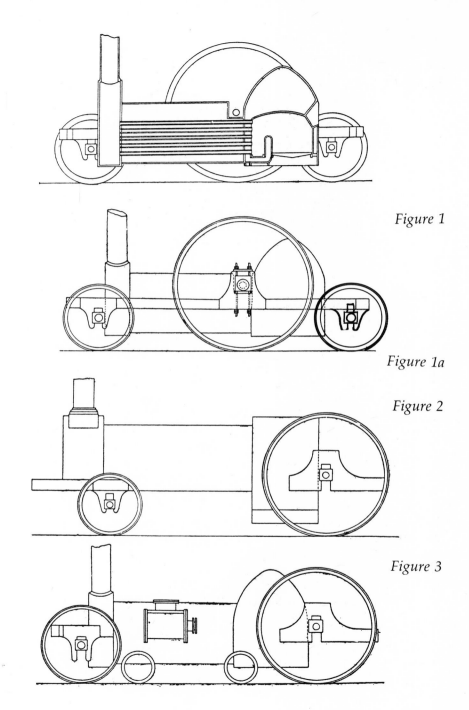

Figure 1

Figure 1a

Figure 2

Figure 3

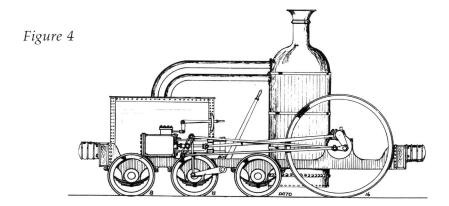

Figure 4

Figure 6 shows a section through the design and the transverse springs.

The patent as seen in *figure 6* also refers to the even firing problems of the wide grate and of the possibility of a second fire door *under* the axle! This would require a hole in the footplate and in all probability a further patent for an articulated shovel!

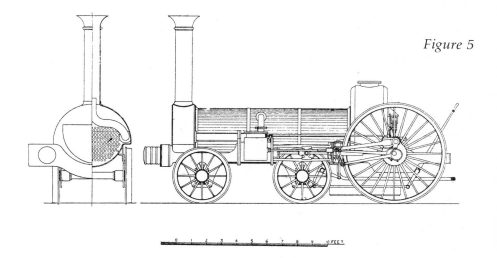

Figure 5

Figure 4 rather contradicts the low centre of gravity theory, but the positioning of the boiler has obviously worried him, as no engineer likes the thought of a pressure vessel with axle-slots running through it. This is of course a tank engine with plenty of carrying wheels but very long rods which would be liable to 'whip' about. We will see how he gets around the long rods later on in the chapter.

Figure 5 shows how the locomotive is now developing into our genuine 'Classic Crampton'. The wheel layout is now pretty much standardised with the cylinders brought closer to the driven axle, so shortening the rods, but making a long curved steam pipe necessary from cylinders to smokebox. The firebox is very like Allan's *Courier* with a wide fore and aft grate (which must have been difficult to fire evenly) and transverse springs bolted to a massive bracket on the firebox assembly which supported the driving wheels. Here also we have his first use of eccentrics on the return cranks to operate the valve gear which in this case are quite small. The ones used on *Liverpool* (to be discussed later) were 2' 9" in diameter. Finally, in among the valve gear one can see the crosshead operated water feed pump which became standard on almost all his engines. These were driven either as seen in the drawing, or mounted in front of the cylinders and driven from a piston rod extension. The whole idea was very sound for the servicing department, as everything was easily accessible.

Figure 6

Figure 7

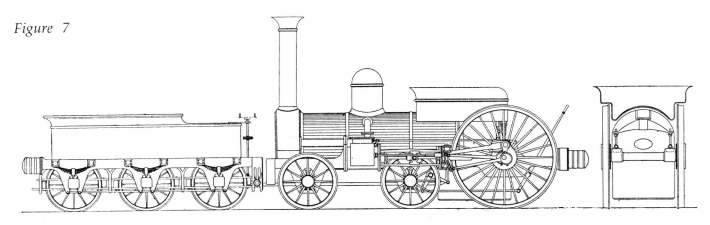

Still about firing, *figure 7* shows this time the utilisation of the draught created by the forward speed of the locomotive. You will note the buffers at the footplate end of the loco, and the large receptacle on top of the firebox to contain the coke. The engine would travel left to right, i.e. drivers leading. One wonders if the fire box door was to be left open all the time the train was moving, or if some form of controllable vents were to be used. The tender was just a water cart in this design. Showing what would appear to be about the worst way to distribute weight is *figure 8a* and especially if one wanted an efficient locomotive. However, several light duty machines did use the front driver system but with a wide variety of cylinder arrangements, from the *Rocket* of

1829 to the vertical cylinders and right-angled cranks of the *Earl of Airlie* of 1833, and this pretty little example I have included here in *figure 8b*. I know she has nothing to do with Crampton but she gives good 'supporting evidence' to the patent. She was built by the Belgian engineer De Ridder in 1841 for the Brussels to Turbize route of the Belgian State Railways. The dimensions are not known, but if one uses the buffer centres to track dimension it makes the driving wheels approximately 6' 6" with the carrying wheels around 3' 9". The valve gear will interest the steam 'buffs' among you, as study of the drawing will show what appears to be an extra valve chest. It was in fact an auxiliary expansion valve driven by a separate eccentric which could be engaged or disengaged actually on the move. It's a shame that efforts to make more efficient use of the steam almost always resulted in a mechanical penalty.

Figure 8b

De Ridder

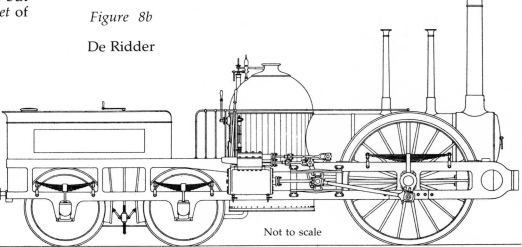

Figure 8a

Patent

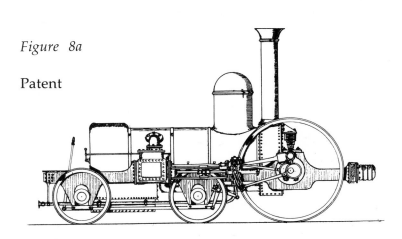

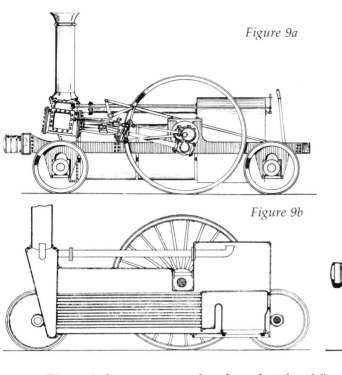

Figure 9a

Figure 9b

Figure 10

Figure 9 shows a more developed style of *figure 1* and has all the basic Crampton features except that the large driving wheel is in the centre and not yet behind the firebox. He has also accepted that to get a boiler big enough for his speed requirements he must allow a cut-out in the top to clear the driving axle, as did Richard Trevithic in his 8' 6" single *Cornwall* built for the Northern division of the London and North Western Railway in 1847. She was first built as seen in *figure 10*, on six wheels, but was very quickly rebuilt with two more as shown in the photograph (*Plate One*) of the model. *Cornwall* had in fact several alterations during her life, with her wheels and frames surviving in her present day preserved state at the National Railway Museum, York. The four large eccentrics similar to *Liverpool's* were originally positioned one each side of the driving wheel, but were both moved outside possibly at the same time as the extra carrying wheels and

frame extensions were added. She was credited with very high speeds (one claim being well over 100 mph) but wishful thinking apart she must have been quite a flyer within the track limitations of the day. In 1858 Mr Ramsbottom restored her to a six-wheeled engine, removing the lovely eccentrics and giving her a more sensible boiler which enabled the locomotive to lead a useful life for many years up to retirement.

Plate 1 A 4mm model of the locomotive No. 173 *Cornwall* in its intermediate form as running about 1847.

5

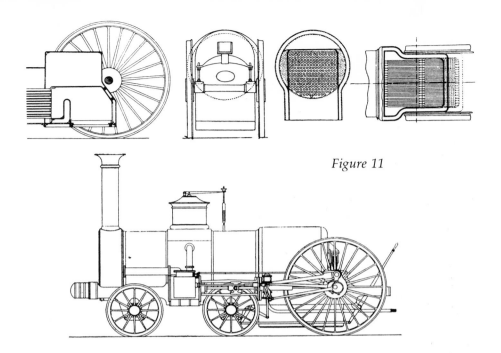

Figure 11

through the firebox soon became the accepted construction technique as we now know.

Figure 12 needs very little comment. It is an early attempt to improve adhesion, with only one tender used as a water tanker. With the coal carried over the driving wheels and presumably only one fireman carried he was cursed with the problem of not knowing if he was coming or going!

The sketches seen in *figure 13a to e* have been taken slightly out of order (relative to the patents evolution in time) but I felt they *were* related, and together they made their study and comparison more interesting. We mentioned long-coupling and connecting rods in *figure 3* and here we can see a whole selection of ideas, culminating in three examples which were actually built. These were the locomotives seen in *figure 13d* and *figure 13e* (to be described in later chapters), and *Fire Queen* illustrated by photographs on *page 8*. They were all experiments to achieve a better adhesion by using single or coupled wheels with various means of getting the energy from the cylinders to the wheels with the least mechanical losses. Sketch *13a* shows four-coupled wheels on a long stable wheelbase with the rear driving wheels still behind the firebox. The outside cylinders drive the rear axle, the dummy crankshaft being simply a centre support to prevent the coupling rods whipping about in service. The small carrying wheels will have taken very little weight, being, I suspect, more an insurance against broken crank axles than a serious weight distribution design. The *Fire Queen* in *plate 2* followed this system quite closely, but apparently did not have problems with the long

The group of patent sketches in *figure 11* show how the standard gauge dimensions available were being stretched to their limits. The firebox for instance has crept rearwards under the driving axle, and the boiler has expanded beyond the rail gauge necessitating some odd kinks in the firebox structure. This system appears again in *Liverpool* as study of the detail drawings in Chapter Two (part three) will show. This 'keyhole' section

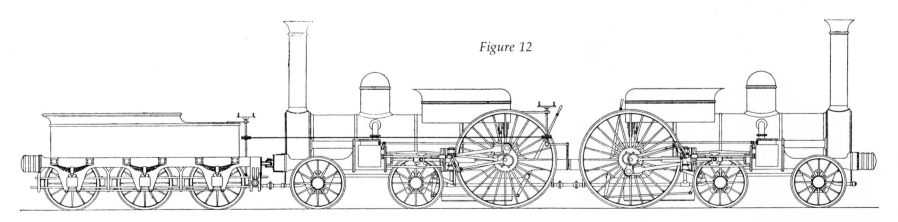

Figure 12

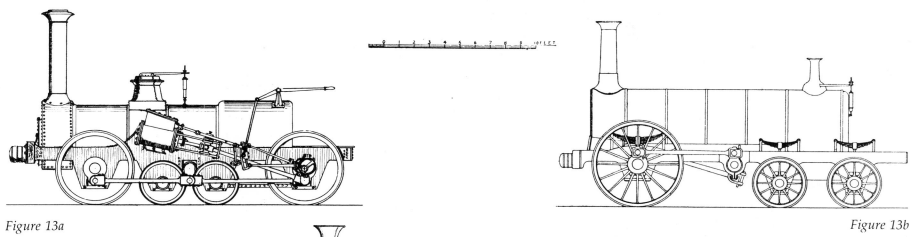

Figure 13a

Figure 13b

Figure 13c

Figure 13d

Figure 13e

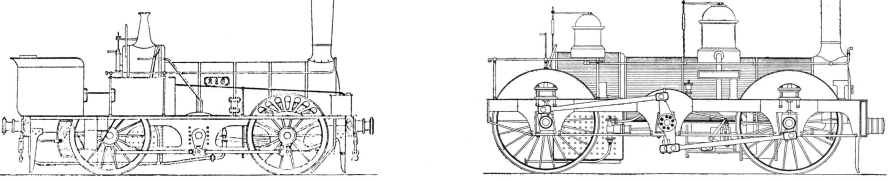

Plate 2

coupling rod. The 'safety' wheels were dispensed with, and both *Fire Queen* and *Lablache* in *figure 13e* seem to have used the main boiler structure as the backbone of the engine. Expansion and contraction would not have mattered in either case as *Fire Queen* had outside cylinders, and the oscillating rods on the locomotive in *figure 13e* would have expanded equally. *Figures 13c, 13d* and *13e* use the dummy crankshaft as the first stage in the drive, the cylinders being connected directly and the drive to the wheels is then 'passed on' via these cranks. Some of the features of *figure 13c* can be traced on the Chatham and Dover and the South Eastern Railway jackshaft engines to be described later on in *pages 22 to 24*. The sketches in *figures 13d* and *13e* are both described with larger drawings in Chapter Seven on the **Coupled Cramptons**. The *plates 3* and *4* are included to give some idea of

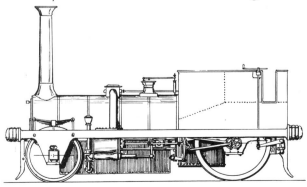

Figure 14

the finish and workmanship put into some of these old engines. Just look how all the rods are beautifully forked and polished, and the crosshead in *plate 3* would be a superb sculpture all on its own!

Figure 14 shows the patent for a tank engine, it puts all the 'reducing' tank weight over the driving wheels but oddly enough, the Egyptian engine on *page 116* (*figure 133*) in Chapter Six does not have this feature.

Plate 3
Plate 4

Chapter Two

The
CRAMPTON
in
BRITAIN

The Cramptons in Britain did not have a very distinguished career, they were an odd and varied lot built by some nine different builders nearly all of whom treated them more as experiments than as serious long term projects. None lasted much beyond 1870 in their original form, the North British Railway No. 55 being the last to be scrapped and that in its heavily re-built form of a 2-2-2. The main reason was of course that although very steady, they lacked adhesion and were hard on the rather weak track of the time. The first batch were those of Tulk and Ley Builders of Whitehaven and were fine looking machines. The 'one off' designs were Allan's *Courier* built at Crewe Works and that majestic monster *Liverpool* built by Bury's. At the time *Liverpool* was built, Bury's were still concentrating on their own 0-4-0 designs for the Midland Railway; it must have been like building a cruiser in a shipyard used to building frigates!

The rest of the engines were only just plentiful enough to call classes, there were quite a few of the 'jackshaft drive' type, spread between the London, Brighton and South Coast Railway, The Great Northern Railway, The South Eastern Railway and the Chatham and Dover Railway. Apart from the pair built by Kitsons for the Midland Railway, the remainder were mainly re-built from other engines of poor performance. There *are* discrepancies; the Bury engines will be discussed in *part 5* and some of the figures for technical detail, pressures etc., will differ on the drawings from some of those given in Gaiser's tables which I have tried to complete up to date. The information given in this table is 'as found' but it would be preferable to consult details as recorded by E. W. Twinings.

This chapter is broken down into parts, one for each builder and only deals with the single wheelers, the Coupled Cramptons follow in Chapter Seven. I have included locomotives *Liége* and *Namur* in this chapter as they were built in Britain, and although some historians feel they never left the country anyway, in fact Dennis did suggest a Belgian livery!

Railway	Name or Number	Builders	Date Built	Works No.	Cylinders Stroke	Cylinders Bore	Wheels Driving	Wheels Carrying	Wheelbase	Shape	Boiler Details Size	Tube Dia	Length	P.S.I.	F'box	Boiler	Total	Remarks
Belgian	Namur	Tulk & Ley	1846	10	20″	16″	7′0″	3′9″	6′4″+6′8″	Oval	4′3″×3′5″	2″	11′	90	62	927	989	May not have left UK.
″	Liége	″	1846	11	20″	16″	7′0″	3′9″	6′4″+6′8″	″	4′3″×3′5″	2″	11′	90	62	927	989	″
LNWR	London	″	1846	12	20″	18″	8′0″	3′9″	7′6″+6′6″	″	4′8″×3′10″	2″	12′	100	91	1438	1592	
Dundee P & A	Kinnaird	″	1847	14	20″	16″	7′0″	3′9″	6′4″+6′8″	″	4′3″×3′5″	2″	11′	90	62	927	989	
South Eastern	81, 83, 85	″	1847	13, 15, 16	20″	16″	7′0″	3′9″	6′4″+6′8″	″	4′3″×3′5″	2″	11′	90	62	927	989	
M'port & Carlisle	12	″	1854	17	20″	16″	7′0″	4′0″+3′9″	6′8″+7′10″	Round	4′1″	1¾″	9′10″	90	76	829	906	
LCDR	27–31	Stephenson	1862	1381–5	22″	16″	6′6½″	4′0″	4′9″+12′4″	″								
LNWR	Liverpool	Bury Curtis & Kennedy	1848	355	24″	18″	8′0″	4′3″+4′0″	4′6″+6′6″+7′6″	Oval	5′1″×4′5″	2³⁄₁₆″	12′6″	120	154	2136	2290	Boiler a double oval. Dimensions approx.
South Eastern	68, 69, 72, 74, 75, 78	″	1848		22″	15″	6′0″	3′6″	8′9″+6′6″	Round								May not have been all same type.
N. British	55	E. B. Wilson	1847		20″	16″	7′0″	4′6″+3′9″	7′6″+7′9″	″				50	59	861	920	Rebuilt 1864 to 2–2–2.
Eastern Counties	108–112	″	1847		20″	16″	7′0″	4′6″+3′9″	7′6″+7′9″	″				50	59	861	920	
Aberdeen Rly	26 & 27	″	1847		20″	16″	7′0″	4′6″+3′9″	7′6″+7′9″	″				50	59	861	920	
LNWR	Courier	Crewe Works	1847		20″	16″	7′0″	4′0″	6′4″+6′9″	Oval	3′10″×3′8″	1⁵⁄₁₆″	10′10″	90	58·7	901·7	960·4	
Gt. Northern	200	Longridge	1851–1852		21″	15″	6′6″	3′6″	4′6″+12′0″	Round	4′0″	2″	10′		97	875	972	
Midland	130 & 131	Kitson	1848		22″	16″	7′0″	4′9″+4′0″	7′9″+8′0″	″	4′0¼″	1⅞″	10′		83	979	1062	
South Eastern	92	Nasmyth	1846		22″	15″	5′6″	3′6″	8′0½″+7′11½″	Oval	3′3″×3′0″		12′6″	90				Rebuilt 2–2–2.
LBSC	56 & 58	Hackworth	1848		24″	16″	5′6″	3′4″	4′0″+9′9″	Round								
South Eastern	136–143	Stephenson	1851	785–794	22″	15″	6′0″	3′6″	4′5¾″+4′6″+7′	″	6′5½″	2″	11′1″	90	94	1059	1153	

Note. Detail blocks are left blank when information is not known.

Chapter Index

THE TABLES

Study of the drawings throughout the book will show that they do not always agree with the figures given in the tables, which are based on **F. Gaiser's** book — *Die Crampton Locomotive of 1909*. I have up-dated these tables where possible, but it is clearly *not* possible after this passage of time to verify all of them, due to the many factors (like re-builds) which affect historical recording. I offer both for your study, but my personal choice would be to believe a drawing backed up by photographic evidence (if possible), *rather* than these tables. Locomotives were *often* built differently from quoted information, especially when wheels or cylinders etc., were sub-contracted.

Part One
The Tulk and Ley Cramptons

Locomotives *Namur* No. 10 and *Liége* No. 11

The first Cramptons to be built on the now recognised 'Classic' pattern were *Namur* and *Liége* (*figures 15* and *16*), commissioned for the Chemin de Fer de Namur à Liége Railway which then passed to the newly formed Chemin de Fer du Nord-Belge Railway in 1854. Retaining their names they were possibly numbered 2 and 3 of that railway. They were built by The Tulk and Ley Co. at Whitehaven in 1846 and were given the works numbers 10 and 11, but were not however the only engines of their kind. Numbers 10 and 11 were the first of a batch of six engines built over a two year period which were all basically the same, having 7 ft driving wheels, and fully accessible cylinders and valve gear mounted between the front and centre carrying wheels. They were in fact fine examples of the type of locomotive Crampton was aiming at, the low centre of gravity combined with, for that period in history, a long steady wheelbase, and large driving wheels to give the high speed. During trials on the London and North Western Railways southern division, *Namur* is credited with taking a train of trucks at just over 51 mph and a passenger train at 62 mph, though the quality of the ride on short fish belly rails must have been good for the digestion if nothing else! There was for a time some doubt about their eventual destinations and the period between their trials and acceptance by the railway seems to have been spent in store in England. On receipt into traffic the main draw-back of these engines was their lack of adhesion. In their acceptance trials this would not have

been apparent as the train loads were light and many of the continental lines added iron blocks under the footplates as the loads got heavier anyway. This of course had its disadvantages, the main one being vibration on the footplate, but set against the stability of the engine compared with the standard 2-2-2 type, this was certainly a lesser evil. The valve gear linkage, though accessible for servicing, seemed to have rather more parts *to* service, with several reversals of movement culminating in a separate regulator on top of each valve chest. This must have

MAIN DIMENSIONS
Driving Wheels 7' 0"
Carrying Wheels 3' 9"
Wheelbase 6' 9" × 6' 3"
Cylinders 16" bore × 20" stroke
Heating Surface
   Tubes 927 sq ft; Firebox 62 sq ft
   Total 989 sq ft
Grate Area 14·5 sq ft
Working Pressure 50 psi
Weight 24 tons
Tender Wheels 3' 6"

Figure 15

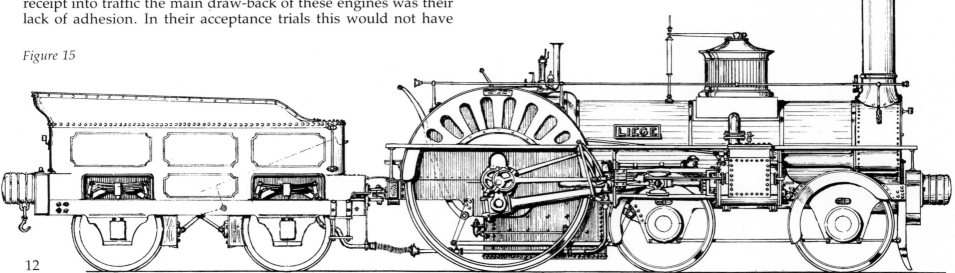

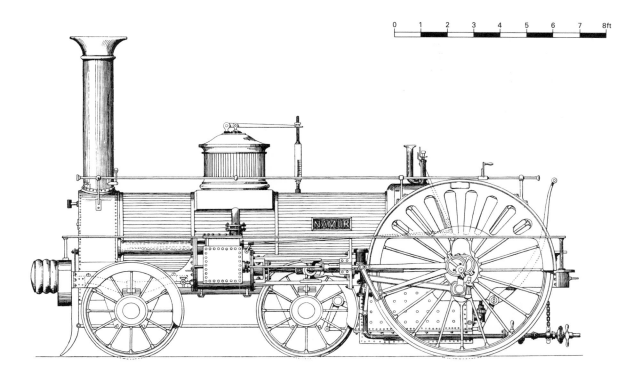

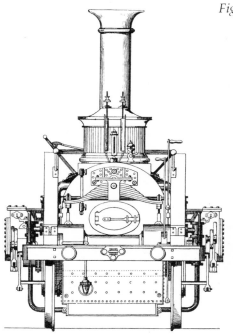

Figure 16

required careful adjustment to get the timing correct on both sides of the engine whilst allowing for all the whip and backlash in the linkage. It is interesting to note that the German and French engines often had a large circular balance weight on the linkage, one wonders why they thought it worth while and we did not?

Tenders for these locomotives are difficult to establish as the builders normally had their own pattern, however in the case of an overseas order, the engine could have been ordered as a separate item and the railway concerned fitted its own style tender. For *Liége* we have shown a standard Belgian four wheel tender of the period. Most of the continental railways seemed to favour a lighter tender than the British style anyway.

Livery. The style suggested as the most likely would be: light chocolate brown for the chassis, boilder and smokebox if lagged, and black for the chimney smokebox front and smokebox if un-lagged, with the number plates at the base of the chimney in bronze. The tender panels were bordered in black with a yellow line separating the black from the brown. The style of the name-plates is shown in *figure 17*.

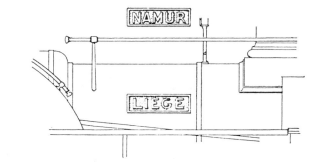

Figure 17

Locomotive *London* No. 12

MAIN DIMENSIONS

Driving Wheels 8' 0"
Carrying Wheels 3' 9"
Wheelbase 7' 6" + 6' 6"
Cylinders 18" bore × 20" stroke
Boiler Double barrel shape
    4' 8" high × 8' 10" wide
Grate Area 17·8 sq ft
Heating Surface Approx. 1350 sq ft
Boiler Pressure 100 psi
Weight 25 tons 12 cwt distributed—
    Front 8 tons 3 cwt
    Centre 5 tons 15 cwt
    Driver 25 tons 12 cwt
Tender Wheels 3' 9"

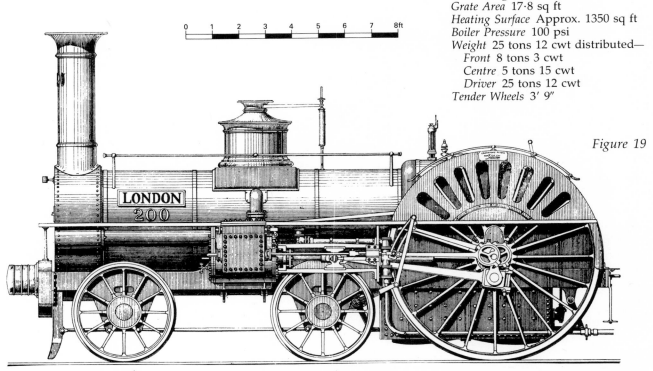

Figure 18

Figure 19

The locomotive *London* (*figures 18* and *19*) was built in 1848 for the southern division of the London and North Western Railway and was the 'odd one out', in having 8' 0" driving wheels, and was built as works No. 12 as a 'trials' engine. Having seen *Liége* and *Namur* perform their test runs on British metals the L.N.W.R. management thought it worth having two engines built, i.e., *London* and *Liverpool*. The northern division did the same but built their own example at Crewe, the engine being named *Courier*. *London* ran very well and was very stable, in fact in one instance her large cylinders fouled the overhang of a station platform at speed demolishing the platform edge without derailing the loco-motive, whose only damage was broken valve gear and a cylinder knocked back out of line. The type was not however continued because it was scrapped or converted fairly quickly as was the Bury built *Liverpool*. The main excuse—or reason, depending on your views—was lack of adhesion and damage to the track caused by the fairly rigid wheelbase of a heavy engine, though, looking back, one cannot help but wonder if railway politics came into it somewhere as the railway 'barons' of the time, when politically tuned, were powerful men in Parliament. Witness the battle of the gauges! Apart from the obvious one of the 8 ft drivers and the fact that the boiler pressure was 50 psi higher than the original

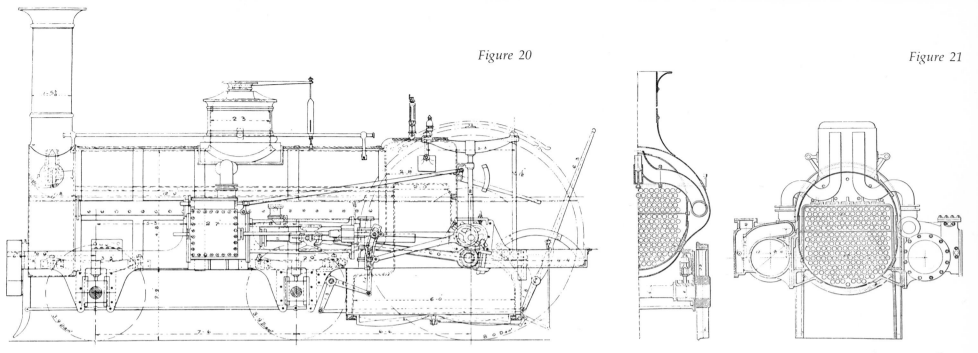

Figure 20

Figure 21

batch, the rest of *London's* technical features were pretty much as described. She had the five point suspension in that the leading and centre wheels were independently sprung, whereas the driving wheels had a single transverse spring which was buckled to a casting on the firebox.

Livery. This is not known for certain but I seem to have deviated on my own model, having finished it in the southern division vermillion which, Mr. Twining says, did not come into use until McConnell's small 'Bloomers'! So the most likely colour scheme

would be: The body colour, a middle chrome green with black bands, lined each side with a fine white line. Boiler bands were also black, lined as the tender panels which had incurved corners. The tender frames and all wheel tyres were grey with 'body' green wheel centres. The smoke box and firebox rings are polished brass as was the saddle beading, safety valve cap and rims.

The chimney was black with a copper cap and the number 200, in brass cut-outs, positioned half way up the chimney front.

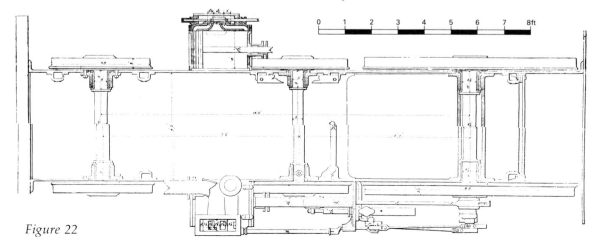

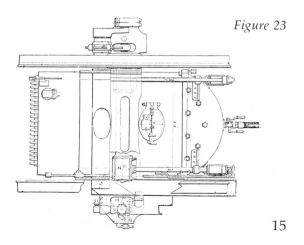

Figure 23

Figure 22

Locomotive *Kinnaird* No. 14

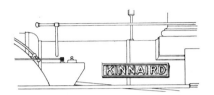

Figure 24

Kinnaird (figure 25) was built in 1847 for the Dundee, Perth and Aberdeen Junction Railway. Her detail differences are only minor and were probably added when she was taken over by the owners. She features in what must be the earliest photograph of a Crampton and, as far as I know, the only photograph *(Plate 5)* of the Tulk and Ley type. This photograph has appeared in many books and has had the usual treatment of the time (and later) of blocking out the background for publicity purposes with the possible subsequent loss of small fittings and often interesting surrounding material! In this case the buffer beam *looks* straight, with just the half-humps on the top for the buffer mountings. As you can see the figure has been drawn with the curved beam to match the others. The dumb buffers *(figure 26)* on these engines comprised a simple metal plate on a shaft mounted to slide in the buffer beam. Horse hair was packed in the space behind the plate, and the whole thing wrapped with a sheet of leather, bound on with iron hoops.

The differences of the locomotive types are well illustrated in the composite drawings *(figures 27, 28 and 29)* on the following page (17).

MAIN DIMENSIONS
As *Liége* and *Namur*

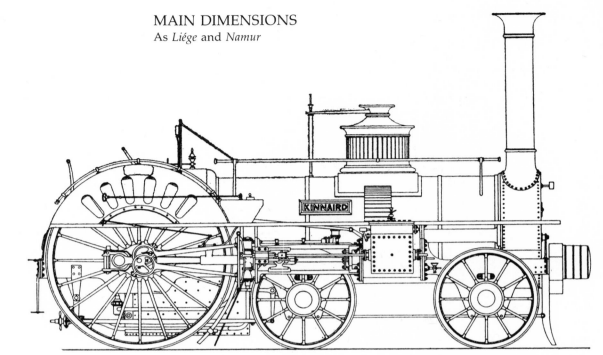

Figure 25

Figure 26

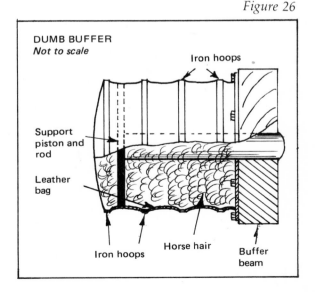

DUMB BUFFER
Not to scale

Iron hoops

Support piston and rod

Leather bag

Iron hoops

Horse hair

Buffer beam

0 1 2 3 4 5 6 7 8ft

Livery. I'm afraid we have not been able to find any! Close study of the photograph of *Kinnaird* shows no sign of any lining at all on tender or splashers, and yet they bothered to make a name plate, so they could not have been too ashamed of her. The base plate for the dome certainly looks polished as does the dome bell mouth, but the chimney has no copper cap. Copper caps were not quite as wide spread as some people believe as, with lining, they were not introduced as standard on the Great Western Railway until the mid 1850s.

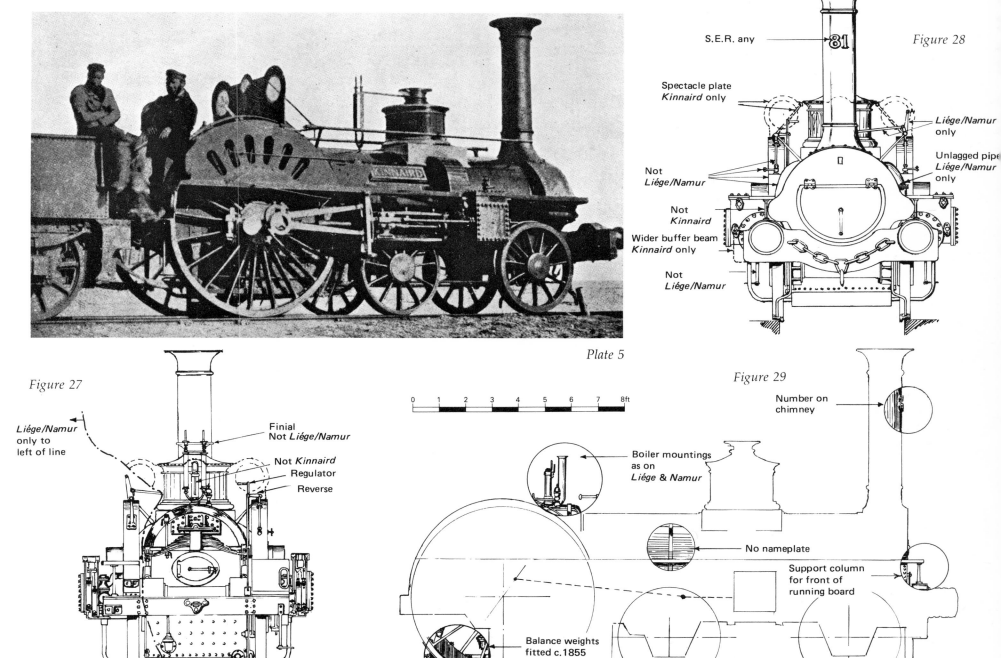

Figure 28

S.E.R. any

Spectacle plate
Kinnaird only

Liége/Namur
only

Unlagged pipe
Liége/Namur
only

Not
Liége/Namur

Not
Kinnaird

Wider buffer beam
Kinnaird only

Not
Liége/Namur

Plate 5

Figure 27

Liége/Namur
only to
left of line

Finial
Not *Liége/Namur*

Not *Kinnaird*
Regulator

Reverse

Figure 29

Number on
chimney

0 1 2 3 4 5 6 7 8ft

Boiler mountings
as on
Liége & Namur

No nameplate

Support column
for front of
running board

Balance weights
fitted c.1855

12 spokes

12 spokes

12 spokes

Composite drawings Tulk and Ley types

17

The South Eastern Railway Locomotives Nos. 81, 83 and 85

This is the last of the 'Classic' batch of Tulk and Ley built Cramptons to be discussed. The drawings in *figure 30* and *figure 31* are by E. Twining, and by comparing the other drawings from *pages 12* to *17* you can compare the small variations. The main dimensions are the same as *Liége* and *Namur*, but apart from what has been described before, and the interesting 'Sherlock Holmes' text on the Bury rebuilds on *page 29*, little more is known specifically about the South Eastern engines.

Livery is as follows: Dark green body colour similar to that of the London and North Western northern division. The chimney and smoke box were black with a copper cap to the chimney, and the locomotive number cut-out in brass and attached half way up the chimney front. The boiler rings between firebox/

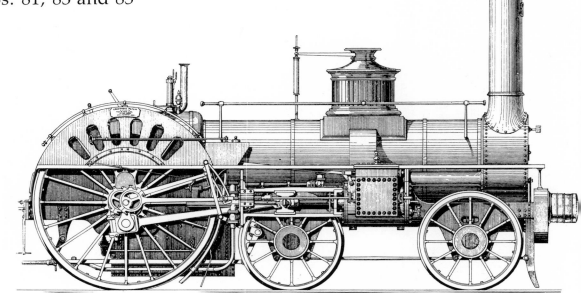

Figure 30

boiler/smokebox were brass, as were the dome and saddle. The splashers and frets were brass beaded, the fronts and tops being painted a dull Venetian red, as were the under frames and cylinders. Wheels were all green with black tyres, and boiler bands were black lined out with fine white lines as were the tender sides and cylinders, but with in-curved corners.

The tender would have been the same for all the English Tulk and Ley Cramptons and is shown on the Maryport engine on *page 20*, but without the lower set of Chauldron buffers.

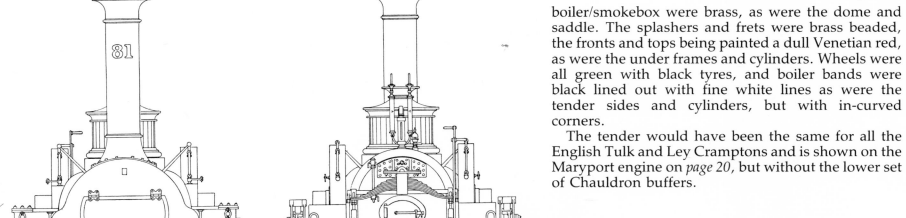

Figure 31

MAIN DIMENSIONS
Driving Wheels 7' 0"
Carrying Wheels 3' 9"
Wheelbase 6' 9" + 6' 3"
Cylinders 16" × 20"
Boiler Pressure 50 psi
Built 1847

18

Figure 32

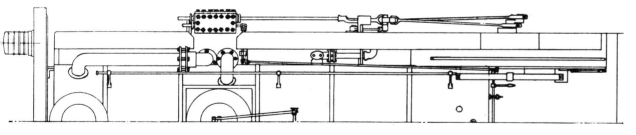

Figure 33

Despite looking superficially the same as the previous engines, the Maryport and Carlisle locomotive is in fact a different engine altogether, and built at a different time.

She was numbered 17 from the Tulk and Ley works which follows on from the South Eastern engines, but was in fact not built until 1854, the building time lag with the consecutive numbering having caused historians much speculation over the years. It was thought that she was built with the original batch, and kept in stock until a bargain hunting buyer came along. However, as Mr. Twining states, 'an old blueprint and a tracing have come to light which show her to have been a totally new engine with many more modern features than were known or used in the 1847-8 period, resulting in an engine on which we have much more information than is usual'.

The main drawings (see in *figure 32*) were completed for my own articles in the May, June, and July 1966 *Model Railway News* by Tom Lindsay, on building the Maryport and Carlisle and the tender having four buffers is quite deliberate! One of the accounts of her later life says the locomotive spent her time working coal trains (probably empties) and, as most of the early coal waggons were Chauldrons with low to nearer central buffers, felt they would be correct for this type of tender. Certainly all the other Maryport and Carlisle Railway goods engines of the period had them.

The cylinder detail drawings (*figure 35*) are by E. W. Twining from his *Model Engineer* article of March 1954 from which I have also taken the accompanying technical details.

MAIN DIMENSIONS

Driving Wheels 7' 0"
Carrying Wheels 4' 0" + 3' 9"
Wheelbase 6' 8" + 7' 10"
Tender Wheels 3' 9"
Cylinders 16" × 20"
Built 1854

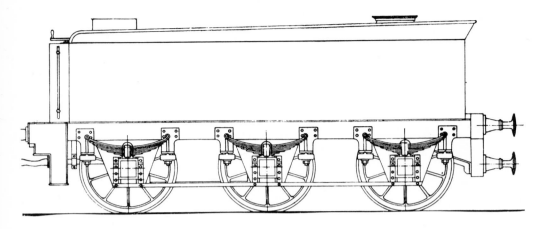

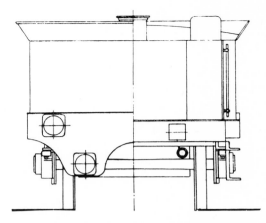

Figure 34

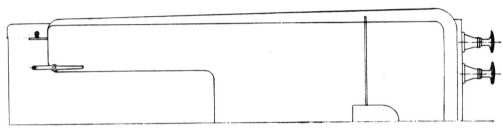

Mr. E. Twining states: The boiler was more modern, notably in the design and construction of the firebox and the barrel was circular instead of being of ovoid section.

For the cylinders, the same foundry patterns were probably used but these, with their coreboxes, were extensively altered. The driving horns, instead of being inverted, were turned down in the normal way and separate springs were provided for each driving axlebox. The reversing gear was much improved, for the doubly cranked arm from the shaft now gave place to a straight arm. There were no eccentric sheaves with straps; instead, the same arrangement was adopted as was used in the L. & N.W. Rly., Crewe-built *Courier*. The return crank, with its two eccentric-pins, the two rods and the expansion link are all shown in the accompanying drawings (*figure 35*) which has, in part, been traced from the old blueprint referred to. The cross-section through the cylinder was not shown in the original and this item (*figure 35*) is a reconstruction by the writer.

In view of the great differences and improvements shown in the drawings, for this works No. 17, the writer believes that it must have been built some years after works No. 16 and that in

the intervening time the firm was engaged upon other engineering contracts which bore different works numbers; for Tulk and Ley were not locomotive builders only. From the point of view of locomotive history it was a most calamitous happening that the old Lowka Works were, in comparatively recent times, entirely destroyed by fire, together with a great mass of Tulk and Ley drawings and records, so that we are never likely to gain any further knowledge concerning the locomotives built by the firm; fortunate it is that certain few drawings have survived which must have been in existence outside of the works.

The principal particulars and dimensions of the engine were as follows: The circular boiler barrel had an outside diameter of 4 ft

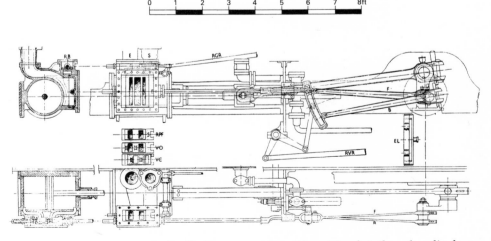

Figure 35 M. and C. Railway, engine No. 12; details of cylinders, motion, valve-gear, etc.

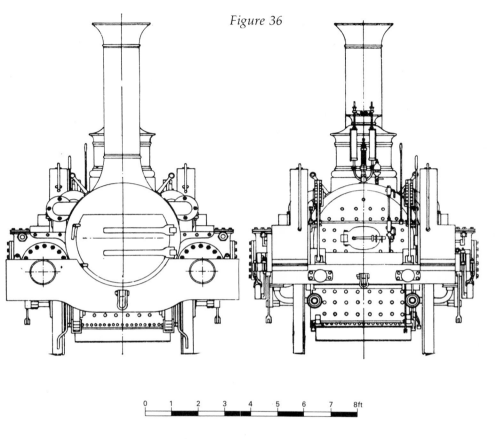

Figure 36

0 1 2 3 4 5 6 7 8ft

10 in long, each of 1¾ in diameter, giving a heating surface of 829.25 sq ft, which, added to 76.75 sq ft in the firebox, made a total of 906 sq ft. The grate area was 14 sq ft. The working pressure is unknown but was probably 90 to 100 lb per sq in.

The regulator was in duplicate, a separate one being provided for each cylinder; each regulator valve in a box cast integral with the cylinder and steamchest. These boxes and valves, with their ports, are shown in detail in *figure 35*. In this drawing the reference letters are: *S*, steam entry; *E*, exhaust; *RB*, regulator box; *RPF*, regulator port face; *VO*, regulator valve open; *VC*, valve closed; *RGR*, one regulator rod. There was a separate rod for each valve and these were led back to a cross-shaft on the firebox immediately over the firehole door; on the shaft was the driver's regulator handle, all as shown in the back elevation (*figure 36*).

The remaining letters in *figure 35* are: *RVR*, reversing rod, which was on the right-hand side of the engine; *F*, the forward eccentric rod; *B*, the backward rod, and *EL*, a back elevation of the expansion link.

The cylinders were 16 in diameter by 20 in stroke. Driving wheels 7 ft diameter. Leading wheels 4 ft 0 in. Intermediate wheels, 3 ft 9 in diameter. The wheel-base was: leading to intermediate, 6 ft 8 in; intermediate to driving, 7 ft 10 in. Total, 14 ft 6 in.

The frames were of plates 1⅛ in thick with a depth, between the front of the cylinders and forward of the driving axle, of 1 ft 3 in. From the cylinders to the front buffer beam the depth was 12 in. The leading overhang was 3 ft 0 in, and overhang at the rear 3 ft 10 in; the total length of frames was, therefore, 21 ft 4 in.

The painting of this Maryport and Carlisle engine No. 12 was dark green and was probably picked out in what became the company's standard style, namely: black with fine vermilion lines. The chimney was all black and the highly ornamental dome wholly of polished brass. Other bright work was: the copper pipes, the brass of the feed pumps, the whistle, safety-valve columns and other fittings. The splashers were probably all painted green though the leading pair may have been of brass.

It would be of interest to model makers to note that the arrangement of the main cranks was for the left-hand crank to lead.

1 in; it was built in four rings, and all joints, both longitudinal and circumferential, were butted and covered by straps, single riveted through each strap and plate. The dome was on the second ring from the front. The barrel plate was carried forward to the front of the smokebox which had an outer wrapper plate flush with the boiler cladding plate. A ring between the two plates carried the chimney. The front tube plate was of the flanged drumhead type, the flange turned forward. The firebox of modern rectangular form was 4 ft 10 in long with a width of 4 ft 0¾ in at the front tapered to 4 ft 0 in at the back; depth from the crown to the foundation ring 4 ft 4 in. The crown was supported by eight girders and these by ten sling stays. There were 184 flue tubes 9 ft

Part Two

R. Stephenson & Co

Folkstone
South Eastern Railway

Coquette
London, Chatham and Dover
Railway

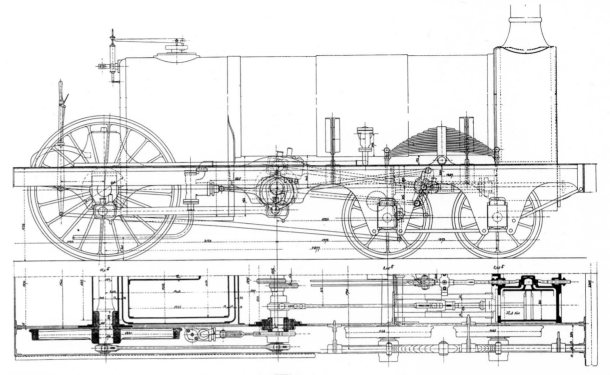

MAIN DIMENSIONS

Driving Wheels 6′ 0″
Carrying Wheels 3′ 6″
Wheelbase 4′ 5¾″ + 4′ 6″ + 7′ 0″
Boiler Barrel Dia. 4′ 2″, length 10′ 9″
Heating Surface 1059 sq ft
Built 1851

Plate 6

Figure 37 Folkstone for the South Eastern Railway.

The Folkstone class was introduced in 1851, and follows quite closely the 1849 patent shown on *page 7, figure 13c.* There are many variations of the theme, but the principle remains. There were ten engines in the class, numbered by the railway Nos. 134 to 143. Although we call it the 'Folkstone' class, I suspect that they had a simple number classification as the class name is usually given to the first locomotive in the series. In this case I suspect she got her name when No. 136 was chosen for the Great Exhibition of 1851 (seen in *plate 6*), and a number is never as impressive as a name, is it?

Plate 7 A very early working photograph of No. 136 on a turntable. Note: no safety rails on the turntable.

The main dimensions are shown on the opposite page, and the main technical features can be obtained from the drawing in *figure 37*.

The idea was to produce a long wheelbase, and therefore stable engine as before, but with inside cylinders instead of the 'Classic' outside design of the Tulk and Ley engines. To do this by driving on an inside crank axle was clearly not possible, so the drive had to be diverted outside the frames to the wheels. The result was the jackshaft drive, a system still used incidentally on our modern diesel shunters today. As the patent drawings show, there must have been a small doubt in the back of Crampton's mind about the results of a possible broken driving axle. He had tried to cover this by adding some extra carrying wheels which, on the final locomotive built, have been omitted! Presumably steel axles had improved from 1849 to 1851 to the point where the precaution was no longer considered necessary.

These locomotives must have been quite successful by the standards of the day as they were not rebuilt into outside frame 2–4–0s until 1869, and one of them, No. 142, lasted in her original form until scrapping in 1874. *Figures 38* and *39* show a 'before and after' sketch of No. 135. The jackshaft has been replaced with a normal crank axle and wheel with also outside frames added.

One interesting account in *Historic Locomotives* tells how there were two classes of locomotive ordered at the same time. The Cramptons, and eight single wheelers of the 2-2-2 type from Sharp, Roberts and Co., having identical cylinders and wheels.

A 'trial' then took place on June 14th 1851 resulting in the Cramptons winning hands down. The Crampton took nine coaches up the New Cross bank of 1 in 100 at 45 mph, did the 25 miles to Reigate in 25 minutes, and covered the 20 miles from Reigate to Tonbridge in 19½ minutes, reaching a maximum speed of 75 mph. The best the Sharp could manage was 61 mph. On a later test, one of the Cramptons took 27 of the light four wheel coaches of the day up the New Cross bank, but unfortunately with no speed recorded.

Livery for the 'Folkstones' would have been the same as that quoted for the South Eastern Railways Tulk and Ley engines on *page 18*.

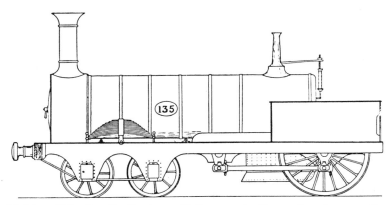

Figure 38 No. 135, South Eastern Railway. A Crampton locomotive, with dummy driving shaft.

Figure 39 No. 135, Crampton engine, converted into a 4-coupled locomotive.

23

Locomotive *Coquette* of the London, Chatham and Dover Railway

Figure 40

This class of five engines were the last singles to be built to the Crampton jack-shaft design by R. Stephenson and Co, but were only similar in outline to the Folkstone class and the Great Northern Railway engine. *Coquette* has many detail difference (*figure 40*), the main one being that rather distinctive bogie. It was, by all accounts, troublesome! It had a central pivot with no castor effect or spring guidance, resulting in the bogie derailing and getting at cross purposes with the track far too often. She has a neat appearance with the spacing and design of the boiler components, which is the same as that fitted to some of the 'Tiger' class coupled Cramptons. Due to lack of adhesion they were soon rebuilt by Martley to four coupled engines, though in model form they way out perform the prototype with the tender (*figure 41*) weight resting on the footplate!

Livery was the standard London Chatham and Dover Railway colour scheme of the period. Body and tender colour was dark malachite green, with wide black banding flanked with a fine white and vermilion line and incurved corners. Smokebox and chimney were black, the chimney having a copper cap. Frames were chocolate lined in red, with green springs and wheels, the wheels having grey tyres.

MAIN DIMENSIONS

Driving Wheels 6' 6½"
Carrying Wheels 4' 0"
Wheelbase 4' 9" + 12'4"
Cylinders 16" × 22"
Tender Wheels 4' 1"

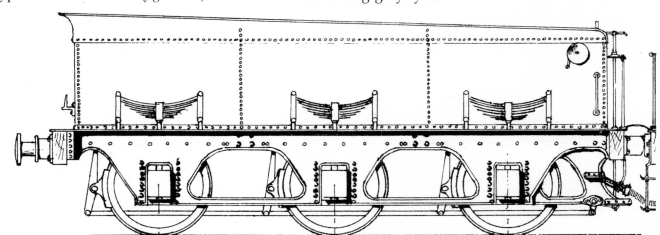

Figure 41

Part Three

Kitson, Thompson & Hewitson

Midland Railway
  Nos. 130 and 131

Locomotives of the Midland Railway, Nos. 130 and 131

These two locomotives were built by Kitson, Thompson and Hewitson in 1848 and numbered 130 and 131 by the Midland Railway. The fine drawings were prepared by Mr. E. Twining from the original works drawings, now in the possession of the Science Museum, London.

As with most of these engines, there are problems interpreting the drawings and any available text, as they quite often differ. In this case two types of valve gear are shown at different periods, and, not being a valve gear expert, I will pass on Mr. Twining's explanations from his *Model Engineer* article of Decembr 1953. 'In the first place, it should be said that the arrangement of the after part of these engines, which had return cranks carrying journals to be taken by outside axleboxes, was such that there was no space available for eccentrics outside of the driving wheels nor yet outside of the inside frames; for there were axleboxes in both inside and outside frames. It, therefore, appeared difficult to fit any of the—at that time—modern gears, and the writer believes that in the January, 1848 drawings an attempt was made to provide something which would overcome the difficulty.

MAIN DIMENSIONS
Driving Wheels 7' 0"
Carrying Wheels 4' 0"
Leading Wheels 4' 9"
Wheelbase 7' 9" + 8' 0"
Cylinders 16" × 22"

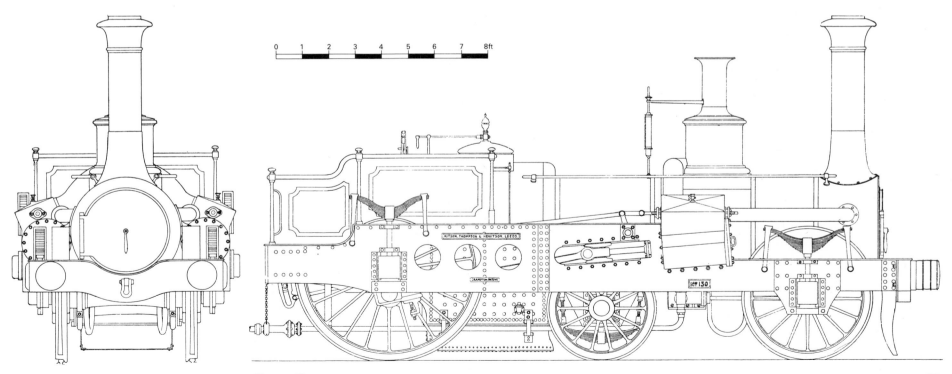

Figure 42

Figure 43

The gear shown, though by no means complete, is Isaac Dodds's wedge motion which, patented in 1839, was obsolete by 1848; it was one which put great stresses on the reversing gear and was very complicated mechanically. There was one eccentric for each cylinder, mounted on a sliding sleeve carrying an oblique wedge, a pair of inclined planes, passing through the eccentric sheave; this wedge was at right-angles to the centre-line of the crank. The driver's gear lever moved the sleeve (*figure 44*) and with it the inclined surfaces of the wedge, longitudinally along the axle and so caused the eccentric to take up positions either in advance of or behind the crank-line, or any intermediate position for expansive working of the valve. As a matter of fact, one sleeve only was fitted and this carried both the wedges at ninety degrees to each other for right-hand and left-hand eccentrics which, although revolving, had to be held literally in order to prevent the tendency to slide on their wedges. This, combined with with complication of shifting the sleeve by means of a reversing lever moving in a plane entirely different from that of the sleeve movement, made the whole gear mechanically inefficient. But the writer believes that the making of the drawing of Dodd's gear revealed, by a natural train of thought and ideas, a way by which it would be possible to fit a link motion, using two eccentrics and an ordinary expansion link together with a rocking shaft and levers, already schemed for Dodds's gear, close to the rear buffer beam.

The works numbers of the two engines were: 130 and 131 and it has been suggested to the writer that the wedge motion and the link motion may have been both used, one gear in each engine. This idea is negatived by the fact that in the elevation the engine bears the number '130' and the Dodds's gear drawings are definitely marked 'No. 130 engine' which clearly shows that there was a change of ideas after January, 1848.

The side elevation of No. 130, reproduced in *figure 43*, is almost a facsimile of the undated original Kitson drawing and has been left unshaded in order to render it a close copy of the same. In the original there are a few little obvious errors and these have been corrected. *Figure 44* is a hypothetical reconstructtion of the link motion valve-gear and *figure 42* a front elevation of the engine; both of these last being by the writer.

Shortly after he commenced to look into this matter of the possible gear, indicated by the elevation drawing, the writer believed that the gear was Gooch's, in which the long valve-rod,

together with the die-block, would be moved up and down in the expansion link by the reversing lever; but this had to be abandoned because it involved either great mechanical difficulties or putting the expansion link outside of the inner frame and there was insufficient lateral space for this. So then it was decided that the gear must have been Stephenson's, with eccentric-rods led

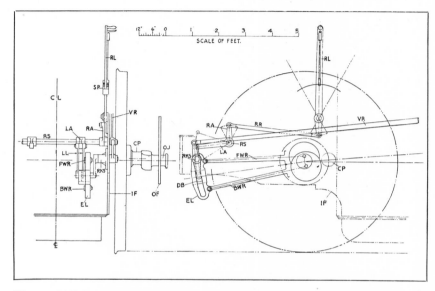

Figure 44 Mr. Twining's hypothetical reconstruction of the valve gear.

backwards instead of forewards and a rocking shaft almost the same as had been schemed for Dodds's gear. The detailed layout was the result.

All the parts shown in *figure 44* have, for convenience, been given reference letters and a list of them is as follows: *CL*, centre-line of engine; *CP*, crankpin; *FWR*, forward eccentric rod; *BWR*, backward eccentric rod; *EL*, expansion link; *DB*, dieblock; *RKS*, rocking shaft; *VR*, valve-rod; *LL*, lifting links; *RA*, reversing arm; *RS*, reversing shaft; *LA*, lifting arm; *RR*, reversing rod; *RL*, reversing lever; *SP*, sector plate; *IF*, inside frame and firebox sideplate; *OF*, outside frame; *OJ*, outside journal. Note that the sideplates of the firebox formed portions of the inside frames. Drawings of other Kitson engines show that this peculiarity was a feature of their standard practice at this time.

The cylinders were 16 in diameter by 22 in stroke. The centres of the cylinders were 6 ft apart, laterally. Driving axle 6½ in diameter. Journals: inner, 6½ in diameter by 7½ in long. Outer: 5 in diameter by 6½ in long. Crankpins 6½ in diameter by 5 in long. These crank-pins were keyed directly into the hubs of the driving wheels. The boiler feed-pumps were of short stroke with rams of large diameter and were driven by eccentrics on the leading axle. In *The Locomotive*, August issue, 1922, Mr. E. A. Forward gave the following particulars of the boiler: The barrel had an outside diameter of 4 ft ¼ in by 10 ft 0 in long, formed of plates 7/16 in thick. Distance between tubeplates 10 ft 5 in. There were 193 tubes of 1⅞ in outside diameter, giving a heating surface of 979 sq ft. The inner firebox was 4 ft 2 in long by 3 ft 4 in wide, by 4 ft 3 in high and added 83 sq ft, so making a total heating surface of 1,062 sq ft. The grate area was 13.9 sq ft.

With regard to the painting of these two engines nothing definite is known, but as they were delivered early in Matthew Kirtley's locomotive superintendency on the Midland Railway, which commenced in 1844, there can be little doubt that they were painted green, picked out in black, with no fine lining. The particular green was a middle chrome, a little darker than that adopted by Mr. S. W. Johnson, Mr. Kirtley's successor. The form of the panel lining, with cut-in corners, is taken from the Kitson original drawing and is in perfect accordance with the Kirtley style of picking out.

Messrs. Kitson's drawing shows the wooden lagging strips on the boiler barrel, although on the firebox they are covered by cladding plate. The writer has ventured to show cladding plate on the barrel as well, for, if there was no such plating when the engines were first turned out, the lagging would not be left uncovered for long. It was at just about this time that the practice of showing the wood, either varnished or painted, fell into disuse and painted thin plate was added to cover it.

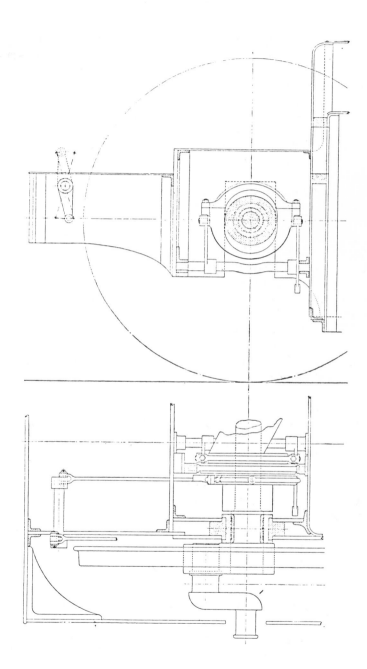

Figure 45 Showing arrangement of 'gear change' levers, to move eccentrics.

Locomotives of the London, Brighton and South Coast Railway, Nos. 56 and 58

Here is the second of the British single wheeler jack-shaft locomotives to be discussed, though the Stephenson designs shown on *page 24* were the last to be built in 1862.

In 1845 the London Brighton and South Coast Railway put out tenders with a view to purchasing another twenty-one passenger engines for their stock. However, this was not as easy as it seemed because all the large established builders were working to capacity, thus resulting in searching around the smaller firms. Timothy Hackworth of Stockton and Darlington fame agreed to build fourteen locomotives at his Shildon Works with an option on seven more. Due to labour shortages and lack of experience the work went far too slowly for the Brighton directors and also was of poor quality, resulting in the locomotives being brought to Brighton for completion often after very severe modifications. These produced the two Crampton locomotives Nos. 56 and 58 being rebuilt from Hackworth 2-2-2s in 1853. Unfortunately they were no more use than the originals, running only a few more miles before being finally converted to 2-4-0s in 1855.

Observation of the drawing *figure 46* shows most of the important features: the rather ornate domes on square saddles with quite elaborate beading, the compensated beams on the carrying wheels with just the one small spring behind and the feedwater pumps driven from the jack-shaft being all quite 'standard' Crampton features. Sanding has been added, and one odd feature—the wood cladding riveted to what (from the rivet spacing) appears to be a twelve spoked or twelve webbed 5' 6" wheel!

Livery. This is not certain, but Hamilton Ellis in his articles chooses the dark green style for his painting, with fine red and white, or red and gold lines with incurved corners, black smokebox, chimney and wheels, and red buffers and beams.

MAIN DIMENSIONS
Driving Wheels 5' 6"
Carrying Wheels 3' 4"
Wheelbase 4' 0" + 9' 9"
Cylinders 16" × 24"

Figure 46

Part Five

Bury Curtis & Kennedy

London and North Western Railway,
Southeren Division
Liverpool

South Eastern Railway
Nos. 68, 69, 72, 74, 75, 78

MAIN DIMENSIONS
OF FIG. 47

Cylinders 15″ bore × 22″ stroke
Driving Wheels 6′ 0″
Carrying Wheels 3′ 6″
Boiler 2″ tubes 13′ 6″ long
Boiler Pressure 100 psi
Heating Surface 965 sq ft
Wheelbase 8′ 9″ + 6′ 6″

Figure 47

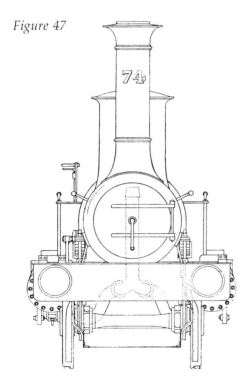

Of the Bury Curtis and Kennedy engines *Liverpool* is fairly well documented and described in *pages 32* to *35*. The South Eastern Railway rebuilds however are another story! The history as set out in the many old accounts is 'delightfully confusing', so to enable you to form your own ideas I will list the various quoted statements with their allied drawings, and offer my own possible solutions on the next page.

The story starts when a batch of six engines were built by Bury's in 1848 for the South Eastern Railway. They were built as 4-2-0 types (see *figure 49*) and numbered 68, 69, 72, 74, 75 and 78 by the Railway, on their receipt into traffic. They had bar-frames among other features, which Mr. Cudworth did not like so he decided to rebuild them on the Crampton pattern, rather like No. 92 in *Part 9* (*plate 75*) but retaining the large dome on the front end of the boiler. They would have plate frames and the driving wheels would be behind the firebox.

Now the plot starts to diverge with a range of quoted 'statements'.

1. All six engines were rebuilt 'in the style' of Tulk and Ley Cramptons.
2. The last four were *believed* to have been rebuilt as illustrated in *figure 47* showing the number 74.
3. The drawing *figure 48* appears in *Die Crampton Lokomotive* by F. Gaiser of 1909 as a South Eastern Crampton No. 85. He also quotes all six engines as being rebuilt.
4. The reproduction of the superb water colour (*plate 8*) by Mr. E. Twining shows No. 92, and the same engine as in *figure 48* also numbered No. 85.

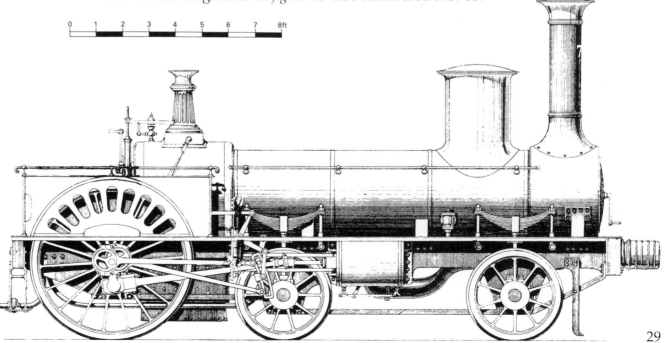

0 1 2 3 4 5 6 7 8ft

5. All the evidence on the Tulk and Ley engines leads us to believe that Nos. 81, 83 and 85 were built as illustrated in *part one* on *page 18, figures 30* and *31*.

6. *Figure 50* is described as a Crampton Engine built for the South Eastern Railway by Tulk and Ley and carries the number 81 on the splasher.

Plate 8

Now we come to conclusion time!

The water colour (*plate 8, figure 47* and *figure 48*) would all appear to be the same locomotive. However, when compared with the Tulk and Ley drawings in *part one* they are only similar in style but not in technical detail. The boiler is certainly much nearer to *figure 37* on *page 22* with its smokebox, door details and length. So, I would suggest that *figure 48* is not a Tulk and Ley engine, so where did it come from and why the numbers 81 and 85?

One possible solution is that all six engines were rebuilt but as two (or more) different types, all in the *style* of Crampton and the numbers could have been a red herring. *Figure 51* is simply a sketch of *figure 47*. A complete comparison of the line drawings of *figures 47, 48, 49, 50* and *51* is strongly recommended.

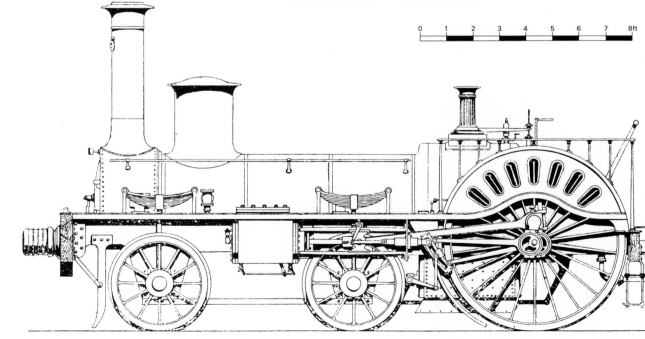

Figure 48

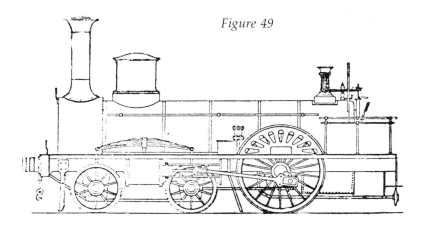

Figure 49

Figure 50

Livery. This would be standard South Eastern dark green for the wheels, boiler, side sheets, tender and springs, with the frames, buffer beam ends, and lower footplate and cylinder lagging, deep indian red. Lining was black with a fine white line each side and incurved corners on the panels. The chimney cap was copper, and the dome, safety valve, firebox and splasher beading were all polished brass. A fine sight in pristine condition!

The leading particulars given are for the locomotive in *figure 47*. However, Nos. 69 and 72 were scrapped in 1865 and Nos. 68, 74, 75 and 78 were given new boilers in 1858. Most of the detail can be seen on the excellent Twining drawings, but one point that is not obvious from the drawings is that the tender brakes were on one side only.

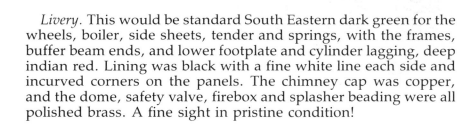

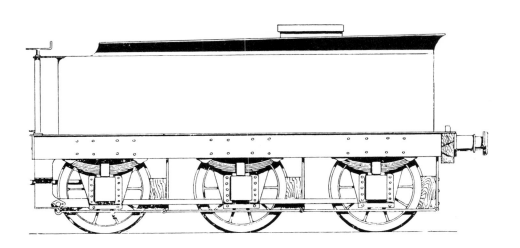

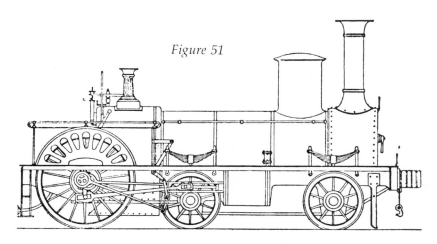

Figure 51

Locomotive *Liverpool* of the London and North Western Railway

MAIN DIMENSIONS
Driving Wheels 8' 0"
Carrying Wheels 4' 3" & 4' 0"
Heating Surface 2290 sq ft
Boiler Pressure 120 psi
Cylinders 18" bore × 24" stroke
Tender Wheels 3' 9"
Wheelbase 4' 6" + 6' 6" + 7' 6"
Weights 8 tons 10½ cwt +
   8 tons 9½ cwt + 6 tons + 12 tons
   = 35 tons

This locomotive must take pride of place in the Crampton saga as she is the most majestic, and the best documented of the fleet. Built by Bury, Curtis and Kennedy in 1848 for the Southern division of the London and North Western Railway, being based mainly at Wolverton and used to work the Euston to Birmingham service until she was despatched to the Great Exhibition, to stand alongside Gooch's *Iron Duke* of the Great Western Railway. The very fine drawings (*figures 52 to 59*) by E. W. Twining really do her justice and from the model builder's viewpoint are superb. She was of course intended as the standard gauge answer to the fine broad gauge engines of the time which were generally superior in steaming capacity and steadiness,

There is an odd mixture of wheels with a 4' 3" leading wheel, 4' 0" flanged and flangeless, with the massive 8' 0" driver, with its 17" diameter boss, and fixed to that a pair of 2' 9" diameter eccentrics. These eccentrics had a vee-groove in them which, unless squirted fairly often with oil, would seize up and shatter into several pieces—the crew must have loved her! As the drawings show, the locomotive has many features of interest several of which might not have been noticed on the usual 'side view only' drawings that railway draughtsmen usually give us. There are two firebox doors and two smokebox doors in the double oval boiler, with two 'normal' springs on long stalks each side of the footplate instead of the single transverse one, on the patents. The front two axles have a common spring each side giving, as well as springing, a degree of compensation which was quite common during this period until the general standard of track settled down to what was accepted as 'normal' on the L.N.W.R., by the 1870s.

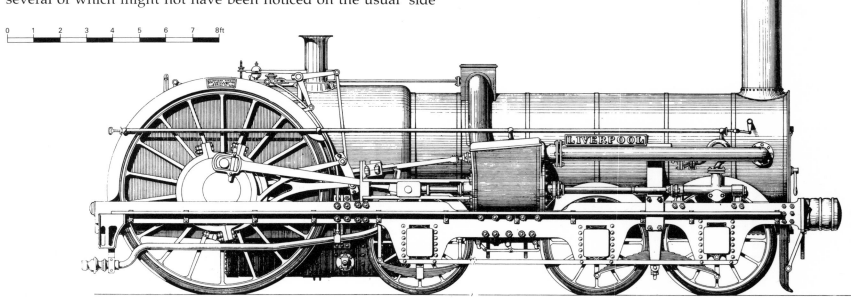

Figure 52

32

As with all Crampton patents, the water feed pumps were driven from the valve gear, only this time with a difference as they are mounted on the outside frame next to the leading wheel splasher, and in line with the cylinder centres. An extension is taken from the piston rod through a bearing in the cylinder end cover, to a universal joint and then to the pump drive rod.

The buffers are the same as those illustrated in *figure 26* on *page 16* with the centre guide spindle. In fact most buffers did not have this feature which is why a lot of old photographs show them with a 'drunken, sagging' look to them.

The six-inch wide, side footplate is interesting if you do make a model of her as it does not fit right up against the frames; the eleven brackets shown on the drawing protrude above and below the footplate and hold it away by the thickness of the metal—about ⅜".

With reference to the drawings, those of you with a fair sized library will find there are several drawings of *Liverpool* available including even a colour print on a post card. There are varying differences among them including taper chimneys, wood lagging on the boiler and carrying wheels of all the same diameter. Now, with all research into railway matters one has to make a choice, and having read the amount of trouble that Mr. Twining went to, to verify and prepare his drawings, I think I would believe his above all others—however, the choice is yours!

As we mentioned earlier, *Liverpool* was built to feature in the battle of the gauges which was fierce and bitter, a lot of politics were involved, which is odd really, as engineers and politics do not usually mix. I feel the engineer quite rightly believes his creative abilities put him above such antics! However, there were bitter words and, as a result, some misinterpretation of facts. It was said that *Liverpool* was heavy on the track and that she spread the rails so that the next train fell in between. But why did not her own train fall in? The long rigid wheelbase was also criticised, but the centre carrying wheels were flangeless so would put no side thrust on the track at all. I suppose, like so many innovations ahead of their time, this locomotive was not appreciated, as it was bigger and heavier than anything else and the track certainly was not ready for her, despite all of which she was credited with 79 mph at one time and did last ten years in service until being broken up in 1858.

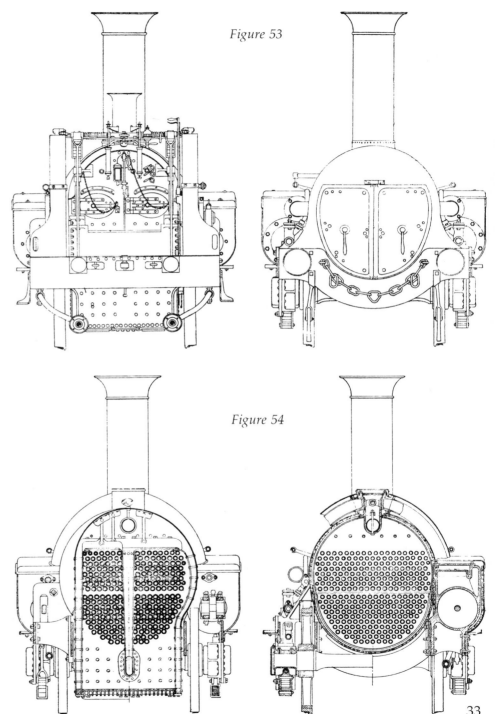

Figure 53

Figure 54

0 1 2 3 4 5 6 7 8ft

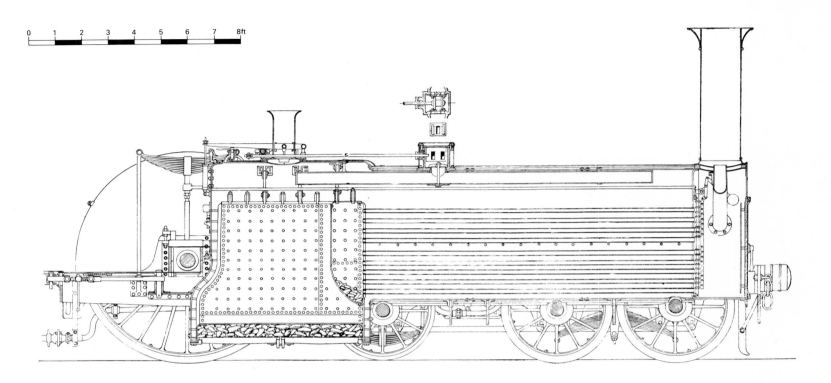

Figure 55

Sectional plan of boiler and frame details in 7mm for the locomotive *Liverpool*.

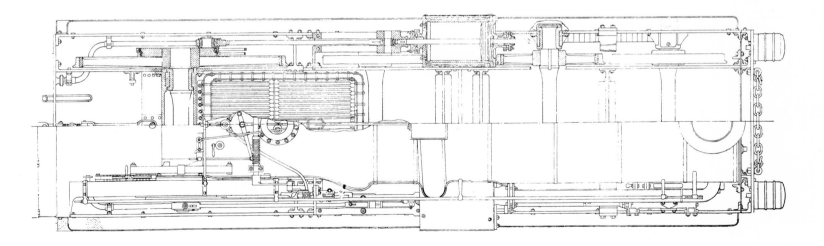

Figure 56

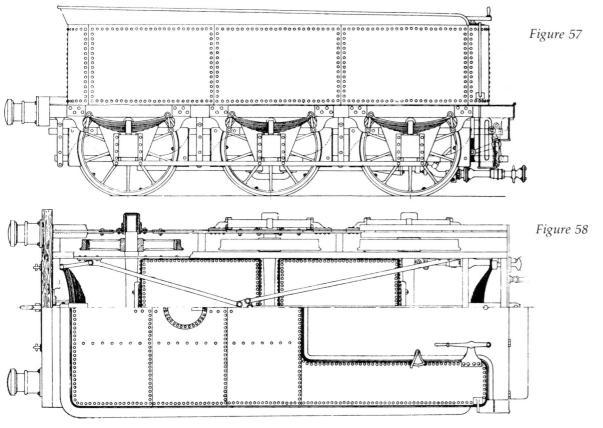

Figure 57

Again Mr. E. Twining has helped in giving us series of tender drawings in *figures 57, 58* and *59*, a rare event in locomotive drawings of long ago. The three views are self explanatory, although I think Mr. Twining has got confused when he says that 4' 0" tender wheels should have 12 spokes, not the 10 as drawn. However, if you scale the drawing, the wheels are in fact 3' 9", which remained the 'standard' on the L.N.W.R. and *should* therefore be 10 spokes. In other words accept the drawings as they stand.

Figure 58

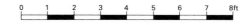

Figure 59

Livery. This is quoted as a middle-chrome green very like the Northern Railway green, with black bands, lined each side with a fine white line. Boiler bands were also black, lined as the tender panels. The frames from the footplate down were grey. The wheels were green with grey tyres.

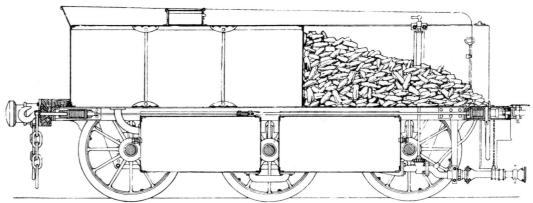

35

Part Six

E. B. Wilson & Co

North British Railway
   No. 55

Eastern Counties Railway
   Nos. 108–112

Aberdeen Railway
   Nos. 26 and 27

MAIN DIMENSIONS

Driving Wheels 7' 0"
Centre Wheels 3' 9"
Leading Wheels 4' 6"
Wheelbase 7' 6" + 7' 9"
Cylinders 16" × 20"

Plate 9

These six engines were to the same pattern, and were built by E. B. Wilson in 1848. Not a great deal is known about them, their main dimensions being as given on this page, but we do seem to have plenty of drawings to peruse! No. 55 was used for the Royal Train in 1860 and was either painted, or draped out in the real material of the Stewart Dress Tartan over a basic colour of green, for the event. This locomotive ran for sixteen years in her original form giving her the British record for un-rebuilt longevity. She was rebuilt in 1864 as a 2-2-2 and completed her career in the form shown in *plate 9* in 1907. The five Eastern Counties Railway engines (*figures 62* and *63*) were re-numbered in 1852 but whether they were rebuilt at the same time is not certain.

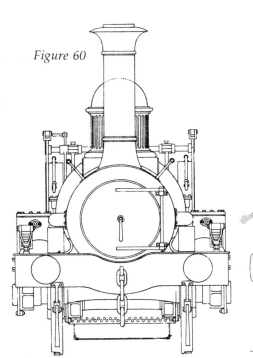

Figure 60

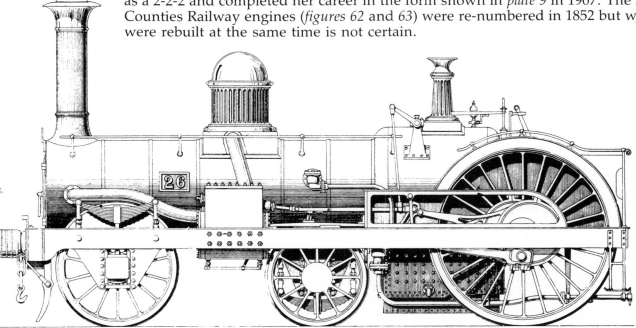

Figure 61

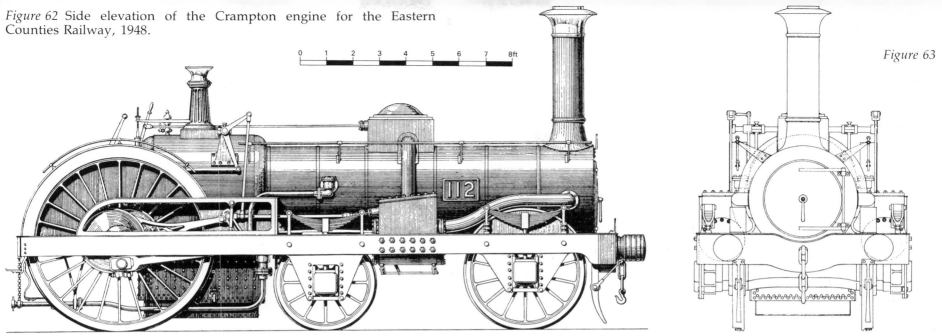

Figure 62 Side elevation of the Crampton engine for the Eastern Counties Railway, 1948.

Figure 63

The Aberdeen Railway Nos. 26 and 27.

These two engines have several grey areas in their ancestry (haven't they all!). It would appear they were built to a continental order in 1849 which later was cancelled, where they remained 'on the shelf' until purchased by the Aberdeen Railway in 1850 and numbered 26 and 27 (*figures 60* and *61*). Apart from the fluted dome they would appear to be a continuation of the Eastern Counties production design, following their main dimensions. However, the line drawing by Mr. Ward (*figure 64*) shows 26 and 27 in a different state! From the Caledonian shed records, it would appear that these two engines were very unsatisfactory in their original state, and were fitted with new valve gear. This gear had smaller eccentrics similar to the Tulk and Ley engines, but would fitting the new valve gear have also required the extensive alterations to the splashers and footplate, or been worth the cost?

Secondly, does Mr. Twining's fine drawings 'assume' a similar-

ity to the earlier ones with perhaps more detail than is warranted, and could not the line drawing by Mr. Ward have been the true original? Finally, why, if the North British engines were so successful, were the rest so poor? And so on!

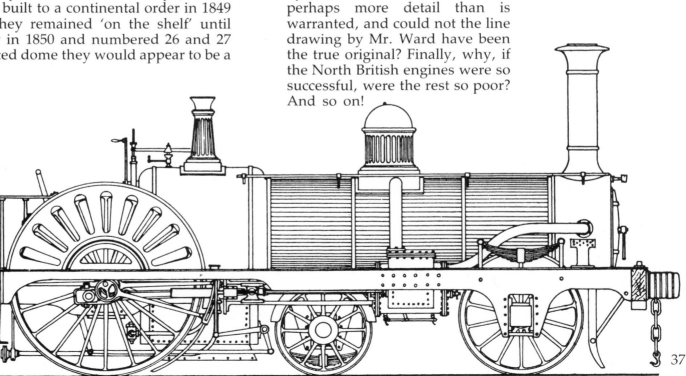

Figure 64 Aberdeen Railway, Crampton type Nos. 26 and 27.

37

Part Seven
Crewe Works
London North Western Railway
Courier

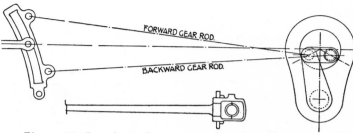

Figure 66 Gooch valve gear showing layout and return crank angles.

Figure 65

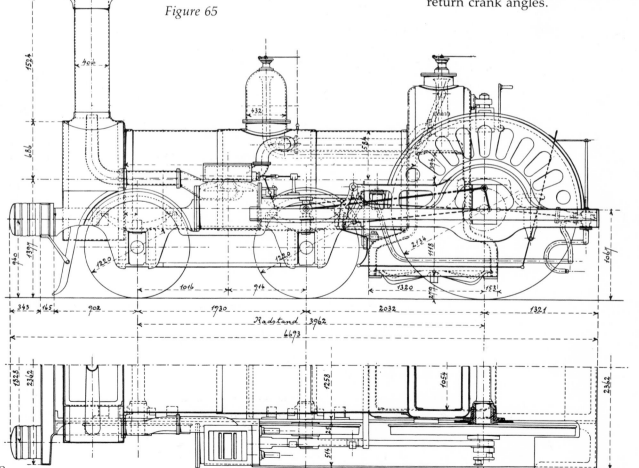

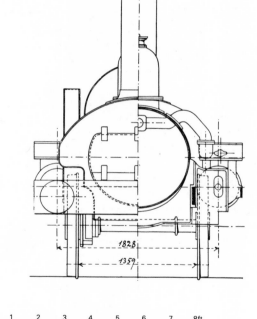

MAIN DIMENSIONS
Driving Wheels 7' 0"
Carrying Wheels 4' 0"
Tender Wheels 3' 9"
Wheelbase 6' 6" + 6' 3"
Boiler Pressure 90 psi

Figure 67

gear used at Crewe. There were no eccentrics of course, but fairly simple return cranks. What was not so simple, was that the gear hung on a swinging link at the front of the valve gear splasher, and then reversed itself on a trunnion on the back of the cylinder and up to the valve on the top. This locomotive had a typically Crampton oval boiler with the transverse spring bolted to it supporting the driving wheels.

One has to presume that this locomotive would have a standard Crewe tender and, as no drawings seem to exist of loco and tender together, Dennis has drawn a possible wooden framed variety below in *figure 68.*

Livery. London North Western Railway Northern division middle chrome green, with black boiler bands, and the tender panels were banded black with incurved corners. It is not obvious that this locomotive was 'picked out' with fine white lines as quoted for *Liverpool,* but was similar to the early 'Problem' class livery. The dome was polished brass as were the front and rear curved corners of the raised firebox. Wheels were green with grey tyres, and buffer beams were red faced with black buffers.

I must confess that this locomotive is a personal favourite. Aesthetically she is just right—the way the chimney, dome and raised firebox casing space out along the boiler, the fine wheel and valve gear splashers, and just for the hell of it, the worst valve gear I have ever tried to model (certainly in 4mm scale). However, though modellers may like her, the railway historians seem to have found this locomotive wanting in many respects.

Courier (figures 65, 67 and *68)* was mostly designed by Crampton, but built at the London and North Western's Railway workshops at Crewe by Alexander Allan in 1847. She had several Allan features which were to become his trademark— the design of the frames in particular. The valve gear previously mentioned was by Gooch, and although a vast improvement on the Tulk and Ley gear by Stephenson, was the only example of Gooch's valve

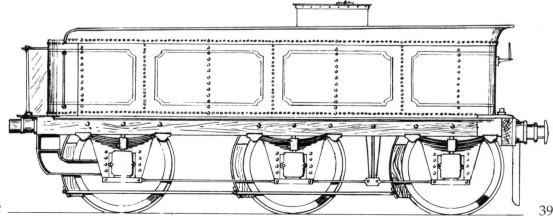

Figure 68

Part Eight
R. B. Longridge & Co
Great Northern Railway
No. 200

Figure 69

MAIN DIMENSIONS
Driving Wheels 6' 6"
Carrying Wheels 3' 6"
Wheelbase 4' 6" + 12' 0"
Cylinders 15" × 21"

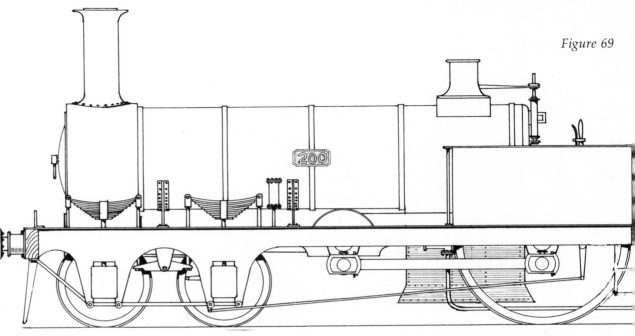

Figure 70 The 'suspect' sketch.

Figure 71

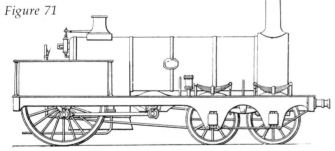

This design presents us with yet another puzzle. All the accounts over the years have led us to believe there were ten engines of this type, Nos. 91 to 99, and 200. They were said to have been built by R. B. Longridge for the Great Northern Railway, to the same basic layout and dimensions as the batch by Stephensons for the South Eastern Railway. The locomotives had small differences, like the spring layout on the front carrying wheels via the compensating beams. The rear transverse spring on the drivers was common to both classes being included to achieve a three-point suspension.

However, Mr. Ahrons states that he has a letter from Mr. Sturrock, saying that there was only 'one' Crampton type on the line, the rest being of the 2-2-2 wheel layout (built by Sturrock) and numbered 91 to 99.

The Locomotive Magazine article on the Great Northern Railway locomotives of 1898 gives sketches of a jack-shaft Crampton No. 91 and a 2-2-2 No. 91, said to have been rebuilt from the Crampton!

It could be that No. 200 (*figure 69*) was in fact built as a trial Crampton engine. It was then found not to be suitable for the Great Northern Railway, so the remainder that were 'planned', were altered to 2-2-2s and built as such, hence the confusion. No. 200 shows up again rebuilt into a 4-4-0 which could support the 'trials' engine theory.

To add further confusion—the sketch (*figure 71*) does not make sense as the buffer heights do not 'scale-out' with a 3' 6" leading wheel, and if it were a 3' 6" wheel it would not have had splashers anyway. I have redrawn the 7mm drawing (*figure 69*) from the sketch and the known information, adding a few Sturrock and Great Northern Railway details to produce, I hope, a more plausible design.

Figure 72

    An enlargement of the Great Northern Locomotive showing in fine detail the link motion, eccentrics, slide valves, and other constructional details which can be compared with the sectional drawing (*figure 37*) on page 22 of *Folkstone*.

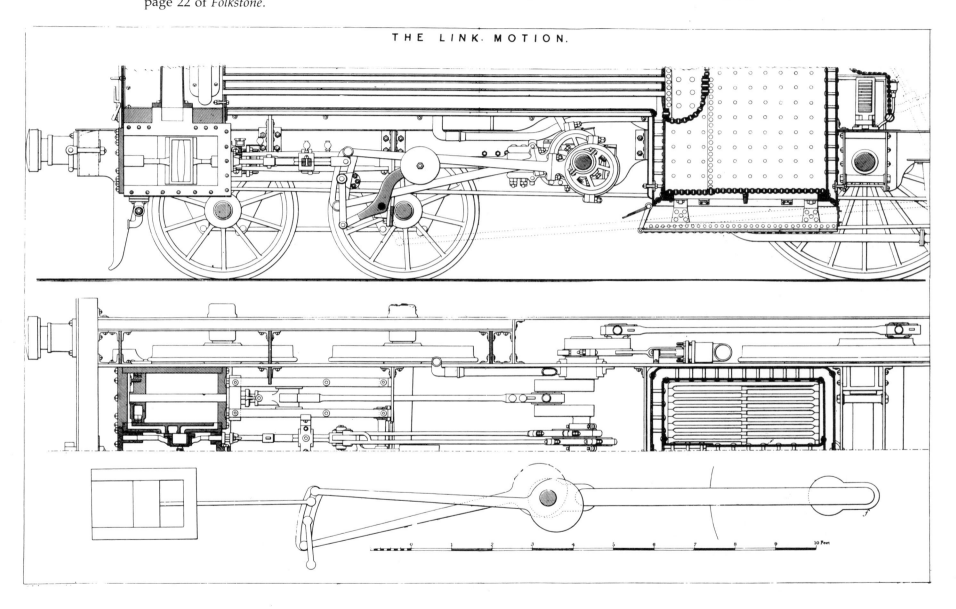

THE LINK. MOTION.

Part Nine

Nasmyth & Co
South Eastern Railway
No. 92

MAIN DIMENSIONS

Driving Wheels 5′ 6″
Carrying Wheels 3′ 6″
Wheelbase 8′ 0½″ + 7′ 11½″
Cylinders 15″ × 22″
Boiler Pressure 80 psi

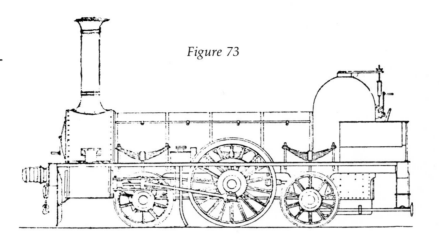

Figure 73

Locomotive No. 92 started life in 1845 as one of a batch of seven locomotives of the 2-2-2 type as shown in *figure 73* built by Nasmyth and Co. They were long boiler singles numbered 88 to 94 (by the railway); the main dimensions are shown in the tables. As 2-2-2s they suffered the common fault of all these short wheelbase types—they pitched and oscillated so violently at times, that they even derailed themselves! All the class were rebuilt in one form or another, but only this one as a Crampton.

The fortunate state with this locomotive is that we have several old prints available from which to produce drawings and trace its history. As usual there appears to be no tender, but Dennis has drawn a 'most likely' type to go with the Twining, side and front elevations. The basic boiler type and shape is shown in *figure 76* and a cross section through some parts of the engine

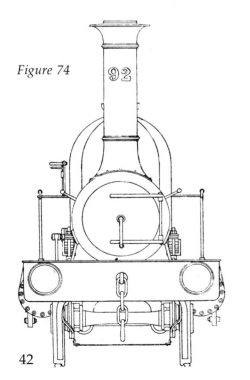

Figure 74

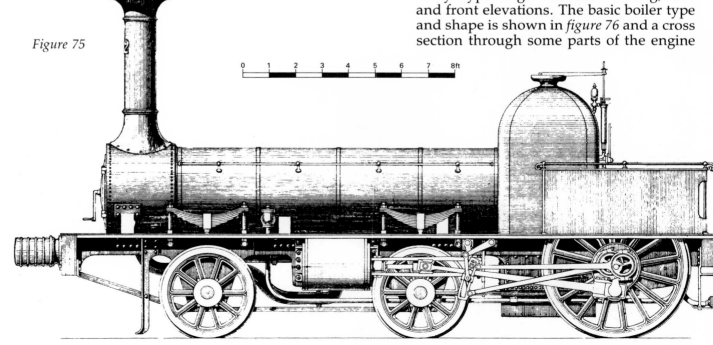

Figure 75

are shown in *figure 77*, in particular, the very distinctive forked drive rods, which are not evident on a side elevation.

No. 92 was rebuilt as a Crampton by Mr. Cudworth at Ashford in 1847, making it one of a grand total of some twenty South Eastern Railway rear-wheel Cramptons, of five quite distinct types. As rebuilt, No. 92 was very successful and worked well, finishing her days in 1875 on the Minster to Deal branch line.

Again we have controversy over dimensions! This time over the driving wheel size and crank throw. Text states— 'the wheels to have been 6' 0" and the cylinder stroke 18", but drawings show 5' 6" drivers and a 22" stroke, so, on building the model, I have taken the logic of the drawing as being more persuasive. The wheels themselves were made up by forging two 'T' section strips of wrought iron back to back, the result shown in the *figure 75*, side elevation. The skills required to finish up with thirty-four parts of bent metal in a good enough concentric circle to receive a tyre, are mind bending!

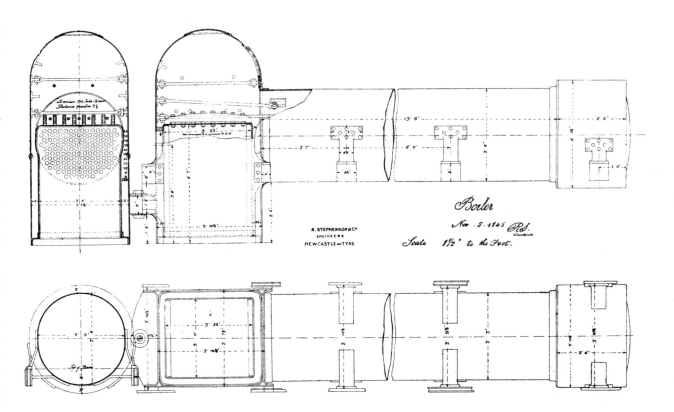

Figure 76

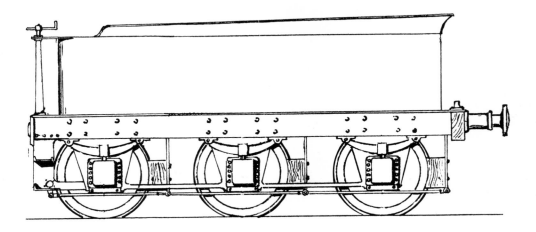

Other features to note apart from the forked rods are: the boiler was not quite round, being 3' 3" high but only 3' 0" across (see *figure 76*); the Stephenson link valve gear with its small eccentrics and return cranks, and the very distinctive 'haystack' firebox, which, in model form is quite hard to shape unless you file it from the solid metal.

The livery is as before and details on *page 18*.

43

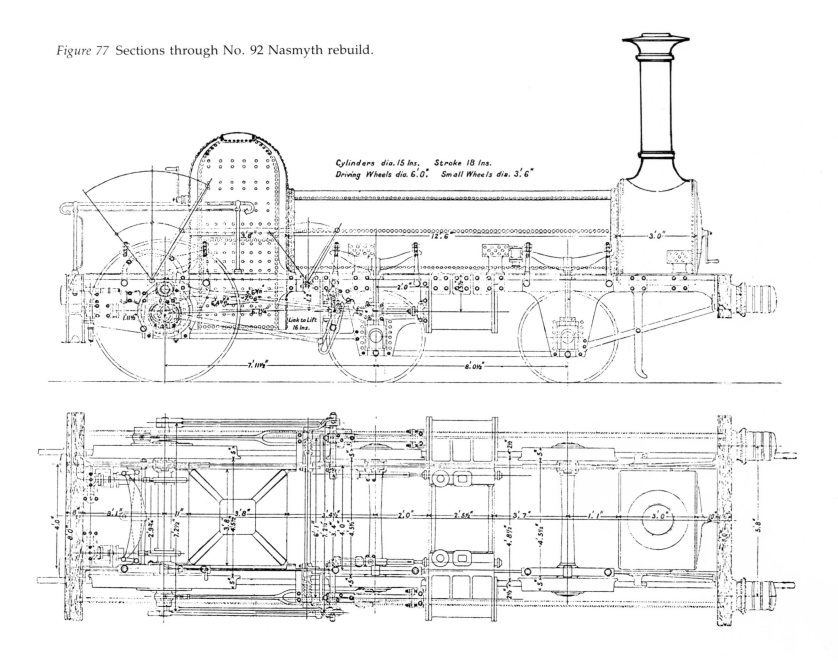

Figure 77 Sections through No. 92 Nasmyth rebuild.

Cylinders dia. 15 Ins.   Stroke 18 Ins.
Driving Wheels dia. 6'.0".   Small Wheels dia. 3'.6"

Plate 10 No. 29 Echo class 4–4–0 (formerly *Flora*).

This is just a random selection of photographs from many sources, to show some of the very many degrees of rebuild carried out over the years on some of the locomotives we have discussed in detail. To cover all the permutations would take another book, and so this is just a selection.

Plate 11 4–4–0 Echo class, locomotive *Echo*.

Plate 12 A later version of the Echo class 4–4–0 is seen here as No. 27.

Plate 13 Tiger class 2–4–0 *Jackall.*

Plate 14 Tiger class *Xanthus* in 1868, as a 2–4–0

Plate 15 Locomotive *Sondes* as a 2–4–0

Plate 16 Sondes class 2–4–0T No. 523 (previously *Chatham*

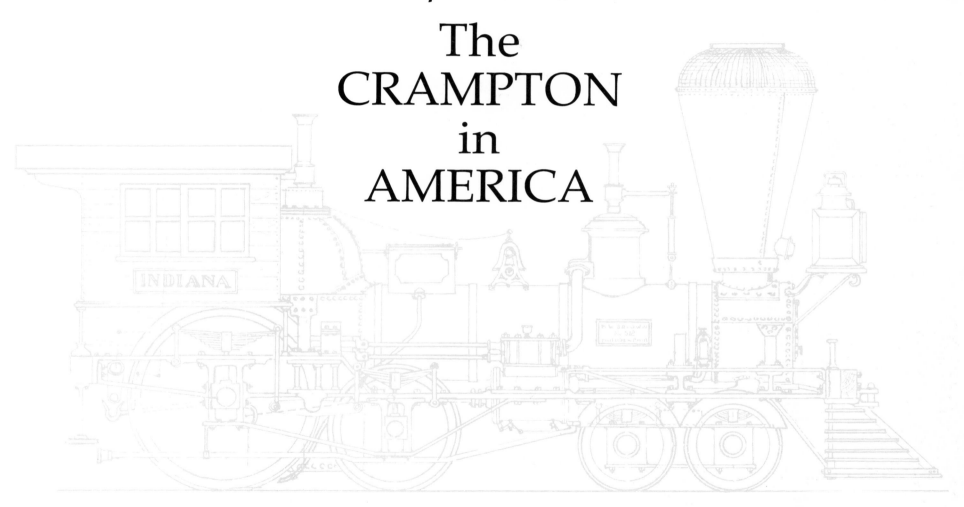

Chapter Three

The
CRAMPTON
in
AMERICA

Chapter Index

By and large America was just not Crampton country. In the 1850s, when the Crampton was making its European impact, transatlantic train tonnage had already passed the Crampton limit. Conversely, the casual American trackage was not equal to the speed potential of the stern wheelers. Finally, the stability of the Crampton chassis, which made it so attractive to French engineers, was if anything inferior to that of the American standard 4-2-2, as offered by Baldwin and Norris. The development of a flexible stable carriage for the sinuous undulations of the early American engineers to the locomotive art in its early years. The American standard 4-2-0, with a light bar frame, Bury firebox and leading bogie, rode as well as any Crampton ever could, while having adequate adhesion into the bargain. In the Norris engines this was obtained by placing the driving axle ahead of the firebox. Baldwin, preferring the longer wheelbase,

placed his driving axle in the Crampton location and made good the traction deficiency by arranging for the front-end weight of the tender to be carried by the driving axle; a patent which has been used very successfully in all of the Crampton models built so far!

The diagrams of *figure 78* compare the Baldwin and Norris designs with the Crampton, and eloquently highlight the foregoing thesis. In the light of all this it may be wondered at that the Crampton ever reached America at all, but it did. From three concurrent but unrelated germinations, the Cramptons were born, reached a total population of no more than a dozen locomotives and departed early and unsung, leaving only exhilarating memories in the minds of throttle artists who, here and there, managed to get the light-footed speedsters wound up. In Britain, and in Europe there was a Crampton era, 'une Belle Epoque'. In America there was 1849—the year of the Crampton.

The Utica and Schenectady Railroad followed a water-level route between its two title towns in the Mohawk valley of upper New York State; later it was to become part of the New York Central's Chicago-bound speedway. The term 'water-level' was sinisterly significant for the U & S paralleled the famous Erie canal, which it had to fight for both bales and bodies to transport. Here was a clear case for speed, and it was this which led the railroad to acquire in 1849 a Crampton called *Lightning*. *Lightning* was designed in England under circumstances which have now gone into oblivion, though clearly stamped with the Crampton brand, she showed only detailed marks of affinity with any of the European Cramptons. She was built in Schenectady by Edward Norris (not to be confused with the famous Philadelphia Norris Co.), who followed her British blueprints to the point of absurdity, providing buffers which would buffer no other item of rolling stock on the line, and conserving a feeble little running

Railroad	Name or Number	BuilderS	Date Built	Works No.	Cylinders		Wheels		Wheelbase	Shape	Boiler Details			Heating Surface			Remarks
					Stroke	Bore	Driving	Carrying			Size	Tube Dia.	Length	Firebox	Boiler	Total	
Utica & Schenectady	Lightning	E. Norris	1849		22" 558	16" 406	7' 2070	48"+40" 1180 985	3'9"+6'9"+6'4"	Round							
Vermont Central Railroad	Governor Paine	Baldwin	1849				6'6"	36"+47"	3'4"+7'4"+5'6"	„							Missing details left
Pennsylvania	3 Locos	Baldwin	1849				6'0"	36"+47"	3'4"+7'4"+5'6"	„							blank where not
Hudson River	Susquehanna	Baldwin	1849				6'0"	36"+47"	3'4"+7'4"+5'6"	„							known.
Camden & Amboy	John Stevens	R. Norris & Sons	1849		34" 864	13" 330	8' 2440	3' 914	3'3"+3'3"+3'3"+ 10'9"	„	3'2" 965	2" 51	12' 3658			1504	

lantern and flimsy guard irons, both inappropriate to the conditions of the American Railroad. *Lightning* was a 2-2-2-0, a little like *Liverpool* but without the latter's massiveness. The locomotive's two front axles were combined in a rudimentary bogie with minimal radial freedom, but fully equalised fore and aft. Her spidery 7 ft drivers (the first solid forged wheels used in America) were equalised with the rear carrying wheels, provision being made for moving the equaliser fulcrum pins so that the load on the drivers could be preselected.

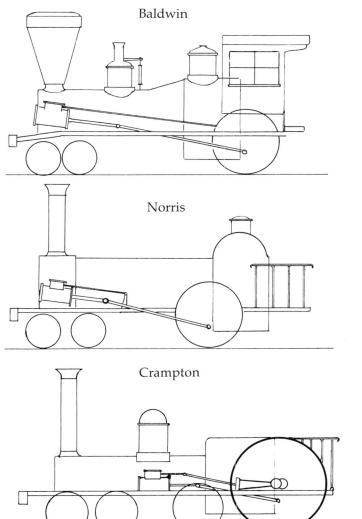

Baldwin

Norris

Crampton

Figure 78

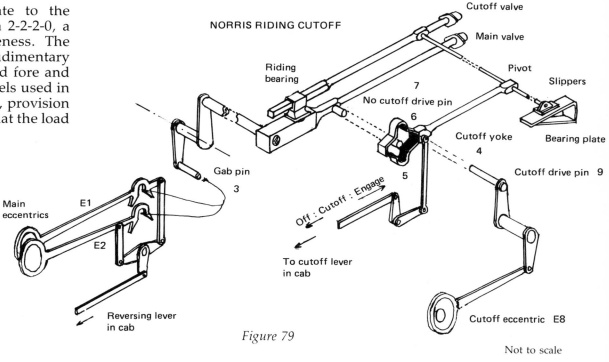

NORRIS RIDING CUTOFF

Cutoff valve

Main valve

Riding bearing

Pivot

Slippers

7

No cutoff drive pin

6

Cutoff yoke

4

Bearing plate

Gab pin
3

5

Cutoff drive pin 9

Main eccentrics

E1

E2

Off : Cutoff : Engage

To cutoff lever in cab

Reversing lever in cab

Cutoff eccentric E8

Figure 79

Not to scale

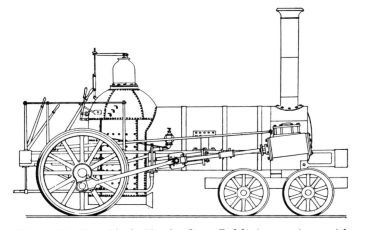

Figure 80 The *Black Hawk*, first Baldwin engine with outside cylinders. Built for the Philadelphia & Trenton Railroad by Baldwin in 1835.

49

Figure 81

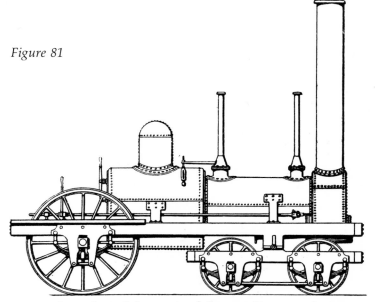

The mere fact that this sort of ingenuity was incorporated suggests some apprehension regarding hauling capacity! Of the total weight of 20 tons, no more than 7 tons was carried on the driving wheels. Although *Lightning* looked like a double frame engine, her outer frames were little more than footwalks—the only bearings they carried were light-duty thrust blocks for the return crank pins. The engine had full Gooch fixed-link motion, and in this respect must have been one of the earliest engines so fitted to run on the far side of the Atlantic. As will be mentioned later, America was very late in adopting the link motion, and the fact that the reversing lever quadrant on *Lightning* carries only three notches suggests that even here there was no intention of using the Gooch gear for expansive working. This, and other details of the same kind, suggests some American influence in *Lightning's* British design.

In service *Lightning* occasionally lived up to her name; on one occasion she is reported to have run sixteen miles at 68 mph with eight cars in tow. When one considers that this means eight heavy timber and truss rod bogie vehicles, the hauling capacity is reasonably creditable—but by 1850 American train weights had passed this level and, as a puller, *Lightning* was woefully inadequate. After only a year she was withdrawn, and no more was heard of her. The locomotive is believed to have been rebuilt as a 4-4-0. The drawing of *Lightning* (*figure 82*) shows her with a six wheel tender of the standard type turned out by her short

lived maker, and is almost certainly what she would have hauled on the U & S. Railway.

Model builders are often cursed by the fact that the tender is the most poorly documented of all railway vehicles, and in this book we have tried wherever possible to rectify this omission, feeling that an authentic reconstruction drawing is infinitely preferable to nothing.

Lightning was a Crampton's Crampton. The next group of engines to be discussed may well have seen light of day had Thomas Russell never existed. They were Cramptons by identification, but whether or not the 'master' provided even inspiration for them is a matter for conjecture. What happened was this: Governor Paine, president of the newly built Vermont Central Railroad, decided out of the blue that his railroad needed a high speed passenger service. Accordingly, in 1848, he approached Matthias Baldwin with an offer of $10,000 for a locomotive capable of operating at 60 mph. The going price of a Baldwin engine at that time was around $6,000, which may have been a factor in the canny watchmaker's acceptance. Anyhow, in 1849 there rolled out of Philadelphia a 4-2-2-0 with 78 inch drivers, protected up to the spark arrester by Baldwin patents, and called (not unpredictably) *Governor Paine* (*figure 83*). This engine, regardless of its origins, had all the required features of a classic Crampton—ergo, it *was* a Crampton. The wheel diameter, though fairly commonplace by English standards, was large for America, where 56″ was typical of express power.

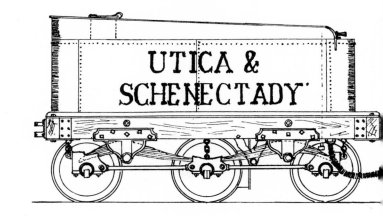

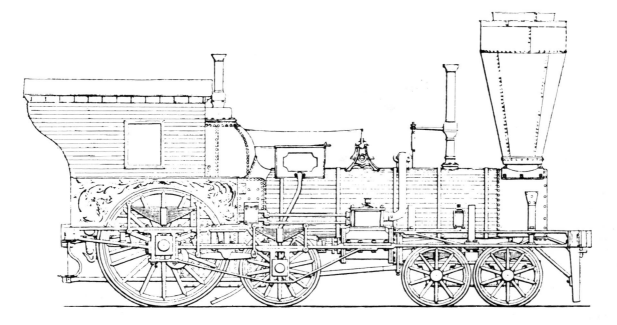

Figure 83

Figure 82

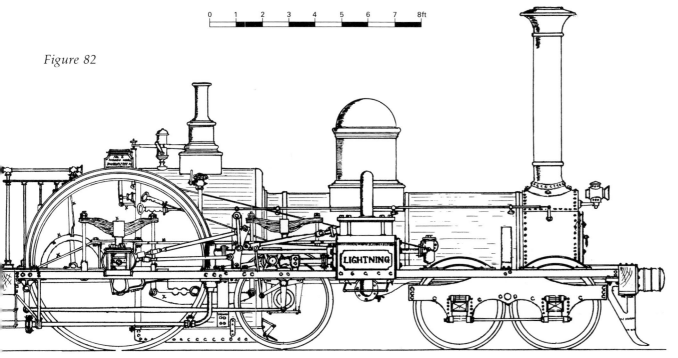

Baldwin immediately put the new type in his catalogue (classified as an 'A' type built to special order only), and got orders for four more. Three of these were for the Pennsylvania Railroad with drivers of only 72 inches, called *Miffin*, *Blair* and *Indiana*. The fourth, *Susquehanna* of the Hudson River Railroad, was almost identical.

Figure 84 shows *Indiana*. The engine has outside bar frames carrying driving and rear carrying axleboxes, the front of the engine is carried on a four wheel bogie. Variable loading equalisation is provided between the driving and rear carrying axles, but while *Lightning* achieved this by permitting the fulcrum pin to be inserted in one of several different positions, on *Indiana* a sliding fulcrum block was provided. Operation of the device allowed the adhesive weight to be varied between 7 and 12 tons out of a total weight of about 24 tons.

Note Items marked 'X' are behind the wheels; there are *no* guard sheets on inside of driving wheel splashers.

Indiana had inside motion using the patented Baldwin 'half crank' axle (*figure 85*) in which the outer crank web was formed by the wheel itself. This device permitted the connecting rods to be spaced widely enough to embrace the firebox, and was a feature of Baldwin practice for many years. Also of interest was that strange American abberation called the 'riding cut-off'. Normal foreward and reverse operation was provided by gab gear giving a fixed cut off of about 70%, and actuated by one or two eccentrics each side. Above the normal valve in the valve chest, 'riding' on it in fact, was an auxiliary valve which could take motion from a separate eccentric giving a lower cut-off of usually 40-50%, or could be immobilised by dropping its drive pin into a slotted bracket on the firebox side. This curious device persisted for many years in the United States, long after link motion had become widespread in the Old World. The drawing of *Indiana* (*figure 84*) was prepared from a document incorporating some degree of artistic licence, and hence full details of the gear are hidden, and a little of what is shown is speculative. This dearth of data is typical of the early years of American railroading when machines were built by private companies intent only on making a precarious 'buck', and with neither the time nor the inclination to keep the meticulous records of the European systems, much data has thereby been lost.

However, in this case the incompleteness should not deter the modeller since the working parts of the gear are in any case concealed. *Indiana* would, in fact, make a most spectacular model, with its copper firebox (iron did not come into general use until 1860) and ornate iron and brass work. Contrasting *Indiana* with its palatial cab, sanding gear, and iron lagged boiler with the antique quaintness of *Lightning*, it is difficult to believe they were both designed in the same year. *Indiana's* tender, with a bogie and fixed axle, is of the type used by Baldwin in connection with the scheme earlier referred to—for transferring part of the tender weight on to the driving axle.

Of these Baldwin Cramptons in service, there are the same flashes of speed, and the same load shyness to report. *Governor Paine* was stated to have run a mile in 43 seconds, but was rebuilt as a 4-4-0 after only three years, and similar tales are told of the Pennsylvania Railroad engines, one of which is said to have hauled a Presidential special at a 60 mph start to stop average, but they too were converted!

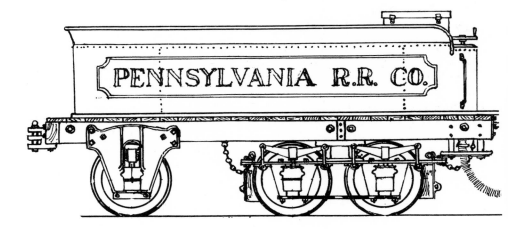

Crampton's Crampton—Baldwin's Crampton—and finally, Steven's Crampton. The Camden and Amboy Railroad in New Jersey stands in the annals of American railroading much as the Stockton and Darlington does in Britain. It was the Camden and Amboy which imported the legendary John Bull from England, to be assembled by a young man named Isaac Dripps who, in spite of having never seen a steam locomotive before, not only assembled the machine and ran it, but made several important modifications which became the basis of the locomotive art in America. Robert Stevens, President of the Camden and Amboy, visited England in 1845 and saw Cramptons at work. Much impressed, he returned to America and in collaboration with Dripps set out to design a Crampton of his own. The result gave the American continent the largest pair of wheels ever to roll thereon, along with what was probably the most 'inaesthetic' silhouette! This horror was called the *John Stevens, figure 87,* No. 28, twenty-five tons of it with eight foot driving wheels running

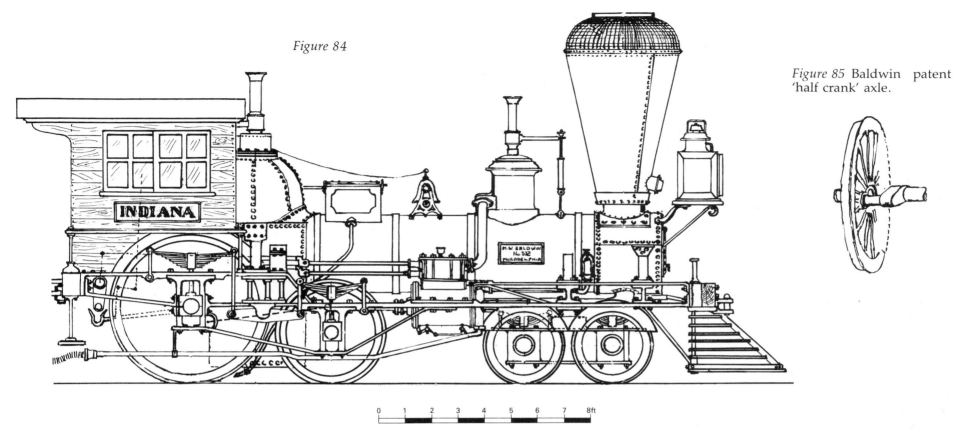

Figure 84

Figure 85 Baldwin patent 'half crank' axle.

INDIANA

0 1 2 3 4 5 6 7 8ft

on the so called 'wide' gauge of 4' 10". No. 28 was a 6-2-0 with massive timber flitched inside bar frames, an anthracite burning firebox whose taper top came right down to driving axle level, and which was fired from a low slung pit which imprisoned the fireman between the drivers while he shovelled coal under the axle into the firedoor. As for the driver, he rode high and proud atop the firebox in a sort of 'howdah' with a promenade deck extending foreward along the top of the very low slung boiler. Even his lofty perch was dwarfed by the great smokestack with its cinder clearing vents sticking out like carbuncles. The safety valves, too, had long extension pipes to raise their outlets clear of the driver's vision. The wrought iron wheels had the spaces between spokes filled in with timber blocks, giving a curiously massive appearance; the connecting rod was trussed, and the valve had the Norris Bros. version of the sliding cut-off, and which is described in *figure 79* at the beginning of this chapter.

Norris Bros. turned out No. 28 in April 1849, the railroad world was not *too* stunned being well conditioned to the Stevens-Dripps team. Both had considerable marine engineering experience which they were fond of adopting for railroad use, both were innovators in the John Craven sense, and neither was plagued by any preconceived ideas as to what a locomotive should look like. But, however different she looked, No. 28 had one trait in common with her breed—she could not pull! The practical Dripps saw to the heart of the problem immediately, but Stevens (shades of Francis Webb) overruled him, though some had the wheel diameter reduced to seven feet. The drawing *figure 86* shows one of the early follow ups. No. 30, with detail differences in framing and boiler mountings to re-distribute the weight rearwards, but still with eight foot driving wheels. The open cab of No. 28 has been replaced by an all weather model, and the woodwork is completed by a standard C & A tender-cum-

53

Figure 86

Figure 87

0 1 2 3 4 5 6 7 8ft

JOHN STEVENS

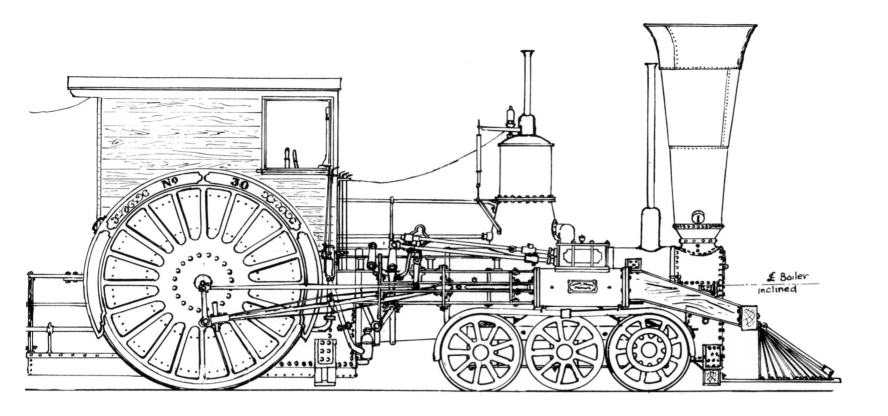

E Boiler
inclined

dosshouse! These engines, in addition to their other traits, were not too particular about staying on the track and derailments were a fairly routine happening in early iron-horse America. They were rebuilt as 4-4-0s within a few years, and in its later form one of them survived until 1865, and, since that shape tends to grow on you, think what a beautiful model could be made of No. 30!

Figure 79 shows a sketch of No. 30's valve gear. Two eccentrics (E1 and E2) inside the driving wheels operate their respective forked rods. The main valve is operated by whichever of the forks or gabs dropped over the gab pin 3 (note that the various elements of the gear have been separated laterally to avoid confusion). Above the main valve is the cut-off valve, capable of independent motion. What the cut-off valve actually does is determined by the position of the pivoted cut-off yoke, with its characteristic closed double gab end. For non-expansive working the cut-off lever is pulled back to the 'off' position, this raises yoke 4 allowing its lower gab 5 to engage the 'no cut-off' drive pin 7. In this condition the cut-off valve is rigidly tied to the main valve, the pair functioning as a single non-expansive valve. For earlier cut-off a third eccentric E8 (in No. 30 this is actually an outside return crank) drives the cut-off drive pin 9, whose motion can be transmitted to the cut-off valve rod by pushing the cut-off lever, allowing the upper gab 6 to engage the cut-off drive pin, and closing the cut-off valve earlier in the stroke. Whichever pin is disengaged, it rides in the open centre portion of the yoke. Note that a slipper and bearing plate is provided to support the off-set loading of the cut-off yoke arm on the cut-off valve rod.

56   *Plate 17* A magnificent photograph of the locomotive No. 30 (*figure 86*) showing the unusual weather cab and enormous chimney.

Chapter Four

The
CRAMPTON
in
FRANCE

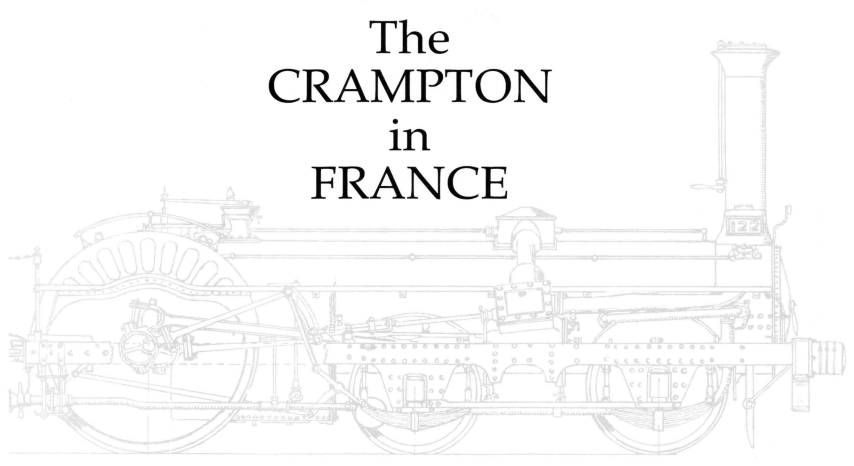

Chapter Index

Part One
Nord

Part Two
Paris, Lyon and Mediterranean

Part Three
Est

Study of the drawings throughout the book will show that they do not always agree with the figures given in the tables, which are based on *F. Gaiser's* book—**Die Crampton Locomotive of 1909**. I have up-dated these tables where possible, but it is clearly *not* possible after this passage of time to verify all of them, due to the many factors like rebuilds which affect historical recording. I offer both for your study, but my personal choice would be to believe a drawing backed up by photographic evidence if possible, *rather* than these tables. Locomotives were *often* built differently to quoted information, especially when wheels or cylinders etc. were sub contracted to other builders.

Chemin de fer	Spécification	Constructeur	Livraison date	Atelier numéro	Cylinder			Roues Secondaires			Diamètre des roues motrice	Dimensions entre roues	Chaundiène				Conduits de Chauffe			Surface de Chauffe		
					Position	Diamètre	Course	Nombre	Arrangement	Diamètres			Forme	Longueur	Diamètre	Pression de la chaundière	Nombre	Diamètre	Longueur	Foyer	Conduits	Total
Ch. d. f. du Nord	122–133	J.F. Cail & Cie., Paris	1849	139–150	zwh	400	550	2	fest	1348 u. 1217	2100	2300+2560=4860	zyl.	1438	1200	6,5	177	50	3615	6,4	92,0	98,4
do.	134–145	do.	1853	—	„	420	560	2	„	1348 u. 1217	2300	2184+2316=4500	„	1605	1279	7,5	180	50	3460	6,1	89,53	95,6
do.	146–161	do.	1855	—	„	420	550	2	„	1348 u. 1217	2100	2360+2570=4890	„	1585	1215	7,5	173	50	3615	6,4	89,9	96,3
do.	162, 163	—	—	—	„	420	550	3	„	1217	2100	1452+1980+1892=5324	Doppel-Kessel	—	—	8	173	50	3657	8,0	91,4	116,3
do.	165–170	Cail & Cie., Paris	1859	—	„	420	550	2	„	1349 u. 1217	2100	2320+2435=4755	zyl.	1585	1215	7,5	167	50	3617	6,15	86,83	92,9
do.	1–12	do.	1859	691–702	„	420	550	2	„	1349 u. 1217	2100	2320+2435=4755	„	1585	1215	7,5	167	50	3617	6,15	86,83	92,9
Ch. d. f. de l'Est	79–90	do.	1852	186–197	„	400	560	2	„	1350 u. 1210	2300	2184+2316=4500	„	1605	1266	8	180	48,75	3460	6,61	90,74	97,3
do.	174–188	Schneider & Cie., Creusot	1855	196–210	„	400	560	2	„	1350 u. 1210	2300	2184+2316=4500	„	1605	1266	8	180	48,75	3460	6,61	90,74	97,3
do.	79–90, 174–188 Umbau	Ateliers d'Epernay	ab 1881	—	„	400	560	2	„	1380 u. 1220	2310	2184+2316=4500	„	1605	1266	9	168	48,75	3458	6,49	84,64	91,1
do.	601–3, 605–12 Umbau	do.	—	—	„	400	600	2	„	1380 u. 1220	2100	2284+2316=4600	„	1605	1266	9	168	48,75	3458	6,49	84,64	91,1
do.	604 Umbau	do.	—	—	„	400	600	2	„	1380 u. 1220	2110	2284+2316=4600	Flaman	1760	1168 u. 780	11	304	40	3100	9,72	111,44	121,1
Paris-Lyon-Méditerranée	1–18	Cail & Cie., Paris	1854	—	„	400	600	2	„	1340 u. 1200	2100	2284+2316=4600	zyl.	1605	1266	7,5	180	50	3460	6,45	90,00	96,4
do.	49–30	do.	1857	—	„	400	600	2	„	1340 u. 1200	2100	2284+2316=4600	„	1605	1266	7,5	180	50	3460	6,45	90,00	96,4
do.	31–40	A. Koechlin & Cie., Mulhouse	1864	820–829	„	400	600	2	„	1360 u. 1220	2100	2284+2316=4600	„	1605	1230	8	180	50	3400	7,1	90,00	97,1

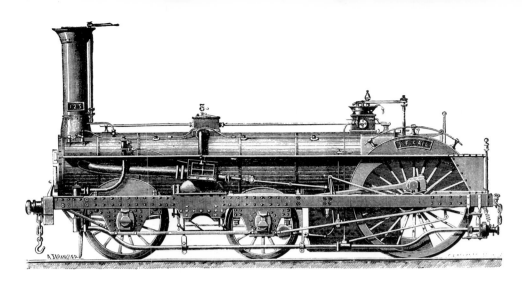

Plate 17a A fine side view of a Flaman-boilered rebuilt locomotive.

Surface de grille	Poids àride	Masse totale en order de marche	Masse d'adhérence	Effort de Traction	
				Cylindre	Maximum
1,424	25,9	28,9	12,6	1770	2520
1,286	26,6	29,8	12,6	2093	2520
1,453	27,5	30,6	12,6	2252	2520
1,409	29,2 / 28,0	32,2 / 31,1	12,6	2402	2520
1,305	25,9	29,1	12,6	2252	2520
1,305	25,9	29,1	12,6	2252	2520
1,3	28,432	31,285	13,24	2026	2648
1,3	28,432	31,285	13,24	2026	2648
1,22	30,1	32,93	13,46	2269	2692
1,22	31,6	34,4	13,74	2674	2748
1,72	39,3	43,7	16,4	3253	3280
1,28	26,14	29,09	12,0	2229	2400
1,28	26,14	29,09	12,0	2229	2400
1,24	27,0	30,2	12,0	2377	2400

59

Part One
Nord

J. F. Cail & Cie
Series Nos. 122–133, 134–145,
146–161, 162–163, 165–170, 1–12

The old paysanterie on the synonymity of 'prendre la Crampton' and 'take the train' has been flogged to death in a hundred otherwise decontextised references to the Crampton era in France, and the only reason for repeating it here is that it does summarise the extent to which the Crampton took hold of the Gallic imagination. A century later the Crampton name still ingered as a qualifying adjective for a dozen bits of steam locomotive hardware. While Britannia flirted inconsummately with Thomas Russell, Marianne across the water took him to her generous heart, for practical reasons not difficult to see. Early Frenche development, strongly influenced by Stephenson, favoured the long boiler design both for passenger and freight locomotives. It had excellent adhesion combined with a short wheelbase. But while in America speeds were low because of casual track, sharp curves and heavy trains, in France they were low because the long boiler could not run fast without violent and damaging oscillation. Thus a French express was never an express by English standards, and the French rapide, destined in due course to become the fastest thing on rails, needed a fast stable engine to bring it into being—enter the Crampton.

On a March day in 1849, France's first Crampton, No. 122 (*figure 88*) of the Nord, ushered in the era by taking a test train out of the Gare du Nord to arrive in Calais exactly five hours later, having reached 62.5 mph across the dripping water meadows of the Somme. The performance was even more notable when one takes account of the fact that, at that time, the route was via Lille, considerably longer than the Golden Arrow route. So the Nord ran the first rapide, acquiring a speed pre-eminence it was to maintain until the advent of main line electrification.

Like all imports, the Crampton never became truly French, never acquired that indefinable quelquechose that hallmarked the French steam. *Lison*, panting below the high facades and low skies of the Rue de Rome, was not—could never have been—a

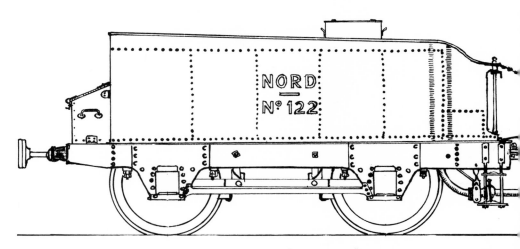

Crampton; literary immortality was not for Thomas. But the fact remains that for well over a generation the fastest trains on three of France's seven great railways were Crampton hauled, and today it is only in France that they can find a Crampton to spew briquette smoke over a centennial celebration.

But back to 1849! No. 122 came out of the Paris works of Ch. Derosne & Cail, the brain child of M. Houel, their chief engineer. He did a better job than he knew, not only were Nord 122-133 the sleekest, most aesthetic Cramptons ever built, but their steam circuit proportions were not to be improved upon until Andre Chapelon rebuilt No. 3566—eighty years later! No. 122 had 83" driving wheels, flush riveted double frames, long high footboards, and a boiler whose lagging extended smooth level, and sparkling apple green from smokebox lamp iron to firebox backhead, and the sleekness was not illusory. Trains of four wheelers in the same light green as the locomotive blazoned with letters of gold-bronze, and weighing no more than 100 tons were whisked away to the black country of Artois at 47.5 mph start-to-stop speeds. In 1850 there was an unofficial but credible report that a Nord Crampton, running light, had attained 93.8 mph!

The Nord, entranced, went back for more, and Cail delivered

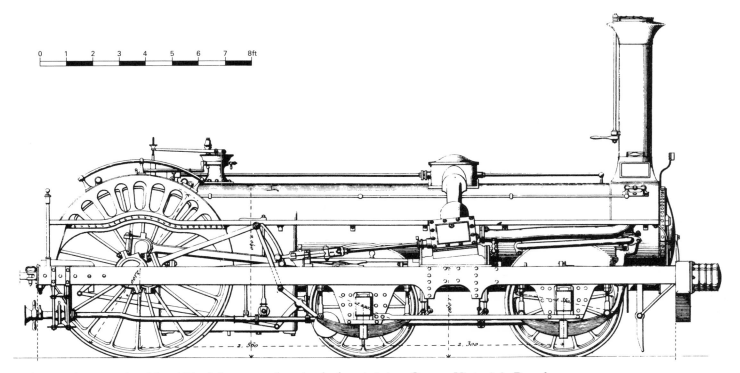

0 1 2 3 4 5 6 7 8ft

MAIN DIMENSIONS
Series 122–133
Driving Wheels 6′ 11″
Carrying Wheels 4′ 5″ + 4′ 0″
Wheelbase 7′ 9″ + 8′ 6″
Cylinders 16″ × 22″
Tender Wheels 4′ 0″

Figure 88

Plate 18 Locomotive No. 137 of the second series before joining Queen Victoria's Royal Train, as seen in *plate 19*.

Figure 89

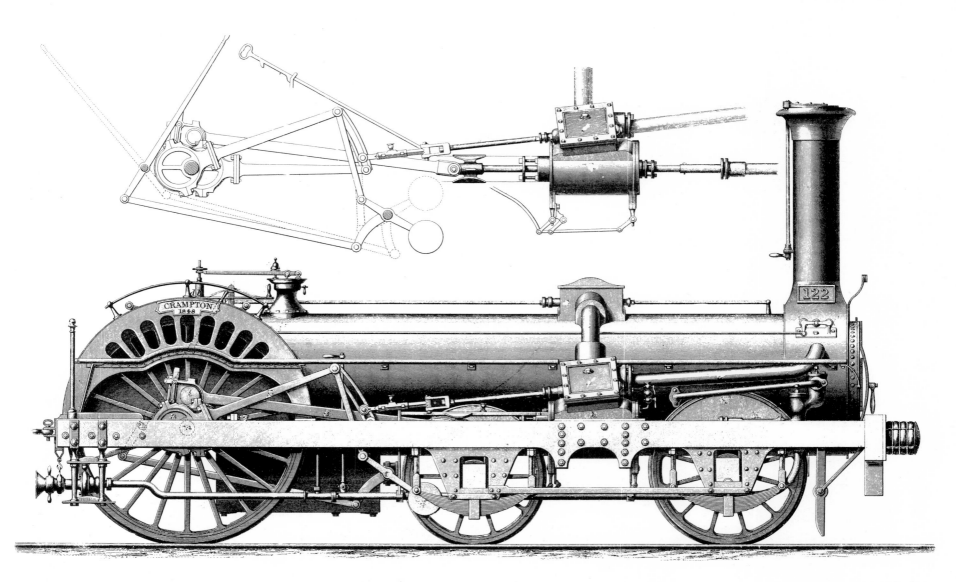

Not to Scale

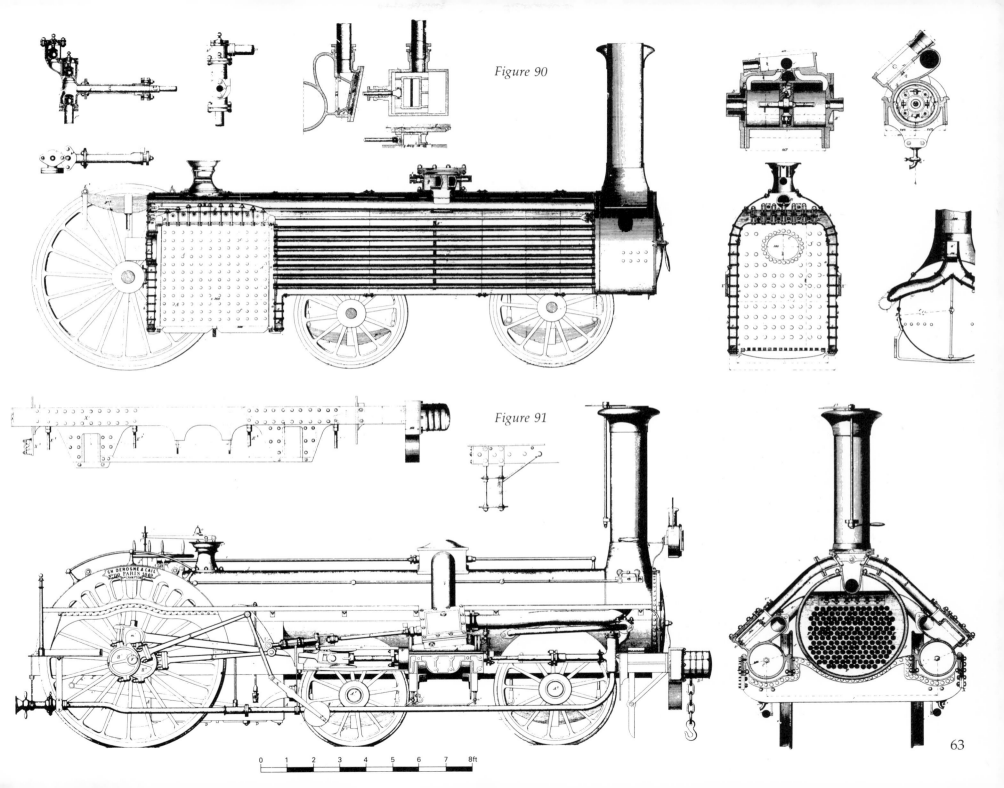

Figure 90

Figure 91

63

Plate 19 The complete Royal Train.

batch two, Nos. 134-145 (*plate 18*) around 1853. The recipe was nearly the same, except for the bigger wheels increased to 91″. One of this batch as illustrated in *plate 19*, had the honour of drawing Queen Victoria's royal train on the occasion of her visit to France in 1855. By then, Napoleon had authorised the Nord Cramptons to run in regular service at the unprecedented speed of 75 mph.

1855 saw the third batch of Nord Cramptons, Nos. 146-161, take to the rails. These were built to more powerful specifications laid down by Jules Petiet, Nord's chief mechanical engineer, but were a little less graceful. The circular smoke box door was replaced by a baker's oven job, and the attractive but hazardous splasher slots were filled in. The boiler was bigger and higher pitched, and the chimney shorter, and the outside frames bristled with engineering acne. It could of course have been worse, Petiet in his time has been responsible for some real visual horrors. This batch had the wheels reduced back to the original 83″, a figure which was to remain for all succeeding batches. The builder was the same company, though by now M. le Chevalier Derosne had

Plate 20 Later 1859 Series 1 to 1

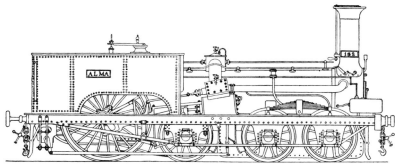

Figure 92

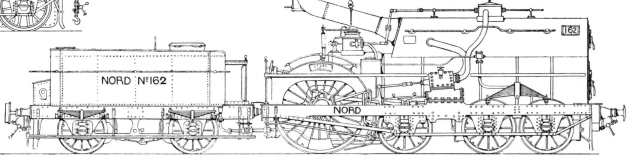

Figure 93 Locomotive No. 162 *Alma*, one of two tank locomotives built in 1855, shown as converted to M. Petiet's steam drying apparatus which was a rather primitive low temperature superheater. They were both withdrawn and scrapped in 1873.

Plate 21

left, and the firm was just Jean-Francois Cail et Cie. In 1856 came an isolated twosome, Nos. 162 (*figures 92* and *93, plate 21*) and 163, heralding a double batch in 1859. These last of the Nord Cramptons, Nos. 1 to 12 inclusive and Nos. 165 to 170 , were again constructed marginally bigger, and from 1859 until 1870, when heavier loads forced the adoption of coupled wheels for express power, the whole north-east corner of France was undisputed Crampton country. Even as late as 1895 you could still get a Crampton, with an iron scroll work cab frame and a Smith ejector atop the firebox, hauling your local through that dreary industrial Lille conurbia.

Figure 94 No. 167 in the locomotive's later years, with the iron scroll cab frame.

Part Two

Paris, Lyon and Mediterranean

Cail & Cie
   Series Nos. 1–18 and 19–30

A. Koechlin & Cie
   Series Nos. 31–40

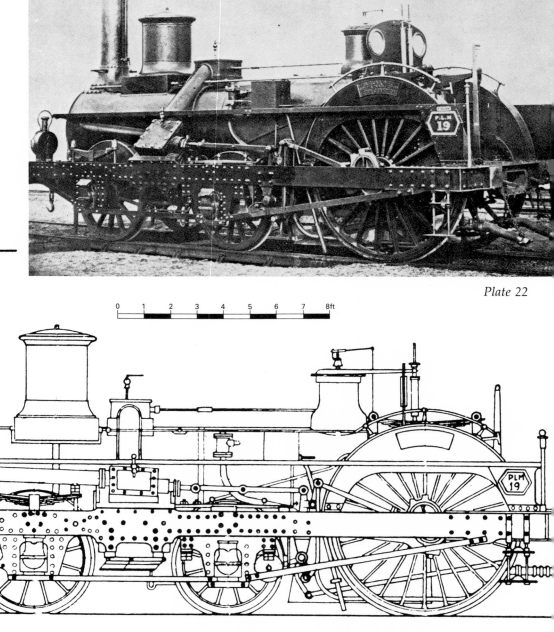

Plate 22

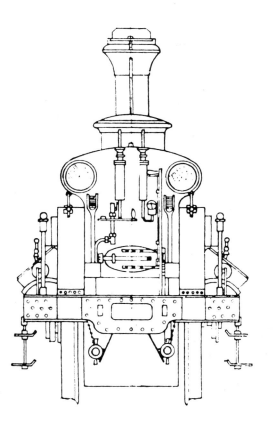

0 1 2 3 4 5 6 7 8ft

Figure 95 No.19 of the second series from Cail of 1857.

As it was in the North, so it became in the South. The Chemin de Fer de Paris à Lyon et à la Méditerranée, to give the proud PLM its full title, came into corporate being as the possessor of forty seven-footers from the Cail Company. They were built in 1853-4 (Nos. 1 to 18) (*figure 96*) and 1857 (Nos. 19-30) (*figure 95*), and differed from the Nord breed mainly in the provision of generously domed boilers. In 1864 came a third batch (Nos. 31 to 40) (*plate 23*), but this time a new name appears on the roll of Crampton builders. This was Andre Koechlin of Mulhouse, the firm that in later years was to become the giant Societe Alsacienne de Constructions Mechaniques. The PLM diagram book of 1868 showed all forty still in existence with cabs and chimneys of pure PLM design. A PLM Crampton, brass bound in olive green, hauling a train of green, brown and yellow four-wheelers down the polychrome Rhone valley, must indeed have been a memorable sight. Mireio could have taken a Crampton across the Crau, and saved herself one hell of a hike; Alphonse Daudet probably did, and the Emperor Napoleon certainly did, his seven-ton two-saloon minitrain was Crampton-hauled from Marseille to Paris at 62 mph overall, and Crampton obtained a Legion d'Honneur

Paris, Lyon and Mediterranean Railway Names

No. 19 *La France*	No. 20 *L'Angleterre*
No. 21 *L'Ecosse*	No. 22 *La Belgique*
No. 23 *La Hollande*	No. 24 *La Norvege*
No. 25 *Le Danemark*	No. 26 *La Russie*
No. 27 *L'Espagne*	No. 28 *Le Portugal*
No. 29 *L'Italie*	No. 30 *La Grece*

These names were removed some time after transfer to C. F. de l'Est, 1869.

MAIN DIMENSIONS
Driving Wheels 6' 11"
Carrying Wheels 4' 5" + 4' 0"
Wheelbase 7' 3" + 7' 6"
Cylinders 16" × 21"
Tender Wheels 4' 0"

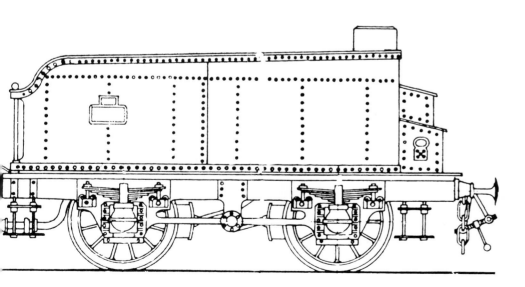

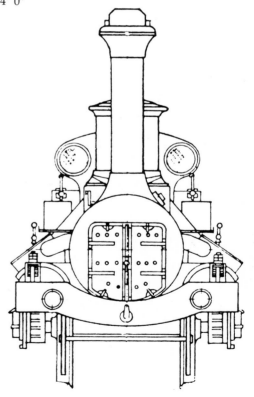

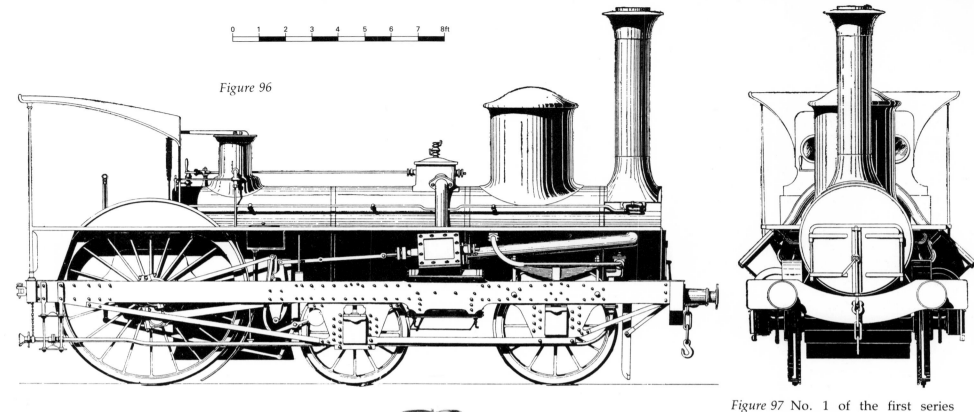

Figure 96

Figure 97 No. 1 of the first series Nos. 1–18, built by Cail in 1853–4.

Plate 23 A side view of PLM No. 40.

ribbon for his button hole. The performance, which reputedly occurred in 1855, is even more remarkable in view of the fact that in that year there was no through rail connection between Paris and Marseille, and the reported date probably anticipates the event by some years. There is, however, no doubt that it did happen. Be that as it may, the Crampton did not haul the PLM prestige trains for as long as they did on the Nord. For one thing, the Ligne Imperiale pioneered bogie stock and its trains got heavier faster; furthermore, there were some cruelly graded stretches of main line; hence the switch to coupled power as early as 1866.

This very pretty series of only three engines was built for the Paris-Lyon or Medietteranian Railway by the Cavé company in 1856. They were only intended for the lightest of duties, weighing only 22 tons in working order, 4.87 tons of this being made up of some 560 gallons of water and 1.3 tons of fuel. The valve gear is a modified form of Stephenson with the eccentrics mounted on return cranks. The well-tank between the frames supplied its contents to the boiler via the feedwater pumps which are driven by extension shafts through the cylinder head covers and on the cylinder centre line. Most of her features are obvious from the drawing (*figure 98*), as are the quite marked differences from the patent drawing on *page 8*, and the Egyptian model on *page 116*!

Figure 98

MAIN DIMENSIONS

Driving Wheels 6' 6"
Carrying Wheels 3' 6"
Wheelbase 10' 10"
Cylinders 12½" × 20"

Part Three
Est

Cail & Cie
   Series Nos. 79–90

Schneider & Cie
   Series Nos. 174–188

Ateliers d'Epernay
   Series Nos. 601–603, 605–612, 604

Plate 24 Locomotive No. 80 *Le Continent.*

Last, the greatest of the Crampton lines, in dedication if not in numbers, was the Chemin de Fer l'Est. In 1852 this line, then still the Paris-Strasbourg Railway, took delivery of a dozen splendid Cail eight-footers. To one of them—No. 80 (*figures 99* and *100*)—fell the distinction of hauling the first Paris-Strasbourg rapide. No. 80 was—no, is—a regal looking engine, long like *Liverpool* but without the latter's tubbiness. The oval section boiler that characterised many English and German Cramptons did not appear on the French variety. French engineers early made an exact science of balancing and suspension resulting in all their know-how going into No. 80 chassis. The result was an engine that ran like the wind and rode like an Imperial salon. It was not only in stability that her meticulous balancing paid off, for the tendency of unbalanced drivers to lift cyclically from the rails was also traction reducing and its elimination, plus the unsprung weight of large eight-foot drivers, made the Est Cramptons better haulers than most. No. 80 and her eleven kin cost the Est Railway Co. 52,000 gold francs apiece; in 1856 the Est was buying its second lot, fifteen engines Nos. 174-188, from the great le Cruesot arms plant. These not only cost more, but were sold at so much per kilogramme!

The EST truly loved its Cramptons and gave them fine heroic names—*Le Continent, Le Globe* (plate 26, *figures 102* and *103*) and *Balaclava*. More than the other French lines, EST modernised and upgraded its Cramptons in 1881 by fitting cabs, domed boilers, and sprung buffers, and then air brakes and spring sanding gear a little later. Adhesion was improved by cast iron slabs under footplates and oversize driving wheel bosses. The sleek lines disappeared under an insouciant mass of epernay piping and gadgets, but the Cramptons still headed the 'rapides' out of Paris—though by now Strasbourg was a German city, and the EST came to an end in rural frontier stops like Avricourt, where the German Elsass-Lothringen Bahn took over. On other lines four-coupled power had won the day but with Cramptons the EST pressed grimly on. When, in 1869, the PLM finally put its Cramptons out to grass, the EST bought the whole of their second batch for only 25,000 francs each, renumbered them Nos. 601-612, and worked another forty years out of them.

No. 604 of this batch, formerly PLM No. 22 *La Belgique*, was fitted-up with an experimental twin drum Flaman boiler and displayed at the great Exposition of 1889. It must surely have looked a little unaesthetic alongside such style setters as Stroud-

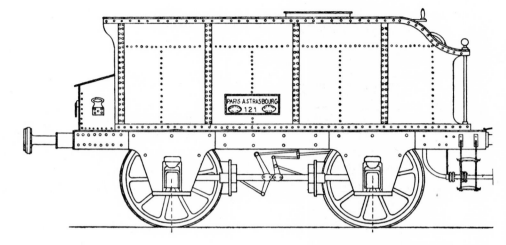

MAIN DIMENSIONS
Driving Wheels 7' 6"
Carrying Wheels 4' 6" + 4' 0"
Wheelbase 7' 2" + 7' 7"
Cylinders 16" × 22"
Tender Wheels 3' 9"

No. 79	*Le Globe*	No. 175	*Kamiesch*
No. 80	*Le Continent*	No. 176	*Balaclava*
No. 81	*Le Océan*	No. 177	*Inkermann*
No. 82	*L'Atlantique*	No. 178	*Sébastopol*
No. 83	*L'Archipel*	No. 179	*Malakov*
No. 84	*La Méditerranée*	No. 180	*Perékop*
No. 85	*La Manche*	No. 181	*Odessa*
No. 86	*La Mer Rouge*	No. 182	*Kertch*
No. 87	*L'Europe*	No. 183	*Iénikalé*
No. 88	*L'Asie*	No. 184	*Anapa*
No. 89	*L'Afrique*	No. 185	*Arabat*
No. 90	*L'Amerique*	No. 186	*Génitschi*
No. 174	*Eupatoria*	No. 187	*Marianpol*
		No. 188	*Taganroc*

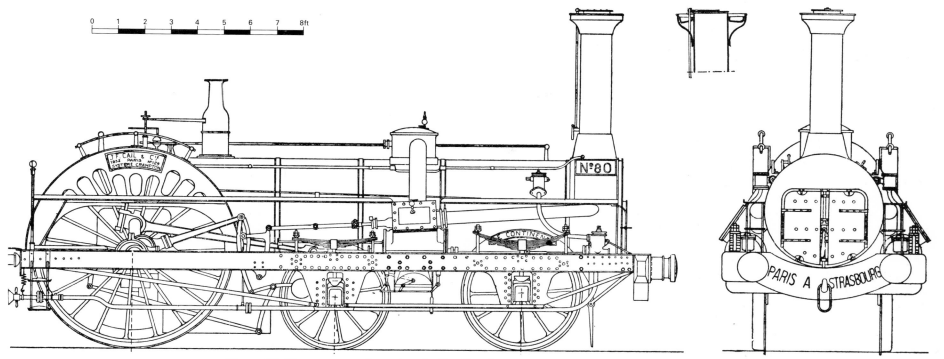

Figure 99 The preserved engine *Le Continent*.

Plate 25 A fine photograph of *Le Continent* standing at the station.

Plate 26 The first Est locomotive *Le Globe*.

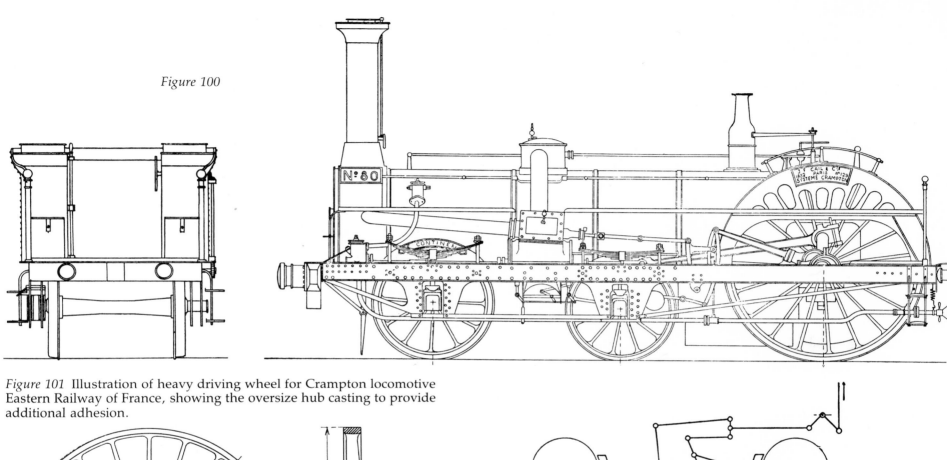

Figure 100

Figure 101 Illustration of heavy driving wheel for Crampton locomotive Eastern Railway of France, showing the oversize hub casting to provide additional adhesion.

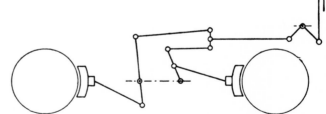

Figure 101a Showing diagrammatic layout of tender brakes.

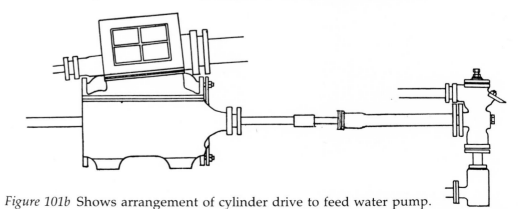

Figure 101b Shows arrangement of cylinder drive to feed water pump.

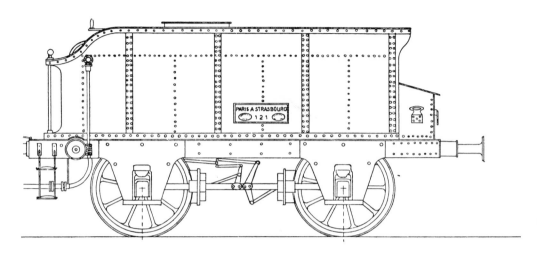

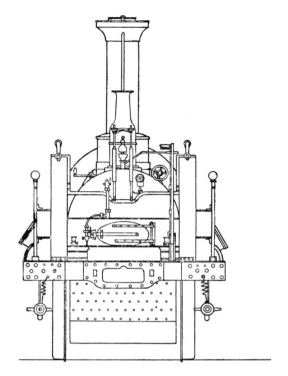

Figure 100a

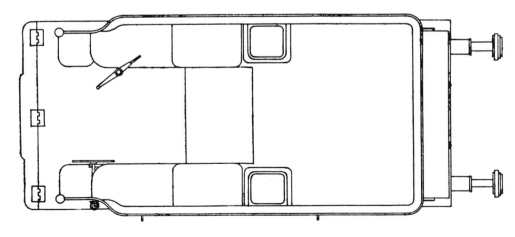

Figure 100b

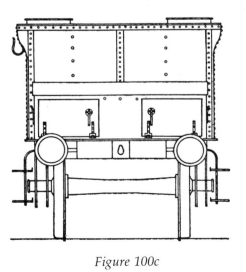

Figure 100c

Locomotive *Le Globe*

MAIN DIMENSIONS
Driving Wheels 7' 7"
Carrying Wheels 4' 6" + 4' 0"
Wheelbase 7' 2" + 7' 7"
Cylinders 16" × 22"
Tender Wheels 4' 0"

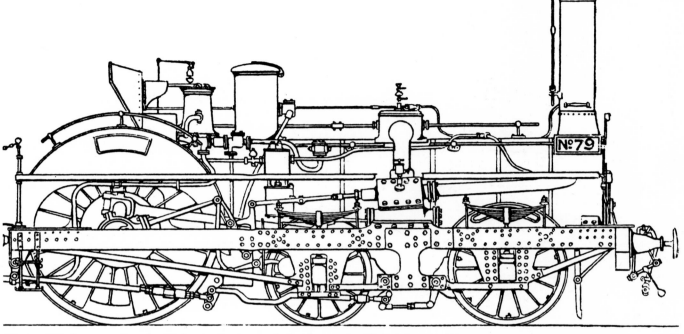

Figure 102 Locomotive *Le Globe*. A photograph is shown in *Plate 26, page 71.*

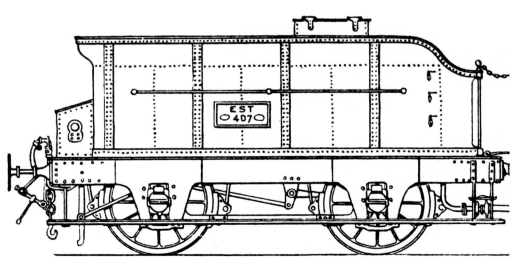

Figure 103

ley's *Edward Blount* and Midland 1853. But came the post exposition speed trials, and No. 604 showed that a Camel could be just as fleet as a racehorse. On the PLM line near Pont sur Yonne she set up a world speed record of nearly 90 mph. No. 604 was a bold experiment but, for all that, was a Crampton 'swan song'. The Flaman boiler added weight to be sure, but little of it came on the driving wheels and without tractive effort even the EST was ready by 1890 to concede that the day of the Cramptons was over. But they were an unconscionable time in dying, for when the new century came in it was still possible to journey from Paris to the great fortress terminals of the EST at Belfort, Epinal, Toul, and Verdun, and in so doing 'prendre la Crampton'.

By World War 1 they were all extinct. No. 80, hidden and half forgotten on a lonely storage track, survived. In the chronic post war motive power shortage she was again fired up, and was in service when the high iron to Strasbourg became once again French. She was definitively withdrawn from service in 1922 after having covered the astronomical mileage of one and a half million (2433298 km as the records have it). Then, lovingly restored to her

74

Figure 104 A Flaman-boilered locomotive, mentioned in Chapter Nine and also portrayed in *Plate 17a* on *page 59.*

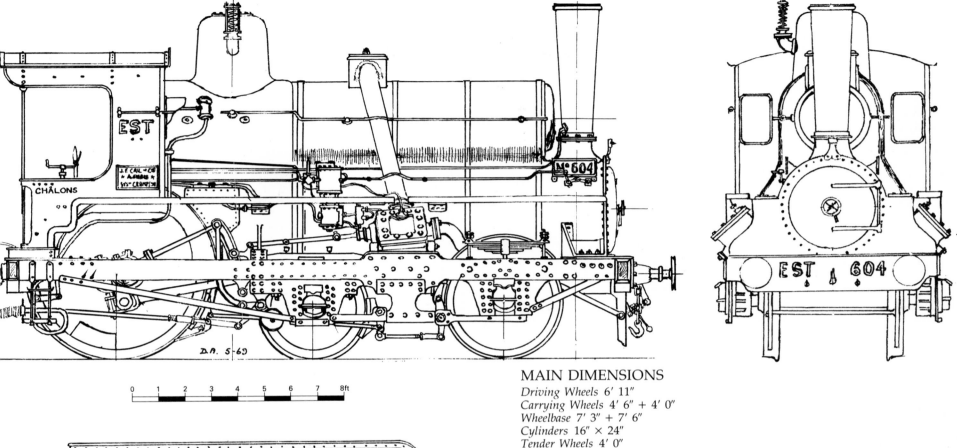

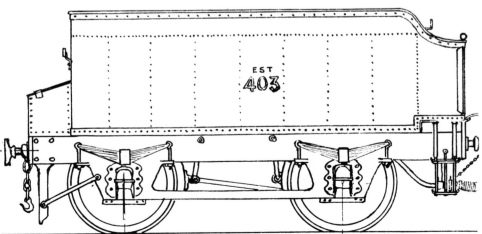

Figure 105

MAIN DIMENSIONS

Driving Wheels 6' 11"
Carrying Wheels 4' 6" + 4' 0"
Wheelbase 7' 3" + 7' 6"
Cylinders 16" × 24"
Tender Wheels 4' 0"

original appearance, she sat proud on a plinth in the Gare de l'Est from 1931 to 1946. Then, back to Epernay, where this time they rebuilt her innards also, enabling the locomotive to go to Switzerland in 1947 for their Railway Centennial, under her own steam. In 1952 she hauled her own centennial train to Strasbourg, and now, after several years of live appearances, but still capable of steaming, she sits in honoured retirement in that vast museum roundhouse at Mulhouse-Nord.

Nord, PLM, Est . . . Almost, but not quite the Crampton story. This chapter is no more than a vignette (peripherally hazy, as vignettes are) of the events and locomotives that made France the premier Crampton country (in spite of Germany's greater numbers) and of J. F. Cail, the Crampton master builder.

There are odd Crampton fringes, like the two Nord Crampton tanks that Petiet rebuilt into even stranger beasts.

Plate 27

Plate 28

Plate 29

The solitary Nord works built Crampton No. 119, hastily rebuilt when Hellemes works found they did not have the Cail touch. Cail's Cramptons were sent to Russia and Egypt with open footplates making them intolerable in Russian winter and African summer. Perhaps the most significant thing about the long Crampton era in France is how few drawings suffice to illustrate this chapter, compared with the significantly greater number necessary for the British breed. The French Crampton, unlike many others, reached the status of a standard product not a quasi-experimental prototype.

76

Chapter Five

The CRAMPTON in GERMANY

Chapter Index

The Cramptons in Germany

Introduction

This chapter very nearly did not materialise as Dennis and myself, in our ignorance, thought that as information in this country was practically non-existent, there could not be enough German examples to be worth worrying about! How wrong we were, on gaining possession of the very rare **Die Crampton Locomotive** by *F. Gaiser* we discovered there were no less than 135 locomotives, in fact more than any other country. France was second with 127, and Britain a sad third with 42.

As Dennis was responsible for compiling the chapter on the French Cramptons, I have found myself with the awesome task of preparing this one with, I might add, a great deal of help from my wife and the German translations. She is good at 'domestic' German but, as some 'scholars' among you will know, domestic German is not the same as 'technical' German, so please bear with our combined efforts.

The next problem was the grouping in this chapter, as I had gathered a great deal of information by now, but not in any uniform pattern or amount. So I decided to offer it in *Parts* by the railway companies supported with information on the background of the location (Germany at that time comprised many separate States), and a more detailed description of any particular locomotive depending on the information available. I have quoted main dimensions for the modeller, but a very full breakdown of technical information is shown in the tables by *F. Gaiser*. I have deliberately left the headings in German as it seemed right somehow, but you can translate them if you look at *Chapter Six* tables which have been translated. The figures in most of the tables are in metric figures so, as a rough guide, I have compiled a small conversion table on *page 81*, to two-places of decimals. As you will see, the examples depicted are classic examples of what one would expect a German Crampton to look like, very solid and business-like. They mostly have outside or double frames, with all the valve gear, cylinders, pumps, etc., in full view, massive domes and strange chimneys, in fact, delightful beasts, with lots of character.

Bahn	B. Nr.	Name	Erbauer
		Bezeichnung Der Lokomotiven	
K.Preußische Ostbahn	20	Dunau	F. Wöhlert, Berlin
do.	21	Gardine	do.
do.	22	Baude	do.
do.	23	Passarge	do.
do.	24	Bahnau	do.
do.	25	Jarft	do.
do.	26	Frisching	do.
do.	27	Pregel	do.
do.	35	England	R. Stephenson & Co.
Magdeburg-Halberstadt	—	Berlin	F. Wöhlert, Berlin
do.	—	Hannover	do.
Aachen-Düsseldorf-Ruhrort	17	Rhein	do.
do.	18	Roer	do.
Hannoversche Staatsbahn	111	—	do.
do.	112	—	do.
do.	113	—	do.
do.	114	—	do.
do.	115	—	do.
do.	116	—	do.
do.	117	—	do.
do.	118	—	do.
do.	119	—	do.
do.	120	—	do.
do.	130	—	do.
do.	131	—	do.
do.	132	—	do.
do.	133	—	do.
do.	134	—	do.
do.	135	—	do.
do.	136	—	do.
do.	137	—	do.
do.	145	—	do.

Lieferungs-Datum	F.-Nr.	Rahmen	Zylinder			Steuerung	Laufachsen			Durchmesser der Treibräder	Radstände	Kessel				Heizröhren			Heizfläche			Rostfläche (Länge × Breite)	Leergewicht	Dienstgewicht	Reibungsgewicht	Zugkraft in kg	
			Lage	Durchmesser	Hub		Zahl	Art der Lagerung	Durchmesser der Laufräder			Form	Mitte über S. O.	Durchmesser	Kesseldruck	Zahl	Durchmesser außen	Länge	Feuerbüchse	Röhren	Gesamt	(0,65)				aus den Zylindern	größte μ = 1/5
1852	12	D.R.	ih	381	508	G.	2	fest	1016	1982	1256+1360+1883 =4499	zyl.	1844	1124	6	154	46	3714	5,8	72,8	78,6	1,07	22,7	24,9	9,6	1452	1920
1852	13	„	„	381	508	„	2	„	1016	1982	1256+1360+1883 =4499	„	1844	1124	6	154	46	3714	5,8	72,8	78,6	1,07	22,7	24,9	9,6	1452	1920
1852	14	„	„	381	508	„	2	„	1016	1982	1256+1360+1883 =4499	„	1844	1124	6	154	46	3714	5,8	72,8	78,6	1,07	22,7	24,9	9,6	1452	1920
1852	15	„	„	381	508	„	2	„	1016	1982	1256+1360+1883 =4499	„	1844	1124	6	154	46	3714	5,8	72,8	78,6	1,07	22,7	24,9	9,6	1452	1920
1852	16	„	„	381	508	„	2	„	1016	1982	1256+1360+1883 =4499	„	1844	1124	6	154	46	3714	5,8	72,8	78,6	1,07	22,7	24,9	9,6	1452	1920
1852	17	„	„	381	508	„	2	„	1016	1982	1256+1360+1883 =4499	„	1844	1124	6	154	46	3714	5,8	72,8	78,6	1,07	22,7	24,9	9,6	1452	1920
1852	18	„	„	381	508	„	2	„	1016	1982	1256+1360+1883 =4499	„	1844	1124	6	154	46	3714	5,8	72,8	78,6	1,07	22,7	24,9	9,6	1452	1920
1852	19	„	„	381	508	„	2	„	1016	1982	1256+1360+1883 =4499	„	1844	1124	6	154	46	3714	5,8	72,8	78,6	1,07	22,7	24,9	9,6	1452	1920
1852	866	„	„	15″ 381	22″ 560	St. o.	2	„	3′6″ 1068	6′ 1830	4′6″+4′6″+7′=16′ 1372+1372+2133 =4877	„	6′5″ 1956	4′2″ 1270	90 6	184	2″ 51	11′1″ 3374	110,33 10,25	979,76 91,02	1090,09 101,27	13,88 1,29	24,4	28,0	11,1	1732	2220
1853	34	„	„	381	508	G.	2	„	1016	1980	1112+1517+1883 =4512	„	—	1124	6	154	46	3400	5,22	66,44	71,66	—	20,0	22,5	9,0	1452	1800
1853	35	„	„	381	508	„	2	„	1016	1980	1112+1517+1883 =4512	„	—	1124	6	154	46	3400	5,22	66,44	71,66	—	20,0	22,5	9,0	1452	1800
1853 Juli	36	„	„	381	508	„	2	„	1220	1980	4642	„	—	1124	6⅔	154	46	3400	5,22	66,44	71,66	—	23,05	26,1	10,6	1614	2120
1853 Juli	37	„	„	381	508	„	2	„	1220	1980	4642	„	—	1124	6⅔	154	46	3400	5,22	66,44	71,66	—	23,05	26,1	10,6	1614	2120
1853 Okt.	42	„	zw h	406	560	G. o.	2	„	1068	2134	1905+2819=4724	„	1473	1220	6	182	47,6	3150	5,7	74,4	80,1	1,28	27,35	30,9	12,7	1687	2540
1853 Okt.	43	„	„	406	560	„	2	„	1068	2134	1905+2819=4724	„	1473	1220	6	182	47,6	3150	5,7	74,4	80,1	1,28	27,35	30,9	12,7	1687	2540
1853 Nov.	44	„	„	406	560	„	2	„	1068	2134	1905+2819=4724	„	1473	1220	6	182	47,6	3150	5,7	74,4	80,1	1,28	27,35	30,9	12,7	1687	2540
1853 Nov.	45	„	„	406	560	„	2	„	1068	2134	1905+2819=4724	„	1473	1220	6	182	47,6	3150	5,7	74,4	80,1	1,28	27,35	30,9	12,7	1687	2540
1853 Nov.	46	„	„	406	560	„	2	„	1068	2134	1905+2819=4724	„	1473	1220	6	182	47,6	3150	5,7	74,4	80,1	1,28	27,35	30,9	12,7	1687	2540
1853 Dez.	47	„	„	406	560	„	2	„	1068	2134	1905+2819=4724	„	1473	1220	6	182	47,6	3150	5,7	74,4	80,1	1,28	27,35	30,9	12,7	1687	2540
1853 Dez.	48	„	„	406	560	„	2	„	1068	2134	1905+2819=4724	„	1473	1220	6	182	47,6	3150	5,7	74,4	80,1	1,28	27,35	30,9	12,7	1687	2540
1853 Dez.	49	„	„	406	560	„	2	„	1068	2134	1905+2819=4724	„	1473	1220	6	182	47,6	3150	5,7	74,4	80,1	1,28	27,35	30,9	12,7	1687	2540
1853 Dez.	50	„	„	406	560	„	2	„	1068	2134	1905+2819=4724	„	1473	1220	6	182	47,6	3150	5,7	74,4	80,1	1,28	27,35	30,9	12,7	1687	2540
1854 Jan.	51	„	„	406	560	„	2	„	1068	2134	1905+2819=4724	„	1473	1220	6	182	47,6	3150	5,7	74,4	80,1	1,28	27,35	30,9	12,7	1687	2540
1854 Juli	54	„	„	406	560	„	2	„	1068	2134	1905+2819=4724	„	1473	1220	6	182	47,6	3150	5,7	74,4	80,1	1,28	27,35	30,9	12,7	1687	2540
1854 Juli	55	„	„	406	560	„	2	„	1068	2134	1905+2819=4724	„	1473	1220	6	182	47,6	3150	5,7	74,4	80,1	1,28	27,35	30,9	12,7	1687	2540
1854 Juli	56	„	„	406	560	„	2	„	1068	2134	1905+2819=4724	„	1473	1220	6	182	47,6	3150	5,7	74,4	80,1	1,28	27,35	30,9	12,7	1687	2540
1854 Aug.	57	„	„	406	560	„	2	„	1068	2134	1905+2819=4724	„	1473	1220	6	182	47,6	3150	5,7	74,4	80,1	1,28	27,35	30,9	12,7	1687	2540
1854 Sept.	58	„	„	406	560	„	2	„	1068	2134	1905+2819=4724	„	1473	1220	6	182	47,6	3150	5,7	74,4	80,1	1,28	27,35	30,9	12,7	1687	2540
1854 Okt.	59	„	„	406	560	„	2	„	1068	2134	1905+2819=4724	„	1473	1220	6	182	47,6	3150	5,7	74,4	80,1	1,28	27,35	30,9	12,7	1687	2540
1854 Okt.	60	„	„	406	560	„	2	„	1068	2134	1905+2819=4724	„	1473	1220	6	182	47,6	3150	5,7	74,4	80,1	1,28	27,35	30,9	12,7	1687	2540
1854 Nov.	61	„	„	406	560	„	2	„	1068	2134	1905+2819=4724	„	1473	1220	6	182	47,6	3150	5,7	74,4	80,1	1,28	27,35	30,9	12,7	1687	2540
1855 Dez.	62	„	„	406	560	„	2	„	1068	2134	1905+2819=4724	„	1473	1220	6	182	47,6	3150	5,7	74,4	80,1	1,28	27,35	30,9	12,7	1687	2540

Bahn	B.-Nr.	Name	Erbauer	Lieferungs-Datum	F.-Nr.	Rahmen	Lage	Durchmesser	Hub	Steuerung	Zahl	Art der Lagerung	Durchmesser der Laufräder	Durchmesser der Treibräder	Radstände	Form	Mitte über S.O.	Durchmesser	Kesseldruck	Zahl	Durchmesser außen	Länge	Feuerbüchse	Röhren	Gesamt
Hannoversche Staatsbahn	175	—	G. Egestorff, Linden vor Hann.	1857 Juli	138	D.R.	zw h	406	560	G.o.	2	fest	1068	2134	1905+2819=4724	zyl.	1486	1220	6	180	47,6	3454	5,5	81,0	86,5
do.	176	—	do.	1857 Juli	141	„	„	406	560	„	2	„	1068	2134	1905+2819=4724	„	1486	1220	6	180	47,6	3454	5,5	81,0	86,5
do.	177	—	do.	1857 Sept.	145	„	„	406	560	„	2	„	1068	2134	1905+2819=4724	„	1486	1220	6	180	47,6	3454	5,5	81,0	86,5
do.	178	—	do.	1857 Sept.	148	„	„	406	560	„	2	„	1068	2134	1905+2819=4724	„	1486	1220	6	180	47,6	3454	5,5	81,0	86,5
do.	179	—	do.	1857 Nov.	150	„	„	406	560	„	2	„	1068	2134	1905+2819=4724	„	1486	1220	6	180	47,6	3454	5,5	81,0	86,5
K. Westfälische Eisenbahn	152	—	Egestorff, umg. in Lingen mit neuem Kessel v. Vulcan	1872	—	„	„	412	555	„	2 „		1014	2134	1905+2828=4733	„	1755	1238	8¾	181	48	3218	6,22	76,43	82,65
do.	150	—	Desgl.	1873	—	„	„	412	555	„	2	„	1014	2134	1905+2828=4733	„	1755	1238	8¾	181	48	3218	6,22	76,43	82,65
do.	148	—	Desgl. v. Borsig	1875	—	„	„	412	555	„	2	„	1014	2134	1906+2828=4733	„	1755	1238	9	181	48	3218	6,22	76,43	82,65
do.	151	—	do.	1875	—	„	„	412	555	„	2	„	1014	2134	1905+2828=4733	„	1755	1238	9	181	48	3218	6,22	76,43	82,65
do.	149	—	do.	1878	—	„	„	412	555	„	2	„	1014	2134	1905+2828=4733	„	1755	1238	10	181	48	3218	6,22	76,43	82,65
Hannoversche Staatsbahn	180	—	G. Egestorff, Linden vor Hann.	1857 Nov.	153	„	„	406	560	„	2	„	1068	2134	1905+2819=4724	„	1486	1220	6	180	47,6	3454	5,5	81,0	86,5
do.	181	—	do.	1857 Dez.	155	„	„	406	560	„	2	„	1068	2134	1905+2819=4724	„	1486	1220	6	180	47,6	3454	5,5	81,0	86,5
do.	182	—	do.	1857 Dez.	„	„	„	406	560	„	2	„	1068	2134	1905+2819=4724	„	1486	1220	6	180	47,6	3454	5,5	81,0	86,5
do.	191	—	do.	1859 Aug.	174	„	„	406	560	„	2	„	1068	2134	1905+2819=4724	„	1486	1220	6	180	47,6	3454	5,5	81,0	86,5
do.	192	—	do.	1859 Okt.	175	„	„	406	560	„	2	„	1068	2134	1905+2819=4724	„	1486	1220	6	180	47,6	3454	5,5	81,0	86,5
do.	193	—	do.	1859 Okt.	178	„	„	406	560	„	2	„	1068	2134	1905+2819=4724	„	1486	1220	6	180	47,6	3454	5,5	81,0	86,5
do.	194	—	do.	1859 Nov.	179	„	„	406	560	„	2	„	1068	2134	1905+2819=4724	„	1486	1220	6	180	47,6	3454	5,5	81,0	86,5
do.	195	—	do.	1860 Jan.	182	„	„	406	560	„	2	„	1068	2134	1905+2819=4724	„	1486	1220	6	180	47,6	3454	5,5	81,0	86,5
do.	196	—	do.	1860 Febr.	183	„	„	406	560	„	2	„	1068	2134	1905+2819=4724	„	1486	1220	6	180	47,6	3454	5,5	81,0	86,5
Wilhelms-Bahn	11	—	F. Wöhlert, Berlin	1854 März	52	„	„	406	560	G.	2	„	1068	2134	4760	„	—	1202	6	182	—	3454	5,17	79,54	84,71
do.	12	—	do.	1854 März	53	„	„	406	560	„	2	„	1068	2134	4760	„	—	1202	6	182	—	3454	5,17	79,54	84,71
do.	15	—	do.	1855 April	63	„	„	406	560	„	2	Drehg.	1068	2134	4812	„	—	1202	6	182	—	3454	5,17	79,54	84,71
Rheinische Bahn	—	Crampton	A. Borsig, Berlin	1854 Juli	516	„	„	406	560	St. o.	2	fest	1204	2132	2125+2295=4420	„	1641	1256	6⅔	180	—	3397	—	—	88,8
do.	—	Humboldt	do.	1854 Juli	517	„	„	406	560	„	2	„	1204	2132	2125+2295=4420	„	1641	1256	6⅔	180	—	3397	—	—	88,8
do.	—	Arago	do.	1854 Juli	518	„	„	406	560	„	2	„	1204	2132	2125+2295=4420	„	1641	1256	6⅔	180	—	3397	—	—	88,8
do.	—	Beuth	do.	1854 Juli	519	„	„	406	560	„	2	„	1204	2132	2125+2295=4420	„	1641	1256	6⅔	180	—	3397	—	—	88,8
Main-Neckar-Bahn	19	Loewe	Mb.-G. Karlsruhe	1855 Dez.	16	„	„	381	560	„	2	„	1218	1980	2298+1986=4254	„	1398	1200	6	197	41	3225	5,4	71,9	77,3
do.	20	Greif	do.	1855 Dez.	17	„	„	381	560	„	2	„	1218	1980	2298+1986=4254	„	1398	1200	6	197	41	3225	5,4	71,9	77,3
Magdeb.-Leipzig	—	Sturm	do.	1857	31	„	„	406	560	„	2	„	1067	2134	2040+2670=4710	„	1545	1236	6	184	46	3399	6,11	80,47	86,58
do.	—	Blitz	do.	1857	32	„	„	406	560	„	2	„	1067	2134	2040+2670=4710	„	1545	1236	6	184	46	3399	6,11	80,47	86,58
do.	—	Pfeil	do.	1857	33	„	„	406	560	„	2	„	1067	2134	2040+2670=4710	„	1545	1236	6	184	46	3399	6,11	80,47	86,58
do.	—	Greif	do.	1857	34	„	„	406	560	„	2	„	1067	2134	2040+2670=4710	„	1545	1236	6	184	46	3399	6,11	80,47	86,58

80

Inches	Millimetres	Inches	Millimetres
0·25	6·35	30	762·0
0·5	12·7	40	1016·0
0·75	19·05	50	1270·0
1	25·4	60	1524·0
2	50·8	70	1778·0
3	76·2	80	2032·0
4	101·6	90	2286·0
5	127·0	100	2540·0
6	152·4	110	2794·0
7	177·8	120	3048·0
8	203·2	130	3302·0
9	228·6	140	3556·0
10	254·0	150	3810·0
20	508·0	160	4064·0

Part One
Main-Neckar-Bahn

Plate 30

Rostfläche (Länge × Breite)	Leergewicht	Dienstgewicht	Reibungsgewicht	Zugkraft in kg	
				aus den Zylindern (0,65)	größte μ=1/5
1,17	24,75	28,5	11,5	1687	2300
1,17	24,75	28,5	11,5	1687	2300
1,17	24,75	28,5	11,5	1687	2300
1,17	24,75	28,5	11,5	1687	2300
1,17	24,75	28,5	11,5	1687	2300
1,50	29,85	32,5	13,0	2488	2600
1,50	29,85	32,5	13,0	2488	2600
1,50	29,85	32,5	13,0	2559	2600
1,50	29,85	32,5	13,0	2559	2600
1,50	29,85	32,5	13,0	2844	2600
1,17	24,75	28,5	11,5	1687	2300
1,17	24,75	28,5	11,5	1687	2300
1,17	24,75	28,5	11,5	1687	2300
1,17	24,75	28,5	11,5	1687	2300
1,17	24,75	28,5	11,5	1687	2300
1,17	24,75	28,5	11,5	1687	2300
1,17	24,75	28,5	11,5	1687	2300
1,17	24,75	28,5	11,5	1687	2300
—	26,00	28,8	9,0	1687	1800
—	26,00	28,8	9,0	1687	1800
—	26,00	28,8	9,0	1687	1800
1,3	27,35	30,25	13,5	1848	2700
1,3	27,35	30,25	13,5	1848	2700
1,3	27,35	30,25	13,5	1848	2700
1,3	27,35	30,25	13,5	1848	2700
0,98	27,65	29,7	12	1601	2400
0,98	27,65	29,7	12	1601	2400
1,25 (1202×1046)	27,35	30,25	12,65	1687	2530
1,25 (1202×1046)	27,35	30,25	12,65	1687	2530
1,25 (1202×1046)	27,35	30,25	12,65	1687	2530
1,25 (1202×1046)	27,35	30,25	12,65	1687	2530

Bahn	B. Nr.	Name	Erbauer	Lieferungs-Datum	F.-Nr.	Rahmen	Lage	Durchmesser	Hub	Steuerung	Zahl	Art der Lagerung	Durchmesser der Laufräder	Durchmesser der Treibräder	Radstände	Form	Mitte über S. O.	Durchmesser	Kesseldruck	Zahl	Durchmesser außen	Länge	Feuerbüchse	Röhren	Gesamt
Bayer. Pfalzbahn	26	König Max	J.A. Maffei, Hirschau b. München	1853	132	A.R.	a h	356	610	„	2	„	1220	1830	1651+2311=3962	oval	1550	c. 1200/ 1140	6,3	144	48	3256	5,3	63,3	68,6
do.	27	Hohe	do.	1853	133	„	„	356	610	„	2	„	1220	1830	1651+2311=3962	„	1550	c. 1200/ 1140	6,3	144	48	3256	5,3	63,3	68,6
do.	28	Die Pfalz	do.	1853	134	„	„	356	610	„	2	„	1220	1830	1651+2311=3962	„	1550	c. 1200/ 1140	6,3	144	48	3256	5,3	63,3	68,6
do.	29	Königin Marie	do.	1853	135	„	„	356	610	„	2	„	1220	1830	1651+2311=3962	„	1550	c. 1200/ 1140	6,3	144	48	3256	5,3	63,3	68,6
do.	36	Ludwigshöhe	Mf. Eßlingen, Emil Keßler	1855	265	„	„	381	610	„	2	„	1220	1830	1638+2322=3960	zyl.	1640	1222	6,2	165	48	3300	5,8	72,7	78,5
do.	37	Madenburg	do.	1855	266	„	„	381	610	„	2	„	1220	1830	1638+2322=3960	„	1640	1222	6,2	165	48	3300	5,8	72,7	78,5
do.	38	Maxburg	do.	1855	267	„	„	381	610	„	2	„	1220	1830	1638+2322=3960	„	1640	1222	6,2	165	48	3300	5,8	72,7	78,5
do.	39	Trifels	do.	1855	268	„	„	381	610	„	2	„	1220	1830	1638+2322=3960	„	1640	1222	6,2	165	48	3300	5,8	72,7	78,5
do.	40	Kalmit	do.	1855	269	„	„	381	610	„	2	„	1220	1830	1638+2322=3960	„	1640	1222	6,2	165	48	3300	5,8	72,7	78,5
do.	41	Drachenfels	do.	1855	270	„	„	381	610	„	2	„	1220	1830	1638+2322=3960	„	1640	1222	6,2	165	48	3300	5,8	72,7	78,5
do.	46	v.d. Pfordten	do.	1856	271	„	„	381	610	„	2	„	1220	1830	1638+2322=3960	„	1640	1222	6,2	165	48	3300	5,8	72,7	78,5
do.	47	Mahla	do.	1856	272	„	„	381	610	„	2	„	1220	1830	1638+2322=3960	„	1640	1222	6,2	165	48	3300	5,8	72,7	78,5
do.	48	Sickingen	do.	1858 Nov.	431	„	„	381	610	„	2	„	1220	1830	1638+2322=3960	„	1640	1222	6,2	165	48	3300	5,8	72,7	78,5
do.	49	E. v. Wrede	do.	1858 Nov.	432	„	„	381	610	„	2	„	1220	1830	1638+2322=3960	„	1640	1222	6,2	165	48	3300	5,8	72,7	78,5
do.	60	Poelnitz	do.	1863 Aug.	621	„	„	381	610	„	2	„	1220	1830	1638+2322=3960	„	1640	1220	7,23	168	48	3340	4,93	74,9	79,83
do.	61	A. Jaeger sp. A.v. Jaeger	do.	1863 Aug.	622	„	„	381	610	„	2	„	1220	1830	1638+2322=3960	„	1640	1220	7,23	168	48	3340	4,93	74,9	79,83
do.	62	Limburg	do.	1864 Jan.	623	„	„	381	610	„	2	„	1220	1830	1638+2322=3960	„	1640	1220	7,23	168	48	3340	4,93	74,9	79,83
do.	63	Ebernburg	do.	1864 Jan.	624	„	„	381	610	„	2	„	1220	1830	1638+2322=3960	„	1640	1220	7,23	168	48	3340	4,93	74,9	79,83
Badische St.-B.	67	Adler	Mb.-G. Karlsruhe	1854 Okt.	3	„	„	405	560	G. o.	2	„	1374 u. 1221	2130	1875+1875=3750	Doppel-Kessel 1410 u.17101302/1104		7	215	42	3090	6,74	75,05	81,79
do.	68	Falke	do.	1854 Okt.	4	„	„	405	560	„	2	„	1221	2130	1875+1875=3750	„	1410 u.17101302/1104		7	215	42	3090	6,74	75,05	81,79
do.	69	Komet	do.	1854 Nov.	5	„	„	405	560	„	2 Drehg.		1221	2130	1875+1875=3750	„	1410 u.17101302/1104		7	215	42	3090	6,74	75,05	81,79
do.	70	Pfeil	do.	1854 Dez.	6	„	„	405	560	„	2	„	1221	2130	1875+1875=3750	„	1410 u.17101302/1104		7	215	42	3090	6,74	75,05	81,79
do.	71	Elz	do.	1855 Jan.	7	„	„	405	560	„	2	„	1221	2130	1875+1875=3750	„	1410 u.17101302/1104		7	215	42	3090	6,74	75,05	81,79
do.	72	Wiese	do.	1855 März	8	„	„	405	560	„	2	„	1221	2130	1875+1875=3750	„	1410 u.17101302/1104		7	215	42	3090	6,74	75,05	81,79
do.	73	Wutach	do.	1855 April	9	„	„	405	560	„	2	„	1221	2130	1875+1875=3750	„	1410 u.17101302/1104		7	215	42	3090	6,74	75,05	81,79
do.	74	Rench	do.	1855 Mai	10	„	„	405	560	„	2	„	1220	2130	1875+1875=3750	„	1410 u.17101302/1104		7	215	42	3090	6,74	75,05	81,79
do.	75	Lahr	do.	1855 Juni	11	„	„	405	560	„	2	„	1220	2130	1875+1875=3750	„	1410 u.17101302/1104		7	215	42	3090	6,74	75,05	81,79
do.	76	Basel	do.	1855 Dez.	12	„	„	405	560	„	2	„	1220	2130	1875+1875=3750	„	1410 u.17101302/1104		7	215	42	3090	6,74	75,05	81,79
do.	1	Loewe	E.B. Hauptwerk-stätte Karlsruhe	1856 Juni	—	„	„	380	560	St. o.	2	fest	1070	1890	1740+1860=3600	zyl.	1580	1230	6²/₃	189	42	3145	5,18	69,09	74,27
do.	2	Greif	do.	1856 Aug.	—	„	„	380	560	„	2	„	1070	1890	1740+1860=3600	„	1580	1230	6²/₃	189	42	3145	5,18	69,09	74,27
do.	4	Mannheim	do.	1856 Okt.	—	„	„	380	560	„	2	„	1070	1890	1740+1860=3600	„	1580	1230	6²/₃	189	42	3145	5,18	69,09	74,27
do.	83	Rheinfelden	Mb.-G. Karlsruhe	1858 Nov.	74	„	„	405	560	„	2	„	1220	2134	1875+1875=3750	„	1590	1276	7	205	42	3085	5,83	72,52	78,35
do.	84	Säckingen	do.	1858 Nov.	75	„	„	405	560	„	2	„	1220	2134	1875+1875=3750	„	1590	1276	7	205	42	3085	5,83	72,52	78,35
do.	85	Laufenburg	do.	1859 Jan.	76	„	„	405	560	„	2	„	1220	2134	1875+1875=3750	„	1590	1276	7	205	42	3085	5,83	72,52	78,35
do.	86	Waldshut	do.	1859 Jan.	77	„	„	405	560	„	2	„	1220	2134	1875+1875=3750	„	1590	1276	7	205	42	3085	5,83	72,52	78,35

Rostfläche (Länge × Breite)	Leergewicht	Dienstgewicht	Reibungsgewicht	Zugkraft in kg aus den Zylindern (0,65)	Zugkraft in kg größte μ=1/5
0,98 (920×1068)	21,35	24,2	9,2	1730	1840
0,98 (920×1068)	21,35	24,2	9,2	1730	1840
0,98 (920×1068)	21,35	24,2	9,2	1730	1840
0,98 (920×1068)	21,35	24,2	9,2	1730	1840
0,99	24	26,4	9,7	1950	1940
0,99	24	26,4	9,7	1950	1940
0,99	24	26,4	9,7	1950	1940
0,99	24	26,4	9,7	1950	1940
0,99	24	26,4	9,7	1950	1940
0,99	24	26,4	9,7	1950	1940
0,99	24	27,25	9,7	1950	1940
0,99	24	27,25	9,7	1950	1940
0,98	24,6	27,25	10,5	2274	2100
0,98	24,6	27,25	10,5	2274	2100
0,98	24,6	27,9	10,5	2274	2100
0,98	24,6	27,9	10,5	2274	2100
1,07	25,9	27,9	—	1968	—
1,07	25,9	27,9	—	1968	—
1,07	26,35	28,5	—	1968	—
1,07	26,35	28,5	—	1968	—
1,07	26,35	28,5	—	1968	—
1,07	26,35	28,5	—	1968	—
1,07	26,35	28,5	—	1968	—
1,07	26,35	28,5	—	1968	—
1,07	26,35	28,5	—	1968	—
0,98 (838×1044)	22,5	25,2	10,0	1864	2000
0,98 (838×1044)	22,5	25,2	10,0	1864	2000
0,98 (838×1044)	22,5	25,2	10,0	1864	2000
0,98 (1005×972)	24	27,7	11,5	1968	2300
0,98 (1005×972)	24	27,7	11,5	1968	2300
0,98 (1005×972)	24	27,7	11,5	1968	2300
0,98 (1005×972)	24	27,7	11,5	1968	2300

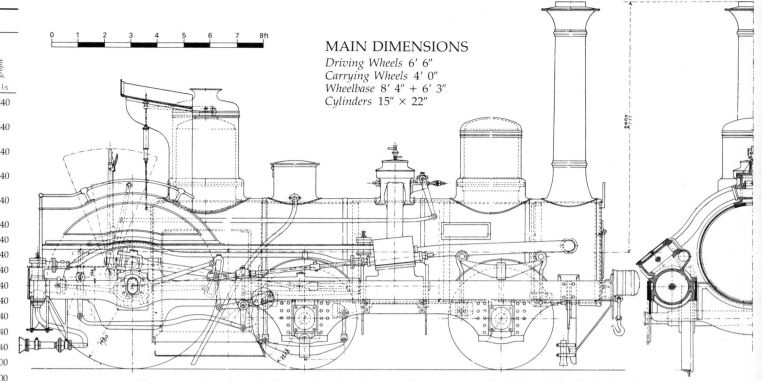

MAIN DIMENSIONS
Driving Wheels 6' 6"
Carrying Wheels 4' 0"
Wheelbase 8' 4" + 6' 3"
Cylinders 15" × 22"

Figure 106

The Main-Neckar Railway had only two Cramptons, built by Mb-G Karlsruhe in 1855. They were named *Loewe* and *Greif* and are illustrated in the photograph (*plate 30*) and the drawing *figure 106* (*above*). As you can see, they differ! I suspect the drawing is later than the photograph in this case, as it shows an extra dome, and sanding gear which must have been fitted soon after the picture was taken.

Now comes the confusion—it always comes sooner or later! If you look at the table on *page 80* you will see the Main-Neck reference. Now turn to *page 82* and about three-quarters of the way down, *Loewe* and *Greif* appear again under the Baden State Railway banner, but built two years later with different driving wheels and wheelbase? It could well be that the two locomotives were built as stated at Karlsruhe in 1855, and then taken into the Baden State Railway in 1856 and rebuilt. There were three locomotives in the Baden State class, Nos. 1, 2 and 4, so No. 4 could have been part of the original batch, and only completed to the same pattern as the re-builds. No. 3 seems to have got lost somewhere but, as often happened in Britain, could have been issued as a 2–2–2 type non-Crampton locomotive. Many of these lines ran in each other's pockets, and there seems to have been a joint administration of the lines to keep them operating during the political changes of the period, resulting in most of them becoming part of the vast Prussian State Railway System.

As for location, both Main and Neckar are rivers which run into the Rhine, Neckar rising in the Black Forest. They serve many towns on their travels—Mainze, Frankfurt, Nurenburg, to name a few—and the Main has links with the canal system down into the Danube. The lines follow the rivers very closely and are still shown on the atlas as secondary lines today.

Bahn	B. Nr.	Name	Erbauer	Lieferungs-Datum	F.-Nr.	Rahmen	Lage	Durchmesser	Hub	Steuerung	Zahl	Art der Lagerung	Durchmesser der Lauf räder	Durchmesser der Treibräder	Radstände	Form	Mitte über S. O.	Durchmesser	Kesseldruck	Zahl	Durchmesser außen	Länge	Feuerbüchse	Röhren	Gesamt
Badische St.-B.	87	Pforzheim	Mb.-G. Karlsruhe	1859 Sept.	89	D.R.	zw h	405	560	St. o.	2	fest	1220	2134	1875+1875=3750	zyl.	1590	1276	7	205	42	3085	5,83	72,52	78,35
do.	88 sp.89	Constanz	do.	1859 Aug.	90	„	„	405	560	„	2	„	1220	2134	1875+1875=3750	„	1590	1276	7	205	42	3085	5,83	72,52	78,35
do.	89 sp.88	Straßburg	do.	1859 Aug.	91	„	„	405	560	„	2	„	1220	2134	1875+1875=3750	„	1590	1276	7	205	42	3085	5,83	72,52	78,35
do.	90	Pfalz	do.	1859 Aug.	92	„	„	405	560	„	2	„	1220	2134	1875+1875=3750	„	1590	1276	7	205	42	3085	5,83	72,52	78,35
do.	7	Badenia	do.	1863 Okt.	195	„	„	405	560	„	2	„	1220	2134	1650+2100=3750	„	1600	1276	8	209	42	3095	5,62	74,17	79,79
do.	8	Carlsruhe	do.	1863 Okt.	196	„	„	405	560	„	2	„	1220	2134	1650+2100=3750	„	1600	1276	8	209	42	3095	5,62	74,17	79,79
do.	9	Mercur	do.	1863 Okt.	197	„	„	405	560	„	2	„	1220	2134	1650+2100=3750	„	1600	1276	8	209	42	3095	5,62	74,17	79,79
do.	10	Meteor	do.	1863 Nov.	198	„	„	405	560	„	2	„	1220	2134	1650+2100=3750	„	1600	1276	8	209	42	3095	5,62	74,17	79,79
do.	11	Vulcan	do.	1863 Nov.	199	„	„	405	560	„	2	„	1220	2134	1650+2100=3750	„	1600	1276	8	209	42	3095	5,62	74,17	79,79
do.	12	Jupiter	do.	1863 Nov.	200	„	„	405	560	„	2	„	1220	2134	1650+2100=3750	„	1600	1276	8	209	42	3095	5,62	74,17	79,79
do.	13	Phoenix	do.	1863 Dez.	201	„	„	405	560	„	2	„	1220	2134	1650+2100=3750	„	1600	1276	8	209	42	3095	5,62	74,17	79,79
do.	14	Offenburg	do.	1863 Dez.	202	„	„	405	560	„	2	„	1220	2134	1650+2100=3750	„	1600	1276	8	209	42	3095	5,62	74,17	79,79
Bayer. Ostbahn	A1	—	J.A. Maffei	1857	296	„	„	394	610	„	2	„	1220	1830	1574+2388=3962	„	1676	1295	6	196	45	3124	6,3	76,9	83,2
do.	A2	—	do.	1857	297	„	„	394	610	„	2	„	1220	1830	1574+2388=3962	„	1676	1295	6	196	45	3124	6,3	76,9	83,2
do.	A3	—	do.	1858	304	„	„	394	610	„	2	„	1220	1830	1574+2388=3962	„	1676	1295	6	196	45	3124	6,3	76,9	83,2
do.	A4	—	do.	1858	305	„	„	394	610	„	2	„	1220	1830	1574+2388=3962	„	1676	1295	6	196	45	3124	6,3	76,9	83,2
do.	A5	—	do.	1858	306	„	„	394	610	„	2	„	1220	1830	1574+2388=3962	„	1676	1295	6	196	45	3124	6,3	76,9	83,2
do.	A6	—	do.	1858	307	„	„	394	610	„	2	„	1220	1830	1574+2388=3962	„	1676	1295	6	196	45	3124	6,3	76,9	83,2
do.	A7	--	do.	1858	308	„	„	394	610	„	2	„	1220	1830	1574+2388=3962	„	1676	1295	6	196	45	3124	6,3	76,9	83,2
do.	A8	—	do.	1858	309	„	„	394	610	„	2	„	1220	1830	1574+2388=3962	„	1676	1295	6	196	45	3124	6,3	76,9	83,2
do.	A9	—	do.	1858	310	„	„	394	610	„	2	„	1220	1830	1574+2388=3962	„	1676	1295	6	196	45	3124	6,3	76,9	83,2
do.	A10	—	do.	1858	311	„	„	394	610	„	2	„	1220	1830	1574+2388=3962	„	1676	1295	6	196	45	3124	6,3	76,9	83,2
do.	A11	—	do.	1858	312	„	„	394	610	„	2	„	1220	1830	1574+2388=3962	„	1676	1295	6	196	45	3124	6,3	76,9	83,2
do.	A12	—	do.	1858	313	„	„	394	610	„	2	„	1220	1830	1574+2388=3962	„	1676	1295	6	196	45	3124	6,3	76,9	83,2
Hessische Ludwigsbahn	14	Ludwig	Mf. Eßlingen, Emil Keßler	1858 Okt.	425	I.R.	a g	381	610	A. o.	2	„	1080	1830	1755+2295=4050	„	1665	1250	6	202	45	2870	6,17	72,81	78,98
do.	15	Mathilde	do.	1858 Nov.	426	„	„	381	610	„	2	„	1080	1830	1755+2295=4050	„	1665	1250	6	202	45	2870	6,17	72,81	78,98
do.	16	Cl. Lauteren	do.	1858 Nov.	427	„	„	381	610	„	2	„	1080	1830	1755+2295=4050	„	1665	1250	6	202	45	2870	6,17	72,81	78,98
do.	17	KarlderGroße	do.	1858 Nov.	428	„	„	381	610	„	2	„	1080	1830	1755+2295=4050	„	1665	1250	6	202	45	2870	6,17	72,81	78,98
do.	18	Maximilian	do.	1858 Nov.	429	„	„	381	610	„	2	„	1080	1830	1755+2295=4050	„	1665	1250	6	202	45	2870	6,17	72,81	78,98
do.	19	Aschaffenbg. A. Humann seit 1861	do.	1858 Nov.	430	„	„	381	610	„	2	„	1080	1830	1755+2295=4050	„	1665	1250	6	202	45	2870	6,17	72,81	78,98
do.	35	Haydn	do.	1863 März	609	„	„	381	610	„	2	„	1080	1830	1755+2295=4050	„	1665	1250	6	202	45	2870	6,17	72,81	78,98
do.	36	Willigis	do.	1863 März	610	„	„	381	610	„	2	„	1080	1830	1755+2295=4050	„	1665	1250	6	202	45	2870	6,17	72,81	78,98
do.	37	Alice	do.	1863 März	611	„	„	381	610	„	2	„	1080	1830	1755+2295=4050	„	1665	1250	6	202	45	2870	6,17	72,81	78,98

Rostfläche (Länge × Breite)	Leergewicht	Dienstgewicht	Reibungsgewicht	Zugkraft in kg	
				aus den Zylindern (0,65)	größte μ=1,5
0,98 (1005×972)	24	27,7	11,5	1968	2300
0,98 (1005×972)	24	27,7	11,5	1968	2300
0,98 (1005×972)	24	27,7	11,5	1968	2300
0,98 (1005×972)	24	27,7	11,5	1968	2300
0,92	24,25	28,5	12,0	2249	2400
0,92	24,25	28,5	12,0	2249	2400
0,92	24,25	28,5	12,0	2249	2400
0,92	24,25	28,5	12,0	2249	2400
0,92	24,25	28,5	12,0	2249	2400
0,92	24,25	28,5	12,0	2249	2400
0,92	24,25	28,5	12,0	2249	2400
1,13	—	26,0	11,0	2018	2200
1,13	—	26,0	11,0	2018	2200
1,13	—	26,0	11,0	2018	2200
1,13	—	26,0	11,0	2018	2200
1,13	—	26,0	11,0	2018	2200
1,13	—	26,0	11,0	2018	2200
1,13	—	26,0	11,0	2018	2200
1,13	—	26,0	11,0	2018	2200
1,13	—	26,0	11,0	2018	2200
1,13	—	26,0	11,0	2018	2200
1,13	—	26,0	11,0	2018	2200
0,97	21,6	24,5	11,5	1887	2300
0,97	21,6	24,5	11,5	1887	2300
0,97	21,6	24,5	11,5	1887	2300
0,97	21,6	24,5	11,5	1887	2300
0,97	21,6	24,5	11,5	1887	2300
0,97	21,6	24,5	11,5	1887	2300
0,97	21,6	24,5	11,5	1887	2300
0,97	21,6	24,5	11,5	1887	2300

The Baden State Railway was a *real* Crampton railway with twenty-nine engines divided into five basic classes. They were full of innovation and solidly majestic to look at.

The line itself covers some very attractive countryside, from Switzerland in the south, spanning out to France and the river Rhine, and including most of the Black Forest. The area was a grand Duchy which turned Republic, but was chopped about and divided up after both world wars, hopefully not to be disturbed again!

Figure 107 Locomotive *Adler* No. 67 Eagle Class (1854).

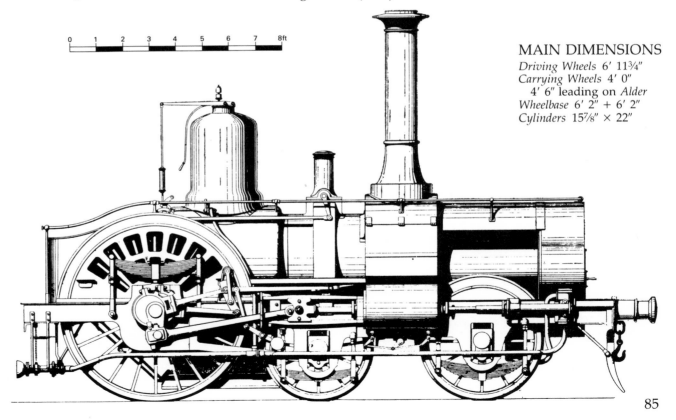

MAIN DIMENSIONS
Driving Wheels 6' 11¾"
Carrying Wheels 4' 0"
  4' 6" leading on *Alder*
Wheelbase 6' 2" + 6' 2"
Cylinders 15⅞" × 22"

Bahn	Bezeichnung Der Lokomotiven: B. Nr.	Name	Erbauer	Lieferungs-Datum	F.-Nr.	Rahmen	Zylinder: Lage	Zylinder: Durchmesser	Zylinder: Hub	Steuerung	Laufachsen: Zahl	Laufachsen: Art der Lagerung	Laufachsen: Durchmesser der Laufräder	Durchmesser der Treibräder	Radstände	Kessel: Form	Kessel: Mitte über S. O.	Kessel: Durchmesser	Kessel: Kesseldruck	Heizröhren: Zahl	Heizröhren: Durchmesser außen	Heizröhren: Länge	Heizfläche: Feuerbüchse	Heizfläche: Röhren	Heizfläche: Gesamt
Nassauische E.B.	3	Dill	Mf. Eßlingen, Emil Keßler	1861	—	I.R.	a g	381	560	A. o.	2	fest	1067	1830	1755+2145=3900	zyl.	—	1275	7,2	160	51	2911	5,82	64,26	70,08
do.	4	Wisper	do.	1861	—	"	"	381	560	"	2	"	1067	1830	1755+2145=3900	"	—	1275	7,2	160	51	2911	5,82	64,26	70,08
do.	7	Aar	do.	1862	—	"	"	381	560	"	2	"	1067	1830	1755+2145=3900	"	—	1275	7,2	160	51	2911	5,82	64,26	70,08
do.	8	Elb	do.	1862	—	"	"	381	560	"	2	"	1067	1830	1755+2145=3900	"	—	1275	7,2	160	51	2911	5,82	64,26	70,08
do.	9	Weil	do.	1862	—	"	"	381	560	"	2	"	1067	1830	1755+2145=3900	"	—	1275	7,2	160	51	2911	5,82	64,26	70,08
do.	22	Rhein	do.	1862	—	"	"	381	560	"	2	"	1067	1830	1755+2145=3900	"	—	1275	7,2	160	51	2911	5,82	64,26	70,08
do.	23	Lahn	do.	1862	—	"	"	381	560	"	2	"	1067	1830	1755+2145=3900	"	—	1275	7,2	160	51	2911	5,82	64,26	70,08
do.	24	Mosel	do.	1862	—	"	"	381	560	"	2	"	1067	1830	1755+2145=3900	"	—	1275	7,2	160	51	2911	5,82	64,26	70,08

Figure 108

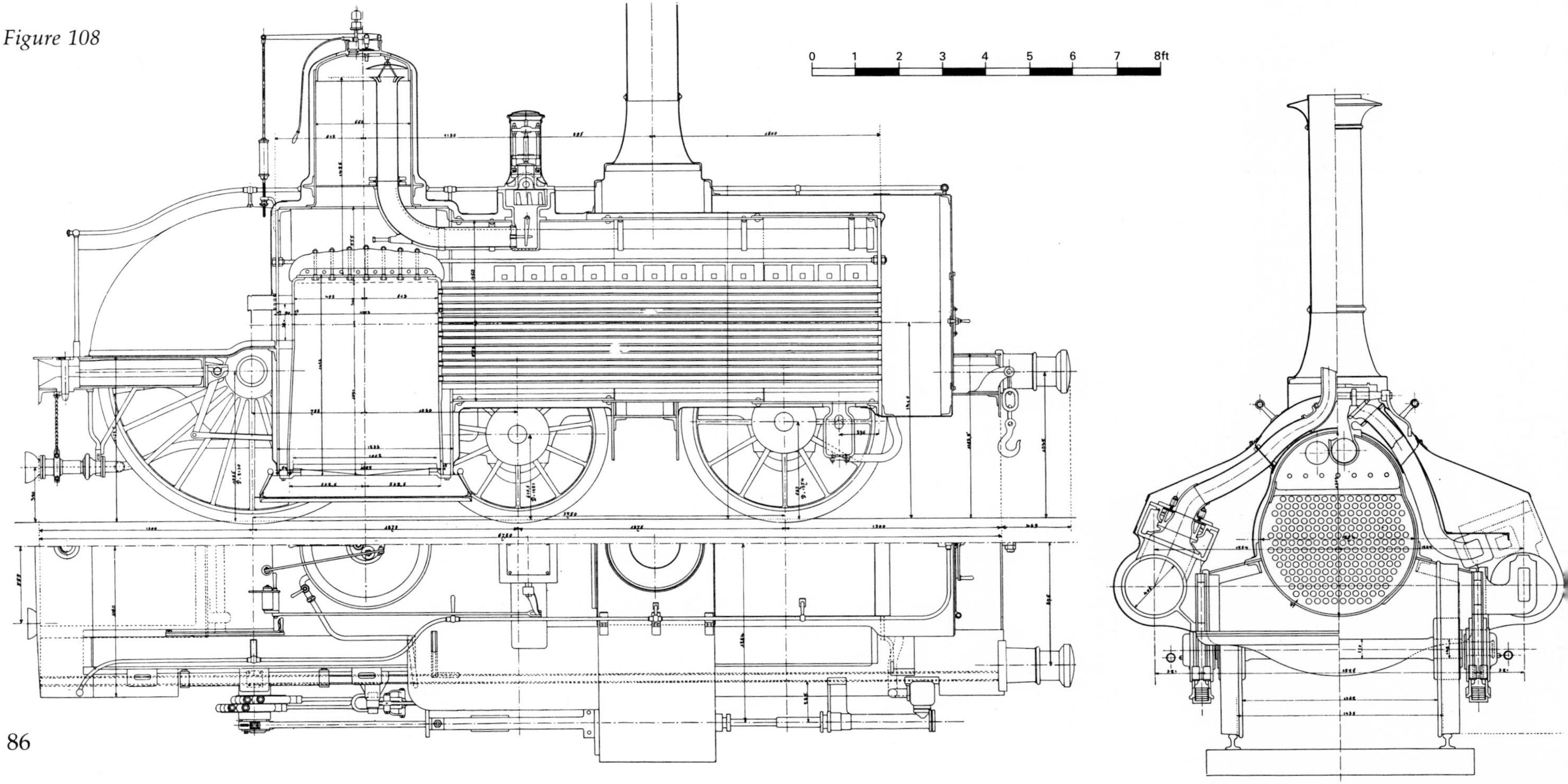

Rostfläche (Länge × Breite)	Leergewicht	Dienstgewicht	Reibungsgewicht	Zugkraft in kg	
				aus den Zylindern (0,65)	größte μ=1/5
,00	24,3	27,0	11,0	2079	2200
,00	24,3	27,0	11,0	2079	2200
,00	24,3	27,0	11,0	2079	2200
,00	24,3	27,0	11,0	2079	2200
,00	24,3	27,0	11,0	2079	2200
,00	24,3	27,0	11,0	2079	2200
,00	24,3	27,0	11,0	2079	2200
,00	24,3	27,0	11,0	2079	2200

These two locomotives were built by Maschinenbau-Gesellschaft-Karlsruhe in 1854 and were very distinctive. They had the 'ultimate' in extended smokeboxes, which did in fact double back over the boiler—Gaiser calls it a 're-entrant smokebox', and may have been influenced by the Black Forest factor, in that it provided a very good spark arrester at the cost of some other adverse boiler characteristics.

They had all the other Crampton features—the pear-shaped double oval boiler, the standard wheel, cylinder, and firebox arrangement. The water feed pumps are driven from a piston rod extension as in *Liverpool*, and an innovation I have not found before—a variable blast pipe cone, which can be adjusted to produce the best fire for the running requirements.

They had, with the 1858-9 class, the shortest wheelbase of any Crampton with an un-Crampton-like front end overhang. The big dome to the rear of the boiler was pure 'Badenese', with the quite large Gooch eccentrics mounted inboard of the connecting rod and piston centres. The buffer beam was not curved like the British engines, but had a large cut-out to clear the smokebox doors. The two engines were not quite the same, in that *Alder* had larger leading wheels than *Falke*—but that was the only difference. It's a bit vague how long they lasted but would appear to have been around in 1875, which was not a bad innings for these types.

Livery. The livery of all the Baden engines was a deep rose red frame, with the boiler, wheels, splashers and tender sides dark green. The smokebox, including the extension on top of the boiler along with the chimney were black with brass beading on the splashers and chimney top.

Figure 109

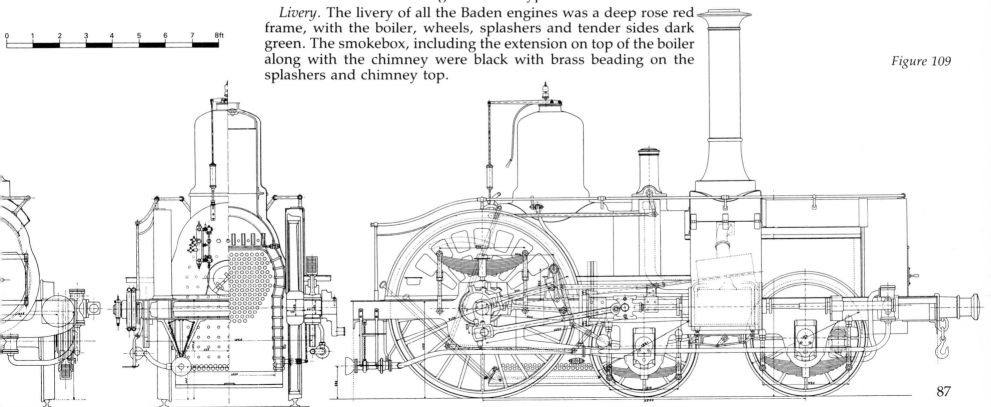

0 1 2 3 4 5 6 7 8ft

87

Locomotives of the 1854 Komet Class

MAIN DIMENSIONS
Driving Wheels 6' 11¾"
Carrying Wheels 4' 0"
Wheelbase 4' 3" + 10' 0"
Cylinders 15⅞" × 22"

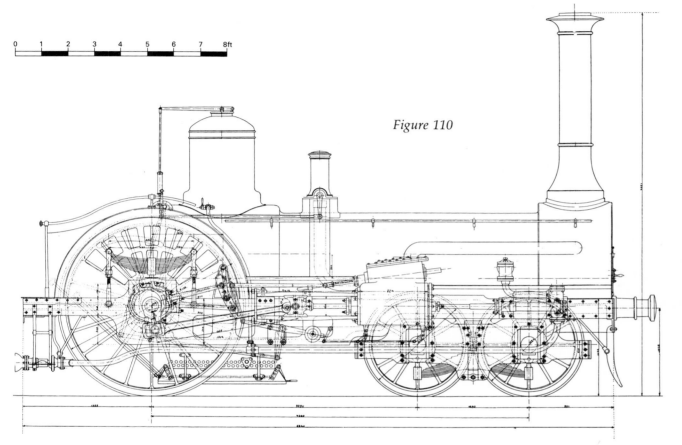

Figure 110

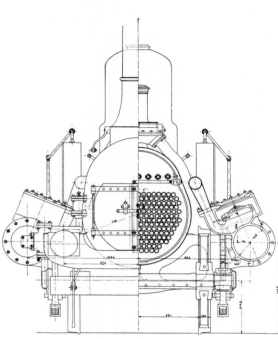

Figure 110a

0 1 2 3 4 5 6 7 8ft

The Comet class of eight engines was built at the same time (1854) and place as the Alder class. The similarities are there to see (in *figure 110*), the large dome, eccentrics and feed pump positions, etc. The most noticeable feature of this locomotive is the very short wheelbase bogie which, on the London Chatham and Dover 'Flirt' class, caused such problems in getting at 'cross purposes' with the track. From the drawing (*figure 110*) it seems that it was not a problem on this locomotive as it was not quite central on its pivot point, but slightly forward, giving a castor

effect. The wheel tyres are almost touching, so it would only be possible to build a proper scale model of this locomotive, as coarse scale 'steamroller' wheels just would not fit!

I have had quite a tussle sorting out the classes of the Baden State Railway as there is a wealth of material to mislead the unwary. The engraving from *F. Gaiser's* book (*figure 112*) shows its name as *Carlsruhe* which is *not* correct, as the name belongs to the last 1863 class which were not bogie types! Unless, of course, someone somewhere knows different!

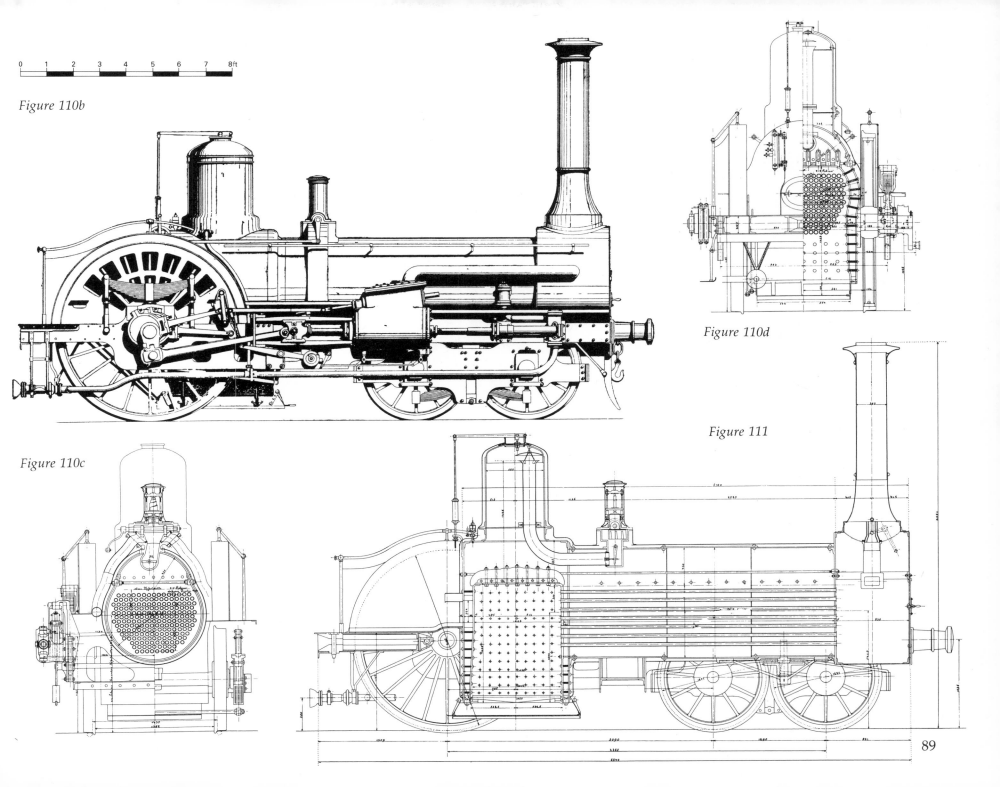

Figure 110b

Figure 110d

Figure 110c

Figure 111

89

Figure 112 The engraving shows the Baden State bogie type but with the name of a later class.

Locomotives of the 1850, 1858-9 and 1863 Classes

This is the 1856 class of three engines built by the E. B Hauptwerkstatte-Karlsruhe and, other than the main dimensions, I have found neither photograph nor drawings of them They were very similar to the final two classes of 1858 and 1863 with minor differences of equipment layout and position, the splashers having six rounded slots in, rather than the more ope type of the others.

The last two classes we can identify as we have photographs o both *Badenia* and *Constance*, and Mr. E. Twining's drawing (*figure 113*) (which he completed from one of his own early photographs is of the final 1863 class. Compared with *Badenia* you can see she has acquired a new rather ugly cab, and an equally ugly stovepipe chimney. She appears, however, to have lost her water feed pump which, on all the other three classes, has moved rearwards to the back of the footplate, and is now driven from a lug on the back of one of the eccentric rods. The weight-operated safety valve is well shown; this had the odd habit of letting-off little spurts of steam as the engine rattled over point-work and crossings. Many of the later classes lasted well into the late 1880s before being scrapped.

Locomotives of the 1856 Loewe Class

MAIN DIMENSIONS
OF 1856 CLASS
Driving Wheels 6' 2"
Carrying Wheels 3' 6"
Wheelbase 5' 8" + 6' 1"
Cylinders 15" × 22"

1856 Loewe Class
No. 1 *Loewe*
No. 2 *Greif*
No. 4 *Mannheim*

Figure 113 The 1863 Class in their final condition, drawn from a photograph by E. N. Twining.

MAIN DIMENSIONS
Driving Wheels 6' 11¾"
Carrying Wheels 4' 0"
Wheelbase 6' 2" + 6' 2"
Cylinders 15⅞" × 22"

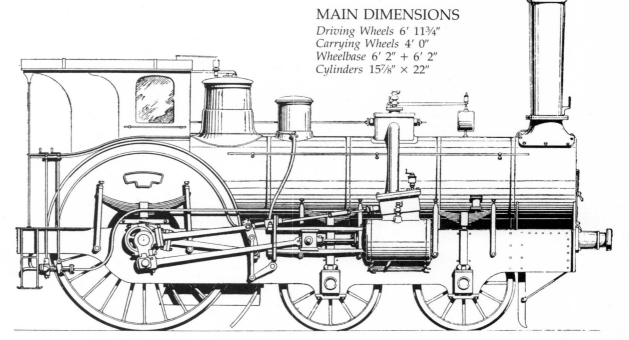

1859–9 Rheinfelden Class

No. 83 *Rheinfelden*
No. 84 *Sackingen*
No. 85 *Laufenburg*
No. 86 *Waldsut*
No. 87 *Pforzheim*
No. 88 *Constanz*
No. 89 *Strassburg*
No. 90 *Pfalz*

MAIN DIMENSIONS

Driving Wheels 6' 11¾"
Carrying Wheels 4'0"
Wheelbase 5' 5" + 6' 10½"
Cylinders 15⅞" × 22"

Plate 31

Plate 32

Locomotives of the 1863 Badenia Class

1863 Badenia Class

No. 7   *Badenia*
No. 8   *Carlsruhe*
No. 9   *Mercur*
No. 10 *Meteor*
No. 11 *Vulcan*
No. 12 *Jupiter*
No. 13 *Phoenix*
No. 14 *Offenburg*

Part Three
Hessische Ludwigsbahn

MAIN DIMENSIONS
Driving Wheels 6' 0"
Carrying Wheels 3' 6"
Wheelbase 5' 9" + 7' 6"
Cylinders 15" × 24"

No. 14 *Ludwig*   No. 15 *Mathilde*   No 16 *Cl. Lauteren*
No. 17 *Karlder Grosse*   No. 18 *Maximilian*
No. 19 *Aschaffenburg, A. Humann* (since 1861)
No. 35 *Haydn*   No. 36 *Willigis*   No. 37 *Alice*

The Hesse-Ludwig-Railway, which was to become part of the Prussian State railways in 1898, had, according to *F. Gaiser*, nine Cramptons on the strength. They were 'maids of all work' passenger wise, working both fast and slow traffic between Frankfurt and Mannheim—running for some way parallel with the Baden State Railway. They were built in 1858 by E. Kessler of Esslingen and, although basically the same, like all classes they had detail differences of smokebox door and buffer beam shape, with not all of them fitted for sanding. They were not very pretty locomotives, looking to me a bit like a mobile set of spare parts. They are one of only two types of Crampton that comes to mind with sloping outside cylinders, the Midland Railway Nos. 130 and 131 being the other. Still, with quite large carrying wheels and smallish (for a Crampton) six-foot drivers, there might otherwise have been clearance problems. The double cylinder monstrosity on the front of the footplate is another later addition and is the Charpentier air brake (*figures 114 & 115* and *plate 33*).

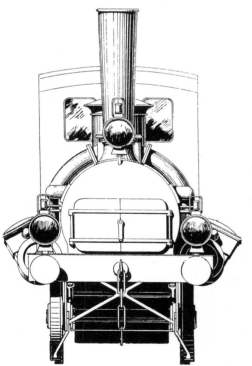

Figure 114

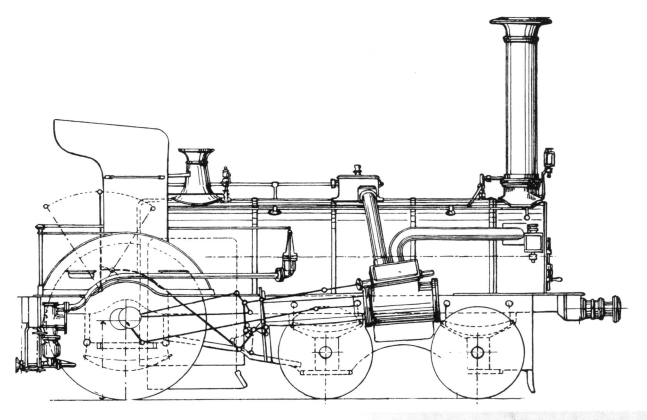
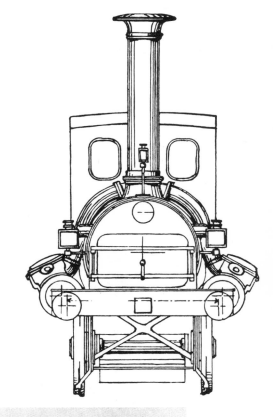

Figure 115

0 1 2 3 4 5 6 7 8ft

Plate 33

93

Part Four
Hannoversche Bahn

The Hannover Railway was one of many railway administrations in this part of Germany which became amalgamated as the political climates changed. Hannover 'State' is part of lower Saxony and has been a principality, an electorate, and a kingdom in its varied history. It ceased to be a kingdom in 1814 when there was union with Prussia, which brings us into our Crampton period.

In the 1850s the City of Hannover was an important industrial centre, with its locomotive works, shipbuilding, and supporting iron works, supplied, materials wise, mainly through the canal port which fed into the vast German canal network. Incidentally, when we talk about a German canal, we mean a full blooded waterway for quite heavy tonnage, not to be compared with our picturesque but industrially puny 'cut'.

The railway started life with some English goods locomotive imports until a Mr. Jahren Kirchweger became Chief Mechanical Engineer in 1850. He was a much respected engineer of the period and is thought to have been responsible for the introduction of Cramptons on to the railway. He quickly recognised that this long wheelbased, steady engine would be ideal for the mainly flat country of the Hannover State, and that the lack of adhesion would not be too much of a disadvantage. He was probably responsible for the basic design also, as the similarities between the two types from two separate builders is just too coincidental!

The first nineteen were built in 1853 to 1855 by F. Wohlert of Berlin, and the remaining fourteen by G. Egestorff from 1857 to 1860; neither series were named.

Figure 116

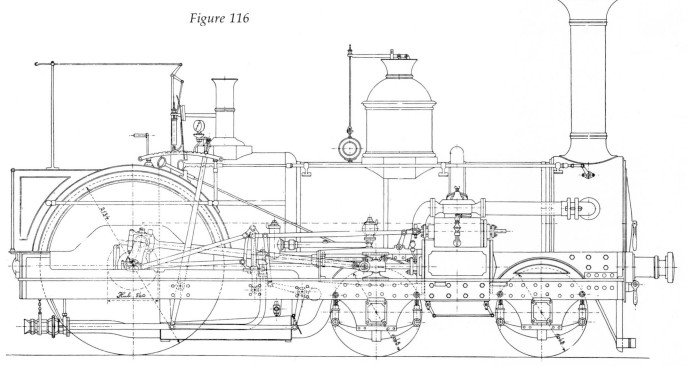

MAIN DIMENSIONS

Driving Wheels 7' 0"
Carrying Wheels 3' 6"
Wheelbase 6' 3" + 8' 3"
Cylinders 16" × 22"
Tender Wheels 3' 3"

94

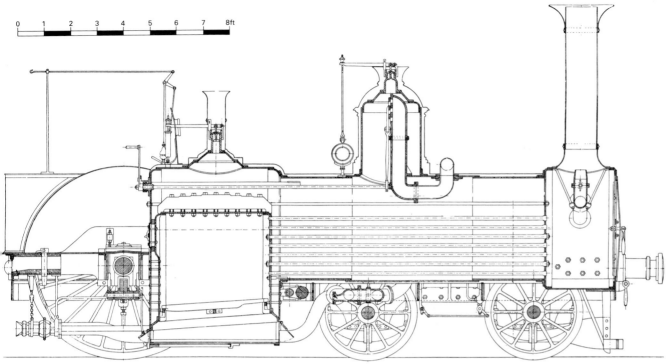

We have quite good drawings of both types of locomotives including the tenders (*figures 116* to *123*), and some more detail of the tender mounted feedwater heater mentioned later in the chapter on the Danish locomotives.

On studying the drawings you can see that they both have a 'bull nosed' appearance which is caused by a rather novel feature. There is no separate buffer beam, but the front plate of the smokebox has been extended to each side of the frames, thereby forming a combined smokebox front and buffer beam, the buffers are then bolted on direct. This would certainly shorten the normal overhang, which, along with the fact that most continental railways had one buffer face flat and one curved, considerably reduced the chance of buffer locking when shunting in industrial sidings.

The Wohlert locomotive had no cabs, as built, which highlights the communication cord arrangement coming in on high stanchions on the left hand side of the locomotive. It is difficult to say whether this applied the brakes direct, or just gave a warning of trouble.

Figure 117 The first batch was built by Wohlert and consisted of nineteen locomotives and were numbered 111 to 145.

Figure 118

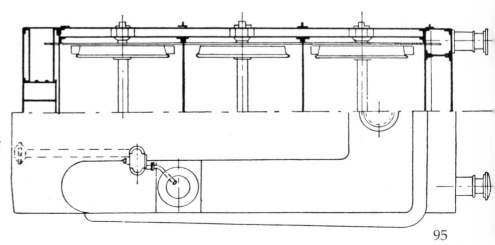

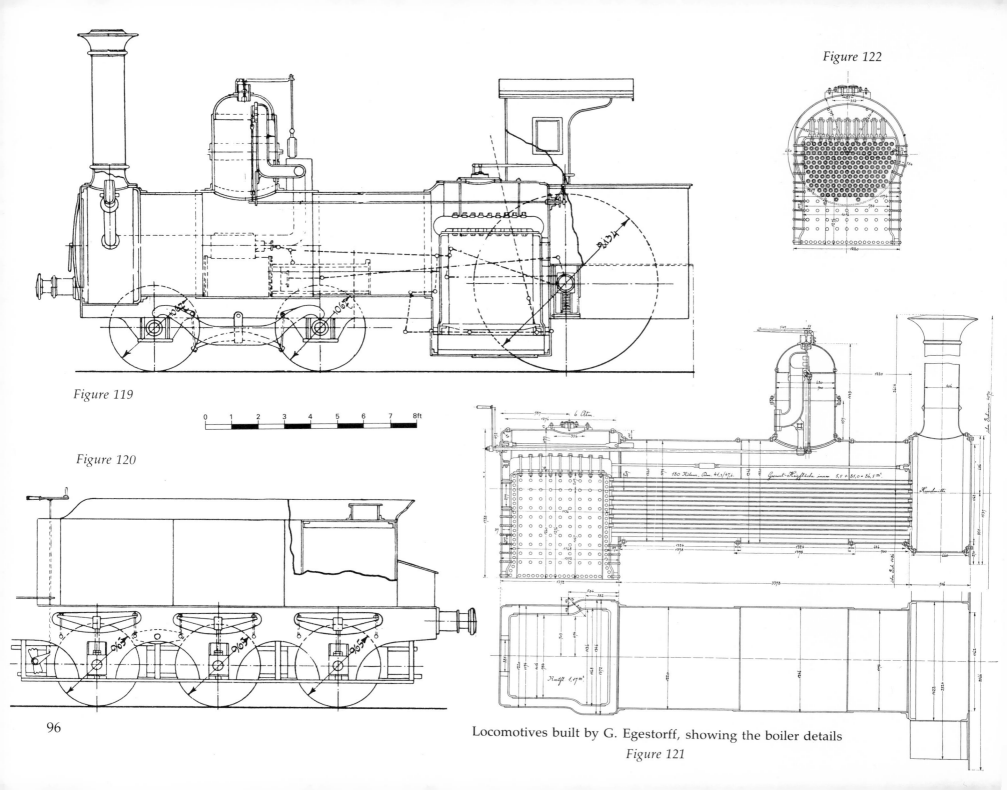

Figure 122

Figure 119

Figure 120

Locomotives built by G. Egestorff, showing the boiler details

Figure 121

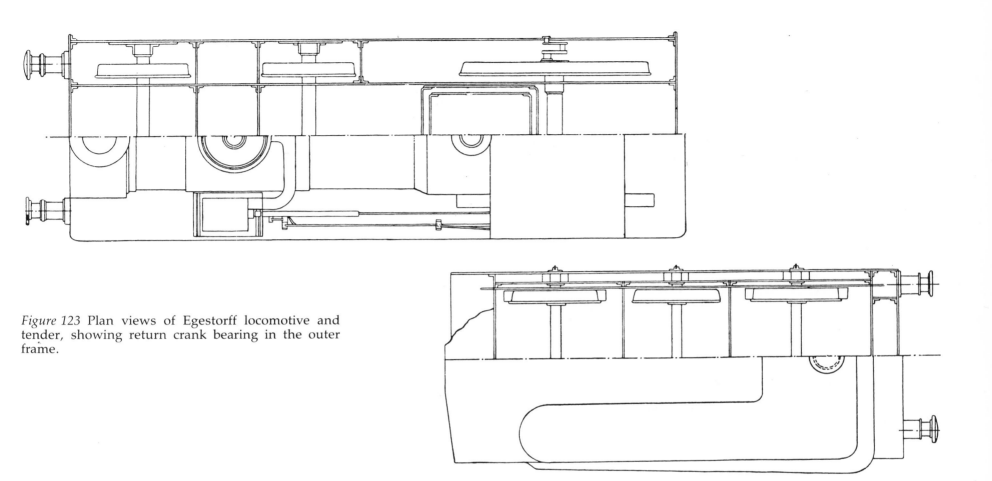

Figure 123 Plan views of Egestorff locomotive and tender, showing return crank bearing in the outer frame.

Apart from the cab, the only other major differences between the two types is that the front carrying wheels are equalised on the Egestorff locomotives but individually sprung on the Wohlert machines. Water feed pumps were driven from inside the cross-heads, and the valve gear, which could have been Hall's, comprised of very neat return cranks mounted with an outrigger bearing in the outside frames. The wheels had quite large 22″ hubs to aid adhesion and were the same size on both locomotives, though, from the drawings, the variable blast pipe control, rather neatly fed through the hollow hand rail, seems to be fitted on the Wohlert locomotive only. Nos. 148 to 153 were transferred to the Westfalia Railway in 1868 and, after reboilering in 1872 to 1878, became among the longest lasting German Cramptons.

Part Five
Rheinischen Bahn

The Rhineland railway metals between Cologne and Aachen near the Belgian and Dutch borders, were one of the major arteries of the various German State railway systems. The City of Cologne on the banks of the mighty river Rhine is, of course, well known. Forty-four miles away Aachen, or Aix-la-Chapelle, not quite so. As the latter it was in early times a French city with some very fine buildings, the cathedral dating from 796 A.D. More modern times brought several international treaties and, alas, widespread destruction in the two world wars to follow. The line had an international importance as it served as a 'border post' and, before the opening of the Austrian Empress Kaiserin Elizabeth railway (Wien-Linz-Salzburg) in 1858-59, anyone who wanted to go from Vienna to Paris had to travel the Rhineland route.

The man responsible for introducing the Cramptons was the then C.M.E., one Paul Camille von Denis, an engineer of French birth and engineering leanings. This was evident in his choice of layout—the French double frame design with a smooth clean 'uncluttered' boiler. The four locomotives were ordered in 1853 from A. Borsig of Berlin and were probably the first locomotives built to the French pattern by Borsig. However, although following the railways basic specification, the makers in many ways put their own individual 'stamp' on the design. The actual cladding of the boiler and dome were a Borsig speciality, and the four large boiler support brackets were a little unusual when three or even two sufficed for most designers.

The valve gear motion driven by two eccentrics was neatly transferred to the cylinders by an arrangement of levers, mounted on two substantial bearings, attached to the frames on each side in such a way that the final valve gear operating link stayed parallel to the cylinder centres with presumably less distortion. The large feedwater pumps were driven from an extension shaft through the front cylinder cover plate via a universal joint, to the pump casings, which were bolted between the frames either side of the smokebox.

The suspension was compensated in such a way that the proportion of weight carried by the carrying wheels was mostly on the leading pair, the centre having a much lighter spring and receiving only about one quarter of the beam weight. There is sadly only the one drawing (*figure 124*) and no photographs, but still giving enough detail to model, I think!

Figure 124

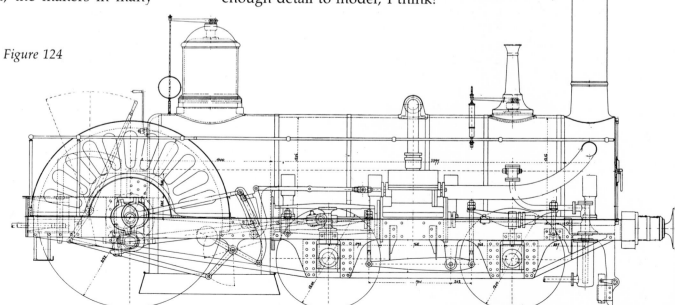

MAIN DIMENSIONS
Driving Wheels 7' 0"
Carrying Wheels 4' 0"
Wheelbase 7' 0" + 7' 6"
Cylinders 16" × 22"

Part Six
Magdeburg-Leipziger Bahn

Plate 34

The two Saxon cities served by this line are both in what is now East Germany, the river port of Magdeburg on the river Elbe being also a railway junction and some 80 miles from Berlin. The other terminus is the old city of Leipzig with its university dating from the 15th century. This city, with its connections with Bach and Mendelssohn, was for many years the centre of the German book publishing trade, and is noted today for its international trade fairs.

There were only four Cramptons on the line, built by Mb-G. Karlsruhe in 1857 and named *Sturm, Blitze, Pfeil,* and *Greif.* There were no running numbers in *Gaiser's* tables so they either had names only, or the records have disappeared with time.

The only pictorial record I could find of the class is shown in the illustration in *plate 34*, and, although not a 'technical drawing, it is quite detailed, showing some interesting and somewhat puzzling features. Although built by the same firm as the Main-Neckar machines, they are very different in style, and one feels the workshops had a field day with their own ideas. Up till now the main contractor for the locomotives had been Borsig who, apparently declined the order? Whether experience of the seven machines they had built for other lines put them off further work, is not known.

Anyway, Karlsruhe obtained the order, and I will try and point out some of the salient features.

They were hung on a basic three point suspension, with the front end very like the Rhineland locomotives with the equalising beam putting most of the carrying wheel weight on the front pair of wheels. The valve gear is the Stephenson type, with very distinctive cylinders having a heavily ribbed valve chest cover plate.

There appears, from the translations from *F. Gaiser's* book, to be a form of patent feed water system which (not being often found in my trade on aircraft) I have not been able to sort out! There is certainly a rotary 'donkey' pump down the rear end with valves and plumbing linked to the thicker than normal dome. I get the feeling that the water was pumped round a double skin on the outside of the dome but I'm not sure. The article refers to a 'waterhead' chimney which may or may not refer to the very thick lip on the chimney itself, though I rather doubt it—I think it must mean the dome.

These locomotives all gave good service in the 1850-60s and were eventually taken out of service in the summer of 1884. *Sturm*, even at this late date, was almost in its original condition. Still cabless but with just a small spectacle plate behind the dome, and a strikingly short cast chimney which must have come from another class altogether. One wonders how *that* came about.

MAIN DIMENSIONS

Driving Wheels 7' 0"
Carrying Wheels 3' 6"
Wheelbase 6' 8" + 8' 9"
Cylinders 16" × 22"

Plate 35

Part Seven
Bayerischen Pfalzbahn

J. A. Maffei Class of Locomotive

Figure 125

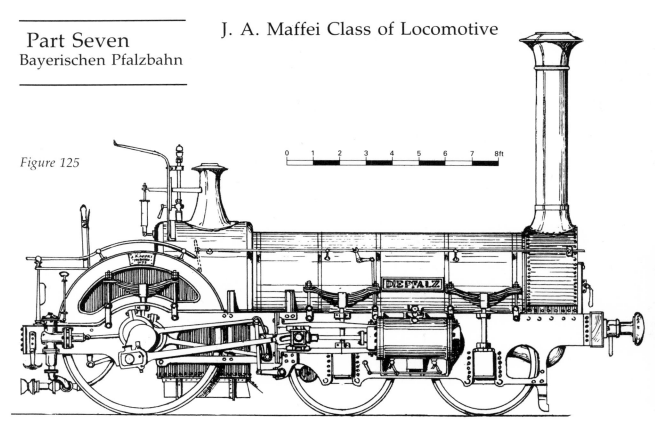

The Bavarian 'Imperial' Railway, as against the Eastern Railway (to be described later), had two classes of Crampton by two different builders as detailed on *page 102*.

The class of four locomotives by J. A. Maffei of Munich were built in 1853, the leading dimensions being as stated above. Dennis has drawn *Die Pfalz* (*figure 125*), and, thanks to the fine 'replica' built in the late 1920s in the Nuremburg Transport museum, we also have some photographs (*plates 36* and *37*) including one very useful one of the cab details (*plate 35*).

As the drawings show (*figures 125* and *126*), this class, like most of the German built Cramptons, differs in detail from both their English and French relations. They appear at first sight to have the French style of double frame, but closer examination of the plan view shows it to be an 'outside frame only', but of double skin 'sandwich' construction, this having a large cut-out between the leading wheels for the cylinder castings to bolt into. These

cylinders were cast in one piece, and designed in such a way that the valve chest lay on the same centre line as the cylinders, i.e. side by side rather than on top of the cylinders, with the valve gear designed by the Englishman, Joseph Hall, on the Stephenson pattern, driven by the eccentrics mounted inside the cranks. The connecting rod from the cranks had a form of 'bayonet' fitting where it joined the crosshead and slide bars, a Maffei 'feature' from about 1853! This may have led to some mechanical gain, but must have made servicing harder—and servicing *was* important, as these locomotives spent quite some time in the Ludwigshaven shops undergoing repairs made necessary by what must be considered a fault in the basic design. The quite flexible sandwich frames with the cylinder castings bolted to them must have flexed quite a lot under load, resulting in the large, heavy, 'Y' shaped steam return pipe to the blast pipe fracturing more often than it should. This pipe had been routed under the smokebox and

Plate 36 Two close-up views of the preserved replica *Die Pfalz* in Nuremburg Museum.

Plate 37 Reconstructed Crampton express locomotive No. 28 *Die Pfalz*, Palatine Railways, which has been placed in the railway collection at the Nuremberg Museum.

between the wheels for purely aesthetic reasons, and were consequently time-consuming to repair. They were later re-routed above the wheels as individual pipes like the other Cramptons, which was a shame as they *did* look very sleek and pleasing to the eye.

The oval boiler/firebox/smokebox 'unit' was fixed at the front end where the smokebox was the full width of the frames, and allowed to expand and contract at the rear via a firebox support bracket. This free steaming domeless boiler was said to be popular with the crews.

The feedwater pumps were mounted in a very accessible position on the rear frames, being driven by a rod attached to one of the eccentric sheaves.

The regulator details I am not sure about. *F. Gaiser* talks about a long cross-shaft operating in the cross-wise steam pipe with a counter weight, but nothing shows on the drawing! Dennis shows rods coming down from the handrail to each cylinder on his *Die Pfalz* drawing in *figure 125*. It should have had a common regulator built into the steam feed pipe under the engine as built, which was converted later to the separate rods to each valve chest as used on the Tulk and Ley engines.

The counter weight mentioned is probably the one on the end of the regulator handle shown in the cab photograph (*plate 35*)—a form of 'dead man's handle'!

The original class ran until about 1880 when they were scrapped.

Livery. Possibly the following. Smokebox, chimney, inner firebox black, with frames and wheels red. Superstructure was dark green with beadings, safety valve and whistle polished brass, and a copper or brass cap to the chimney.

Builder J. A. Maffei

No. 26 *Konig Max*	No. 27 *Hohe*
No. 28 *Die Pfalz*	No. 29 *Konigin Marie*

Builder Emil Kessler

No. 36 *Ludwigshohe*	No. 37 *Magdenburg*
No. 38 *Maxburg*	No. 39 *Trifels*
No. 40 *Kalmit*	No. 41 *Drachenfels*
No. 46 *v. d. Pfordten*	No. 47 *Mahla*
No. 48 *Sickingen*	No. 49 *E. v. Wrede*
No. 60 *Poelnitz*	No. 61 *A. Jaeger*
No. 62 *Limburg*	No. 63 *Edernburg*

Figure 126

MAIN DIMENSIONS

Driving Wheels 6' 0"
Carrying Wheels 4' 0"
Wheelbase 5' 4" + 7' 6"
Cylinders 14" × 24"

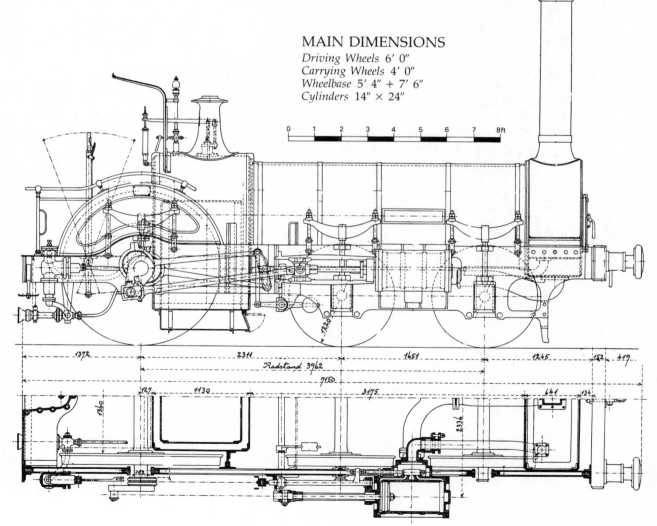

Plate 38 Locomotive No. 38 *Maxburg* shown in 1870 'on shed' at the Weissenburg depot.

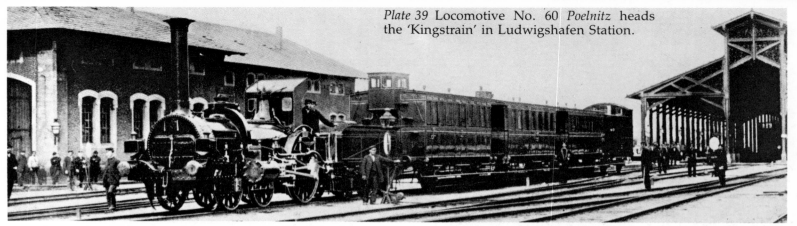

Plate 39 Locomotive No. 60 *Poelnitz* heads the 'Kingstrain' in Ludwigshafen Station.

This group of very imposing machines was supplied in four basic batches by E. Kessler over the 1855-64 period, locomotives No. 40 *Kalmit* and No. 38 *Maxburg* being the first delivered and the locomotive seen in *plate 39*, *Poelnitz*, being the last. They were apparently modified internally over the building period to keep them in line with the proven and well liked French style of construction, though Kessler added their own touches, as we shall see later. The external differences of cab and chimney etc., are, I think, simply the variations of rebuild and overhaul style over the approximately forty years of very useful life these engines had.

The main dimensions are given on this page, and, of course, more comprehensive details in the tables at the beginning of the chapter.

As mentioned, the French 'visual' style of long clean boiler was used (though I'm not happy with the aesthetics of that cab!) with the regulator mounted half way along and controlled from one side via a long cross shaft and linkage. This was presumably to avoid routing it through the safety valve case and safety valve weights which, as mentioned before, were fitted to replace the somewhat suspect coil springs of the period. Some or all of these engines could have been built with springs initially but *Kalmit* has no weights, as seen in the *plate 40*. She could have been converted during her rebuilding.

The construction of the boiler was pure Kessler, and quite sophisticated for the time. The smokebox was circular (*not* a Crampton characteristic!) and quite a bit bigger than the boiler barrel, to which it was joined by several large rings. The smokebox casing was rigidly held between the frames at the front of the engine, and the rear was supported, not by the conventional cross frame half brackets, but was hung between a form of 'drop

arm' allowing it to expand, contract, and absorb the jolts of normal service. This allowed it to flex slightly thereby hopefully reducing fatigue stresses and prolonging overhaul life, though what happened to the steam joints at the cylinders is not mentioned—did they have high pressure flexible couplings in those days, I wonder?

Stephenson valve gear is again used, but the Maffei system of valve mounting inboard has been abandoned. The valve chests are once again mounted on top of the cylinders and angled downwards with their centre line just inboard of that of the cylinders, and operated from the eccentrics by sturdy forked rod-ends and bearings.

The pipe going into the side of the large rear valve casing is, I think, indication of a similar type of feedwater heater to that discussed on the Magdeburg locomotives. The feedwater pump driven from a lug on the rear of one of the eccentrics, supplied the water via a double skin in the safety valve casing to give it a degree of pre-heating before entering the boiler. Both the short stroke pumps and plumbing have gone on the photograph of No. 38 *Maxburg* (*plate 38*), to be replaced by the more efficient Giffard injector. Gone also is the elegant chimney now replaced by an ugly 'stovepipe', the larger cab with side windows has become 'standard', and, not yet shown on any of the photogrphs, sanding gear is to be fitted with the sand-bin mounted between the shapely casing and regulator, with twin pipes down to the front of the driving wheels.

These locomotives seemed to have quite a universal usage, in that they seemed just as happy on the steeply graded mountain lines around Neustadt and Bexbach as on the level Rhine plain, and, as a result, were popular with their crews who, when interviewed in 1909, spoke of them with nostalgia.

Plate 40 Shows locomotive No. 40 *Kalmit* 'posed' for the camera, as built in 1855.

MAIN DIMENSIONS
Driving Wheels 6' 0"
Carrying Wheels 4' 0"
Wheelbase 5' 5" + 7' 7"
Cylinders 15" × 24"

Part Eight
Bayerischen Ostbahn

The Bavarian Eastern Railway was a quite small organisation especially in its locomotive department, but covered quite a lot of ground—linking towns and cities like Nuremburg, Geiselhoering, Passaue, Furth, Munich, Regensburg and many more.

The line was built by P. Camille von Denis in 1856 who also choose the motive power which remained almost unchanged until the late 1860s. This consisted of twenty-four locomotives over the 1865-1858 period from the firm of J. A. Maffei, the first twelve being on the Crampton pattern numbered A 1 to A 12, and the rest A 13 to A 24, very similar in appearance, but to the 2-2-2 design. The Cramptons, however, were the favourites, and were used on the 'top link' passenger trains up to 1875 when the 'Eastern' was absorbed into its larger neighbours. By then increasing train loads made the lack of adhesion of both classes critical enough to necessitate double heading, which caused the railway to embark on a rebuilding programme whereby they were all converted to 2-4-0 types, with all the existing driving wheels shared out! What happened was that half the Cramptons received

the 6' 0" wheels of the other half making six 2-4-0s, then a new batch of wheels was produced for the remainder. The same sequence of events happened to the 5' 0" wheels of the 2-2-2s.

In design the Cramptons were similar to the Bayerischen Pfaltsbahn locomotives except that the valve chests were raised and angled in a more conventional (for Crampton) form, the boiler was now round with a safety valve casing half way along, and a feedwater 'donkey engine' pump added to the left hand side of the cab.

The one fundamental and obvious difference is high-lighted by the spark arrester 'balloon' chimney. The locomotives 'as built' were intended for turf- or peat-burning with a special stepped grate, and the balloon chimney. As you can see in the section drawing *figure 127*, the sparks would be guided outwards by the cone to catch under the lip of the chimney and fall back. However, although the 2-2-2s stayed on turf-burning, the Cramptons only ever used normal steam coal and, when rebuilt as 2-4-0s, had an ugly, quite heavily tapered stovepipe chimney.

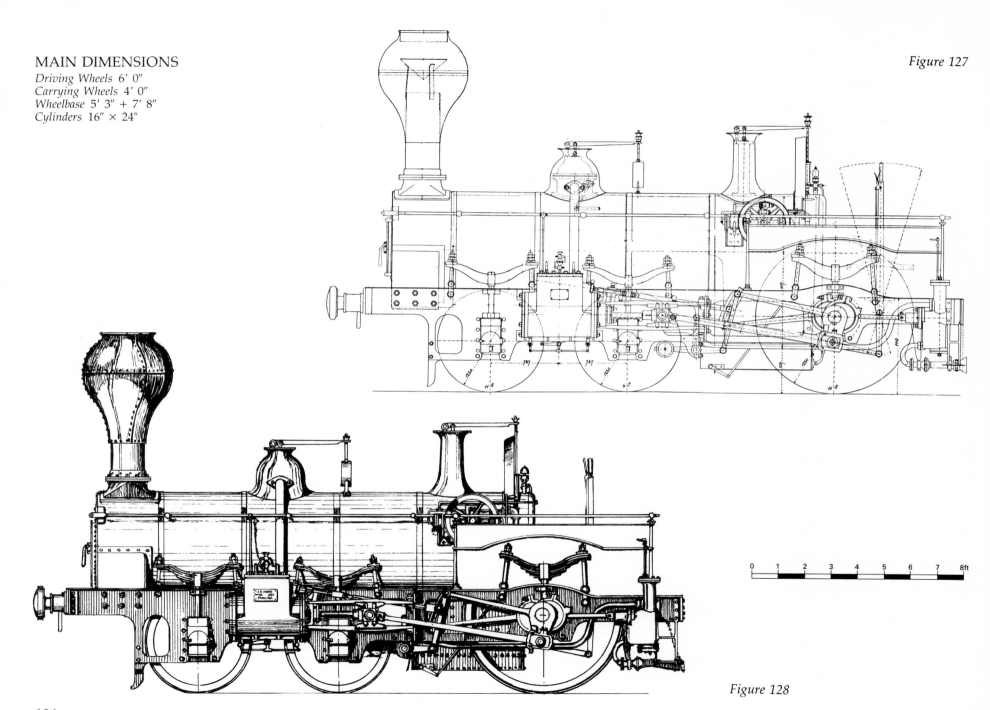

MAIN DIMENSIONS
Driving Wheels 6′ 0″
Carrying Wheels 4′ 0″
Wheelbase 5′ 3″ + 7′ 8″
Cylinders 16″ × 24″

Figure 127

Figure 128

0 1 2 3 4 5 6 7 8ft

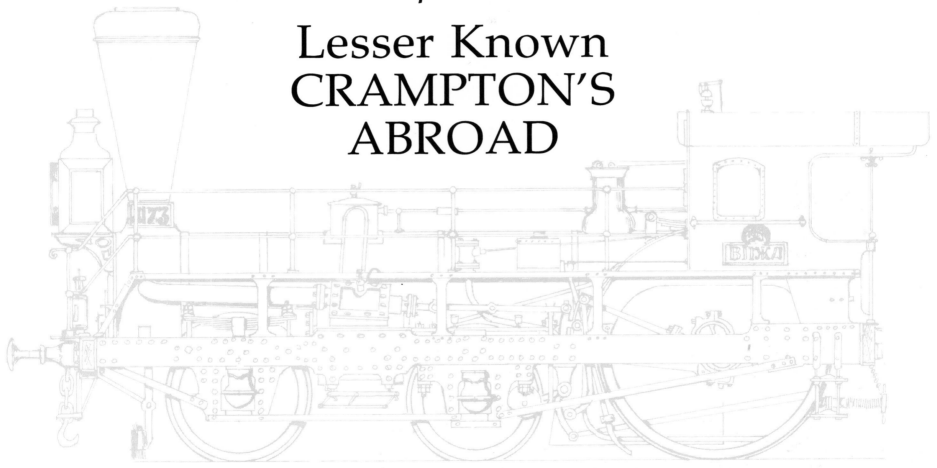

Chapter Six

Lesser Known CRAMPTON'S ABROAD

Chapter Index

Railway	Name or Number	Builders	Date Built	Works No.	Cylinders			Wheels			Drivers	Wheelbase	Boiler Details				Tube Details			Heating Surface			Firegrate Area	Empty Weight	Service Weight	Adhesive Weight	Tractive Effort	
					Position	Bore	Stroke	Number	Arrangement	Carrying			Shape	Length	Diameter	Pressure	Number	Diameter	Length	Firebox	Boiler	Total					Cylinders	Maximum
DENMARK																												
Seeländische Bahn	Thor	A. Borsig, Berlin	1854	553	zw h	381	560	2	fest	1072 u. 942	1544	2119+2040=4159	zyl.	1635	1256	7	180	47	3251	6,4	76,3	82,7		28,75	13,0		2395	2600
do.	Niord	do.	1854	554	„	381	560	2	„	1072 u. 942	1544	2119+2040=4159	„	1635	1256	7	180	47	3251	6,4	76,3	82,7		28,75	13,0		2395	2600
do.	Baldur	do.	1854	555	„	381	560	2	„	1072 u. 942	1544	2119+2040=4159	„	1635	1256	7	180	47	3251	6,4	76,3	82,7		28,75	13,0		2395	2600
do.	Fenris	do.	1854	556	„	381	560	2	„	1072 u.942	1544	2119+2040=4159	„	1635	1256	7	180	47	3251	6,4	76,3	82,7		28,75	13,0		2395	2600
do.	Skirner	do.	1855	557	„	381	560	2	„	1138 u. 1072	1830	2119+2040=4159	„	1635	1256	7	180	47	3251	6,4	76,3	82,7		29,5	13,5		2021	2700
do.	Vidar	do.	1855	558	„	381	560	2	„	1138 u. 1072	1830	2119+2040=4159	„	1635	1256	7	180	47	3251	6,4	76,3	82,7		29,5	13,5		2021	2700
do.	Roeskilde	R.&W. Hawthorn Newcastle	—		„	15″ 381	22″ 560	2	„	3′7″ 1092	6′1½″ 1866	6′7″+7′1″=13′8″ 2007+2159=4166	5′2½″ 1587	4′ 1219	100 7	186	1¾″ 44,4	10′ 3048	73,2 6,81	761,2 70,71	834,4 77,52	14,3 1,33		25,5	11,0		1982	2200
do.	Ringsted	do.	über —		„	15″ 381	22″ 560	2	„	3′7″ 1092	6′1½″ 1866	6′7″+7′1″=13′8″ 2007+2159=4166	5′2½″ 1587	4′ 1219	100 7	186	1¾″ 44,4	10′ 3048	73,2 6,81	761,2 70,71	834,4 77,52	14,3 1,33		25,5	11,0		1982	2200
do.	Soró	do.	nommen 1856		„	15″ 381	22″ 560	2	„	3′7″ 1092	6′1½″ 1866	6′7″+7′1″=13′8″ 2007+2159=4166	5′2½″ 1587	4′ 1219	100 7	186	1¾″ 44,4	10′ 3048	73,2 6,81	761,2 70,71	834,4 77,52	14,3 1,33		25,5	11,0		1982	2200
do.	Slagelse	do.			„	15″ 381	22″ 560	2	„	3′7″ 1092	6′1½″ 1866	6′7″+7′1″=13′8″ 2007+2159=4166	5′2½″ 1587	4′ 1219	100 7	186	1¾″ 44,4	10′ 3048	73,2 6,81	761,2 70,71	834,4 77,52	14,3 1,33		25,5	11,0		1982	2200
do.	H.C. Oerstad	Mf. Eßlingen, Emil Keßler	1858	424	a g	381	610	2	„	1080	1830	1755+2295=4050	„	1665	1250	7	165	51	2978	7,0	70,2	77,2	0,97	22,5	9,5		2201	1900
NEW ZEALAND																												
Oreti Railway	Nos. 2 & 3	Robinson Thomas & Co.	1864			10½″ 226	22″ 560			3′6″	4′6″ 1380	12′9″																
RUSSIA																												
Warschau-Petersburg		Cail & Cie., Paris	1858		zw	400	600	2	fest	1200 & 1360 4′5″ & 4′0″	2100 6′10″	7′4″+7′9″	zyl.		1346	8							123,51	1,58	27,1	30,8	12,0	2377	2400
EGYPT																												
Aegyptische E. B.	49	Cail & Cie, Paris	1859		zw	400 15″	600 23″			1200 & 1360 4′5″ & 4′0″	2100 6′10″	7′4″+7′4″																
do.		Robert Stephenson & Co.				6″	10″			3′4″	4′6″	9′																

108

Please note—Where information is not known, the Table blocks have been left blank.

Denmark

MAIN DIMENSIONS
Driving Wheels 6′ 1½″
Carrying Wheels 3′ 7″
Wheelbase 6′ 7″ + 7′ 0″
Cylinders 15″ bore × 22″ stroke
Total Weight 25·5 tons

Figure 130

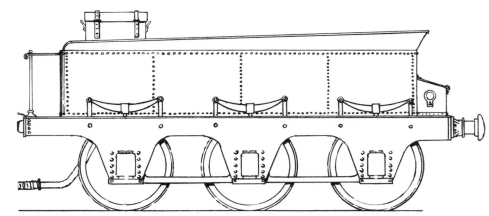

Figure 129

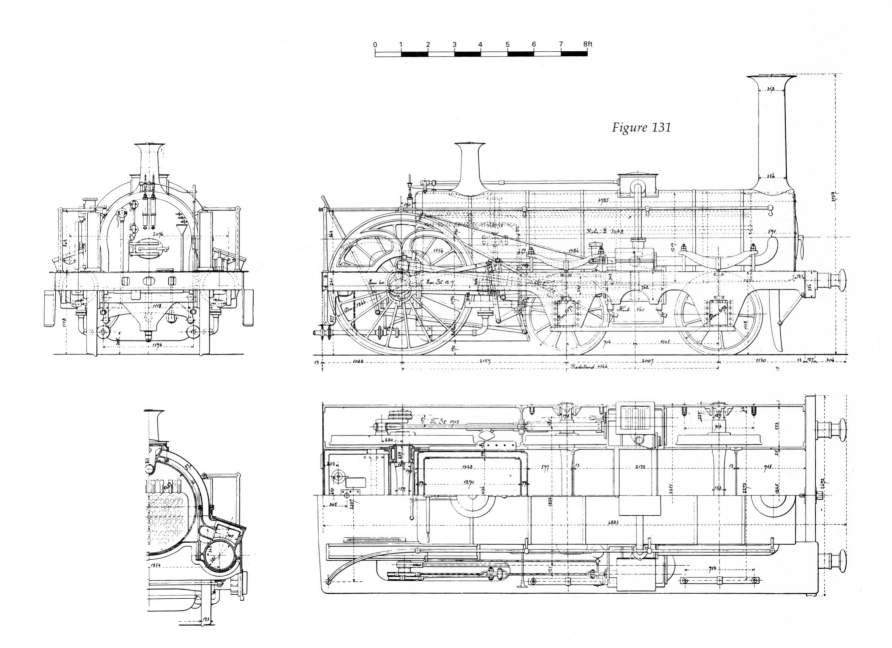

Figure 131

Plate 41

One of a class of four locomotives built by Hawthorns of Newcastle in 1856. She has the standard type of Hawthorn cut-out splasher but not their usual large dome. When they went to Denmark is not certain as one source quotes Crampton as having four 'Trial' engines which he lent to prospective buyers but, bearing in mind the cost of such a venture, it does seem much more likely that they were simply ordered for Denmark, and someone misread some correspondence. The locomotives seem to have given fairly good service until 1864 when it appears that three of the four locomotives were withdrawn in the 1864-1867 period. The faults noted were boiler defects—unspecified, and cracked frames.

The class (*figure 129*) is a little unusual in that the engines were built in the earlier style with mixed framing rather like *Liverpool*, but some eight years later when, in England, the inside cylinder jackshaft type was evolving. The chimney on the tender (*plate 41*) was a fairly common sight on certainly the German railways around this period. It was a system for pre-heating the feed water before it left the tender, and was fitted in 1863. The chimney is presumably just a steam exhaust, and has been seen fitted to various parts of the tender tanking.

Livery. Little is known of the livery except that engines were black, with polished brass chimney caps and dome covers etc. The wheels *could* have been red in line with the rest of the locomotive fleet which came from German builders.

Of the other two types, the H. C. Oersted seems a twin to the ones on the Hessische Ludwigsbahn, but the Borsig locomotive seem to have much smaller driving wheels, perhaps train speeds in Denmark were in general slower than in Germany.

Half a lonely world from Whitehaven, the Southern Cross glares out of a sky of black velvet over the remote southern tip of New Zealand's south island. There the last rails in all creation ended at buffer stops on the quay at Invercargill. There, too, were the last Cramptons, certainly in space and possibly in birthtime, as strange a pair of the breed as ever became hardware. The Oreti Railway was built on the 'cheap' by an impoverished provincial government using the system of one, J. R. Davies of Australia. The rolling stock had flangeless wheels running on wooden track, being kept (most of the time) on the track by inclined vee groove pulleys riding on the top inner corners of the rails. The system was neither new nor original, but was virtually identical with that Arnoux scheme which, on steel rails, guided the flange squealing cars of the Ligne de Sceaux through such improbable Parisian suburbs as Robinson and Gate-of-Hell, as late as 1890. Davies' system differed only in its use of wooden rails, attractively and fatally cheap!

The eight mile Oreti Railway from Invercargill north to Makarewa was built in 1864, and locomotives Nos. 2 and 3 (*figure 132*) were shipped from Australia in time for the official opening in October of that year. Built by Robinson, Thomas and Co., of Ballarat, Victoria, they were 2-2-0s whose general lines were not unlike those of the South Eastern rebuilds, but were considerably smaller. They weighed only 13 tons, of which not more than six tons could have been borne by the driving wheels. Why the design was chosen is not precisely known; it is possible that the attraction of the Crampton four-wheeled layout was that it located a wheel very close to the four corners of the chassis, i.e.

close to where the guide wheels would have to be located. It is also possible that the design followed from that of the tiny contractor's engine *Lady Barkley*, used in building the railway, since that had all the specified requirements of a Crampton design even though its driving wheels were no more than three feet in diameter. Be that as it may, the accounts all refer to Nos. 2 and 3 as Cramptons, so presumably Thomas Russell collected his royalties on them, even though the patentee's plug plate, on the side sheets, credited J. R. Davies.

Only No. 2 was ever actually placed in service on the railway. The 20 mph speed she occasionally got up to, certified by no less an authority than Charles Rous-Marten, caused considerable damage to the somewhat impermanent way! In fact, the whole Davies system was a notable 'flop' since rain, mud or snow so reduced adhesion on the slippery baulks, that trains came to an impotent standstill, even on level track! The railway went predictably bust in 1867, to be followed soon after by the provincial government itself; the two Cramptons went to two different saw mills in Makarewa, one in 1869, the other in 1873. The latter one was still in locomotive service in the 1880s and its cannibalised boiler supplied steam to a corn-crusher until 1917.

Livery. This was a basic three-colour plan. The chimney had a copper cap but was otherwise black, as was the smokebox. The boiler, side sheets, and tender top were green lined out in black with a fine white line either side which had incurved corners. The frames below the footplate were a red brown, and safety valves, dome covers, and whistle were brass. The fleet numbers were painted on in yellow.

MAIN DIMENSIONS

Driving Wheels 4′ 6″ (1380)
Carrying Wheels 3′ 6″
Cylinders 10½″ × 22″
Valve Gear Stephenson

Figure 132

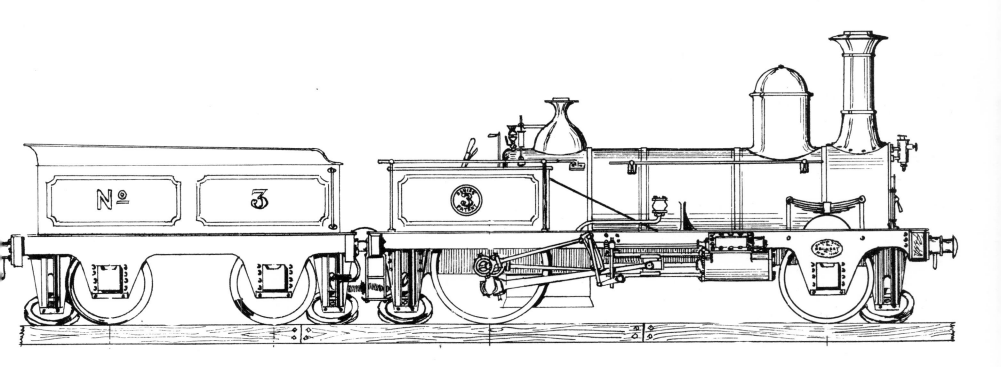

Russia

1861. Warsaw-Petersburg Railway, Russia.
Crampton Locomotives Nos. 171-174. Built by Jean-François Cail et Cie, Paris, France.

This is a standard Cail export design similar to the Egyptian locomotive as depicted in *figure 135*. Details are a bit scarce, but Dennis has based the drawing on a mixture of known facts, and the engineering 'fashions' of the time. We have some choice on building dates and running numbers, so I will quote what *we* think and what could be, in brackets.

There were three locomotives in the order, numbered by the railway Nos. 171-174 (170-173) and were built in 1861 (1858?).

They were delivered to the Warsaw Petersburg Railway with simple spectacle plates and no cab, very like the photograph (*plate 42*), and were immediately fitted with the large enclosed cab as seen in the *figure 133*. We are not sure if the cab extended to the tender like the design of the Russian locomotives, so on the drawing we have left these lines dotted. When the locomotives were delivered, the railway was owned by a French company which, in the 1890s, was taken over by the government. The

Figure 133

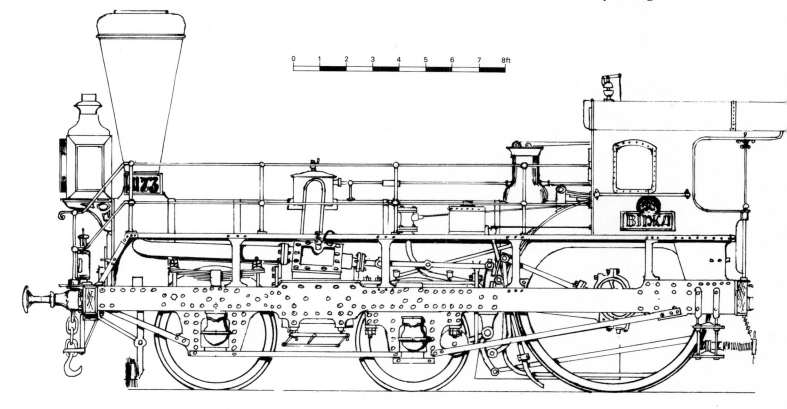

MAIN DIMENSIONS

Driving Wheels 6′ 10″
Carrying Wheels 4′ 5″ + 4′ 0″
Wheelbase 7′ 4″ + 7′ 9″
Cylinders 15″ × 23″
Valve Gear Stephenson
Total Weight 29·09 tons
Adhesive Weight 12 tons

drawing is based on how the locomotive would have looked at this time. In addition to the wide cab, they have the railed gallery (required by Imperial law after 1872) and a standard Russian headlamp as shown. The four-wheel tender has the very high rails needed to contain the vast loads of wood required for fuel. The problem was that, although at that time cheap and plentiful, wood burns very fast. These particular locomotives were in service until 1905.

Plate 42 Showing the 'basic' Cail design of P.L.M. No. 19. With the large dome removed and Russian fittings, we have the same locomotive as seen in the drawing in *Figure 133*.

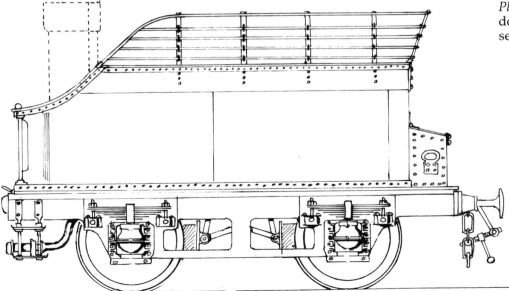

0 1 2 3 4 5 6 7   8ft

Livery. The livery is not known, but green/black and red brown/red were common Russian liveries of the Tzarist days.

Egypt

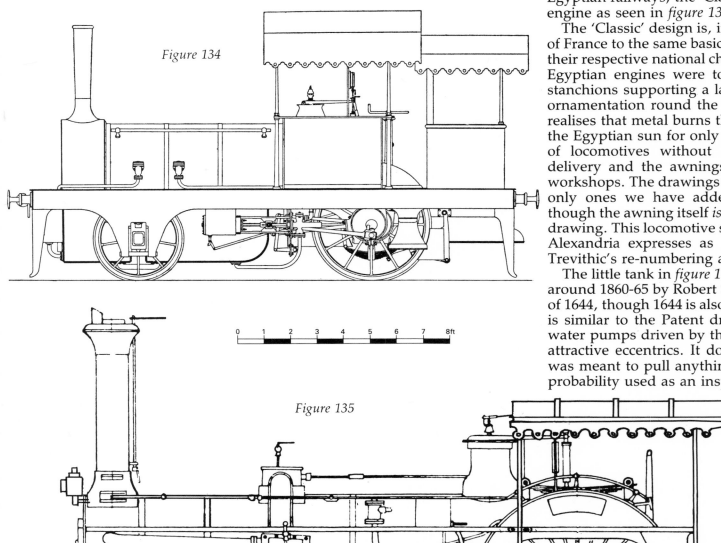

Figure 134

Figure 135

0 1 2 3 4 5 6 7 8ft

We could find only two variants of Crampton's influence on the Egyptian railways, the 'Classic' one, and this delightful little tank engine as seen in *figure 134*.

The 'Classic' design is, in fact, a standard Cail and Cie product of France to the same basic design as the Russian locomotive with their respective national characteristics added. The awnings on all Egyptian engines were to the same basic design of four light stanchions supporting a large area roof with varying degrees of ornamentation round the edge. These were essential when one realises that metal burns the hands quite badly when exposed to the Egyptian sun for only a few minutes. The early photographs of locomotives without awnings were, I suspect, taken on delivery and the awnings soon added in the company's own workshops. The drawings (*figure 135*) and the Russian one are the only ones we have added detail to without direct evidence, though the awning itself *is* taken from an Egyptian railway official drawing. This locomotive spent her early life working the Cairo to Alexandria expresses as No. 49, was re-numbered No. 22 in Trevithic's re-numbering and eventually broken up in 1892.

The little tank in *figure 134*, No. 137, appears to have been built around 1860-65 by Robert Stephenson and Co., to a builder's No. of 1644, though 1644 is also attributed to a six-coupled engine! She is similar to the Patent drawing in **Chapter One** *Figure 14*. The water pumps driven by the crossheads are there, as are the very attractive eccentrics. It does not look as though the locomotive was meant to pull anything as there are no hooks, so was in all probability used as an inspection saloon.

Livery. I am not sure of the very early livery, but in 1889 it was a dark red brown base colour, with black lines edged with fine vermillion lines. The roofs I would expect to be a lighter colour to reflect the heat.

Chapter Seven
The
COUPLED-CRAMPTON

THE COUPLED CRAMPTONS

Railway	Builder	Date	Name or No.	Cylinders Bore	Stroke	Driving Wheels	Carrying Wheels	Wheelbase	Country of Origin	Remarks	Page
Midland	E. B. Wilson	1848	*Lablache*	16"	22"	7'0"	—	16'	Britain		118
Belgian	Urban	1866	30 locos			6'11"	3'11"	8'4"+7'8"	Belgium		120
Est	Epernay	1878	10 locos	16"	26"	7'6"	4'7"	9'5"+8'4"	France		121
Midi		1885	36 locos	15¾"	23½"	6'6"	5'0"	10'0"+7'9"	France		122
S. Eastern	Stephenson	1851	5 locos	16"	24"	4'6"	—	12'4"	Britain	One tender engine	123
L.C.D.R.	*See text*	1861 to 1862	21 locos	16"	22"	5'6"	3'6"	4'0"+5'6"+5'6"	Britain	3 builders	124
G.N.R.	E. B. Wilson	1849	1–3	11"	18"	5'0"	—	10'11"	Britain	Former Ambergate, Nottingham & Boston	125
Y. & N.M.	E. B. Wilson	1850	273	11"	18"	5'0"	—	10'11"	Britain		125
L.C.D.R.	Hawthorn	1858	*Sondes*	15"	20"	5'6"	3'3"	3'9"+7'0"+6'9"	Britain		127
Est		1867	318						France	Photograph only	127
	Woolwich Arsenal			15"	18"	7'0"	4'6"	5'11"+5'6"+5'11"	Britain		128
Private	Soc. de la Meuse		37						Belgium	Photograph only. No other information	130

0 1 2 3 4 5 6 7 8ft

Figure 136

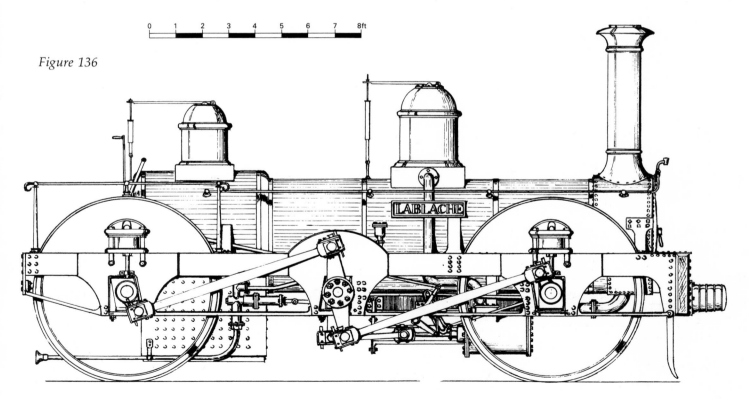

This chapter I'm afraid is in even more disarray than the previous ones, as the problems were—what to call the chapter, and, how to categorise such a mixed bag? Apart from the Woolwich tank, they *are* all coupled in one form or another, but one would hesitate to refer to any of them as conventional! They are a mixture of British and Continental design and are simply described as they come in no order of preference, starting with *Lablache* (*figures 136 and* 137).

This locomotive was built very closely to the Crampton patent illustrated on *page seven* (*figure 13E*) by E. B. Wilson of Leeds, for trials on the Midland Railway. She had many novel features all of which were aimed at producing an engine that overcame many of the design drawbacks current in the 1850s, i.e. basic instability often induced by the thrust of the pistons heaving alternately on each side of the locomotive. The object here was to mount the locomotive very firmly on four large wheels spaced well apart, and try to balance the action of the pistons so that the load 'pulses' transmitted more evenly to the wheels. This was achieved by having a dummy crankshaft which did *not* rotate, but produced a rocking motion. The centres of the outer cranks were set at 1' 9" diameter whereas the wheel crank throw was only 12". This meant that, while the drive shaft rocked, the wheel crank rotated. Sadkt ahe was not used in this form for very long and was rebuilt in a more conventional form soon after, although a similar engine on the South Yorkshire Railway, the *Albion*, had transverse cylinders and a similar rocking drive, and lasted some fifteen years giving good service! So perhaps our old friend 'Prejudice' had crept in again!

MAIN DIMENSIONS

Driving Wheels 7' 0" Note 6' 0" and
  6' 6" have also been quoted!
Wheelbase 16'
Cylinders 21" × 16"

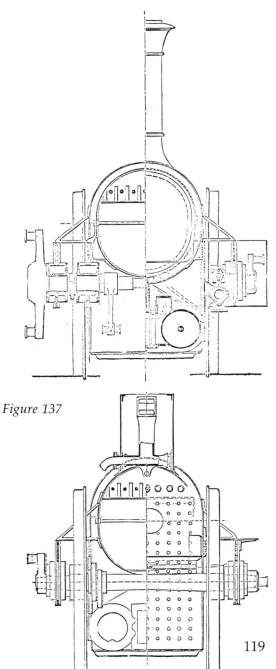

Figure 137

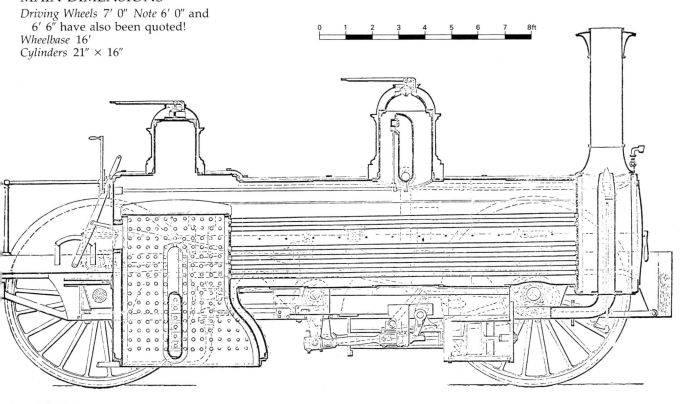

119

Grand Central Belge Urban 2–4–0

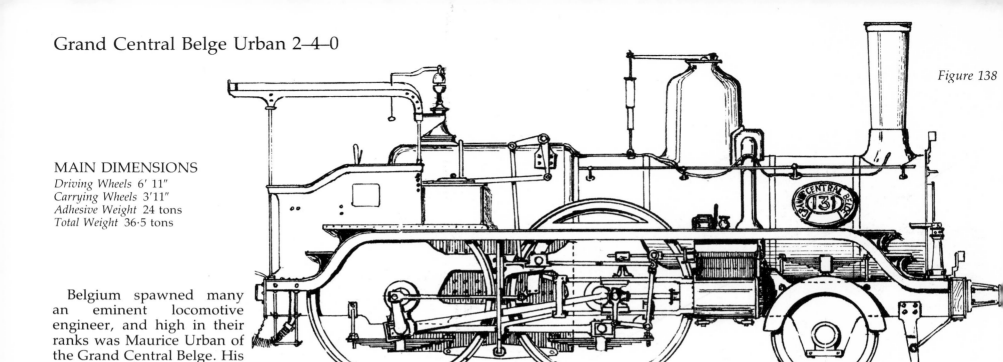

Figure 138

MAIN DIMENSIONS
Driving Wheels 6' 11"
Carrying Wheels 3'11"
Adhesive Weight 24 tons
Total Weight 36·5 tons

Belgium spawned many an eminent locomotive engineer, and high in their ranks was Maurice Urban of the Grand Central Belge. His coupled Cramptons derived not from classic Cramptons of his own system, but most probably from the Cramptons of the Nord-France, with which system the Grand Central made frontier connections in a number of places. Be that as it may, in 1866 Maurice Urban turned out the first of what the Belgians still call the Urban type, shown in the drawing (*figures 138* and *139*) in its original state. Over the period 1866-1877 a total of thirty engines were built in three slightly differing sub-series, Nos. 117 to 130,

131 to 137, 138 to 147. They were built by the Société St Leonard of Liége and the Société Anonyme de Marcinelle et de Couillet, of Hainault, and they had a grace and rakishness in sharp contrast to the cubism of Belpaire over on the Etat Belge. They had big 2100 mm driving wheels, Belpaire fireboxes, and sweeping three level valances. Their original Grand Central livery was a deep chocolate brown, bordered with black and lined in vermilion. The chassis was vermilion, bordered with black. And those great domes were polished brass, gleaming in the thin sooty sunlight of that ghastly Charleroi black country. Etat Belge pounced on the GCB on New Year's Day, 1897, and acquired all the Urban 2-4-0s, decking them out in a more sombre brown with all black chassis. In this guise, and fitted with Westinghouse brake gear, they could be seen on the light, fast Brussels-Antwerp express runs even as late as 1921. In either GCB or Etat Belge colours, the Urbans would make fine, impressive models.

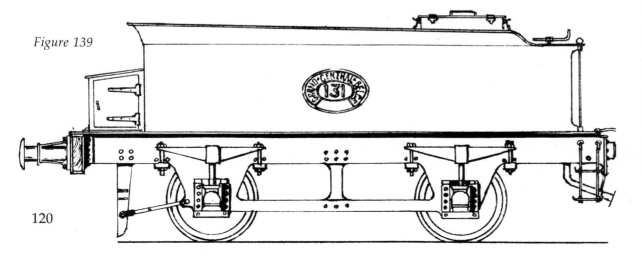

Figure 139

0 1 2 3 4 5 6 7 8ft

Note
Tender as for Crampton
604 in Chapter Four

MAIN DIMENSIONS
Driving Wheels 7' 6"
Carrying Wheels 4' 7"
Adhesive Weight 30 tons
Total Weight 42 tons

Figure 140

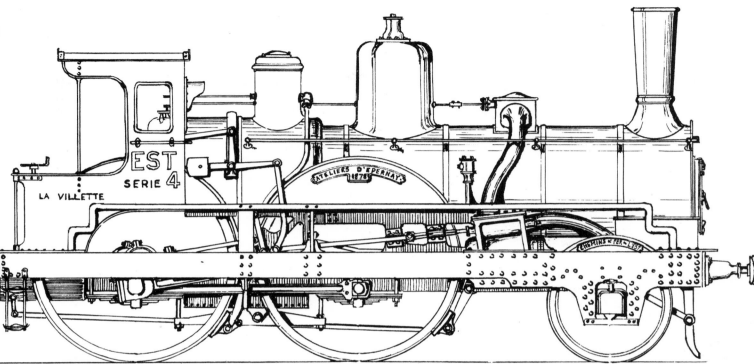

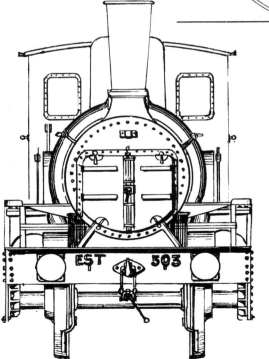

On the Est, the overdue demise of the conventional Crampton was followed by a directly-derived 2-4-0, series 501–510, designed by A. Salomon and built at the company's Epernay works, in 1878. These engines preserved all the Crampton features, as the drawing (*figure 140*) shows: massive double frames, lowslung wayback cylinders, the Crampton boiler and regulator with outside steam pipes, leading wheels in the main frames, and 2300 mm (90 inch) driving wheels. The coupled axle, just ahead of the fire-box, was equalised with the rear driving axle, giving a reliable 30 tonnes adhesive weight out of an overall 42 tonnes. These engines made quite a name for themselves on the Paris-Belfort runs (Strasbourg, the original Est terminal, was by now German), and to one of them fell the honour of hauling the inaugural Orient Express in 1883. Two of them, No. 508 and No. 509, went the way of Crampton No. 604 (q.v.) and acquired Flaman twin drum boilers. Some were converted to 4-4-0s in 1896, and from then on any claim to Crampton derivation is highly questionable.

The drawing brings out the massiveness of the breed, and also highlights some points of detail interest. One of these is the disposition of the reversing gear. Since rocker shafts could not pass through the firebox, transmission of link motion to the non-driving side could be done only over the firebox top or under the ashpan! The former was the preferred arrangement. The Est 4-wheel tender shown with No. 604 was used with this series also.

Livery. Est livery was black, polished bands, and liberal fine red lining round frame contours, cab sheets, running boards, and tender body. Front buffer beam red, bordered in white. Cabside letters white, shaded red. Not beautiful, the 501s—but definitely Est!

MAIN DIMENSIONS

Driving Wheels 6′ 6″
Carrying Wheels 5′ 0″
Tender 4′ 0″
Cylinders 15¾″ × 23½″
Total Weight 45 tons
Adhesive Weight 32 tons

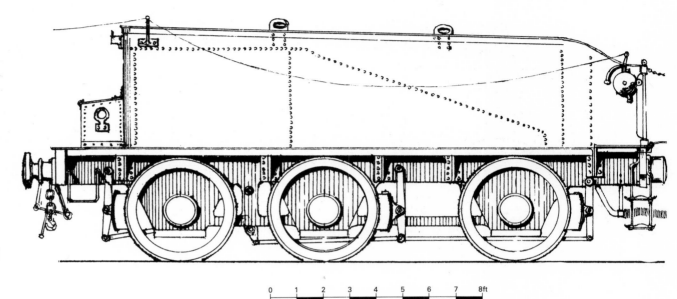

Figure 141

0 1 2 3 4 5 6 7 8ft

The Midi never had a Crampton of its own. Its lines that probed the Pyrenean heights out of the rose pink city of Toulouse, were neither lightweight nor known for their high speed. But in 1883 M. Millet of the Midi took the Urban design and made of it something closer to a Crampton than Urbans had been. Thirty-six locomotives were built between 1885 and 1893, and they did fine service for over a decade, hauling light expresses at 50 mph from Bordeaux to the Spanish frontier. Nos. 1601 to 1636 had much original Crampton design about them, including the Gooch link motion, Crampton regulator, and lagging extending unbroken over the smokebox as in the early Nord engines. The smokebox extended well forward of the big 1400 mm leading wheels, and the visual effect was enhanced by the six-wheel tender which

(rare in a French locomotive) had inside frames. The aesthetics suffered somewhat because the Midi was more than unusually insouciant as to how it distributed the gadgetry over the engine, even hanging the Wenger air pump on the vestigial side sheets. These locomotives were the last of the coupled Cramptons in service, being still in use in 1939.

Livery. In contrast to the Urbans, their livery was sober and honest—plain unlined satin black, with not even a red buffer beam. The boiler bands, however, were polished, as were the bronze number plates and the Midi road plate that sat partway up the severe smoke stack. But look at the drawing (*figure 141*) again—this sort of thing grows on you.

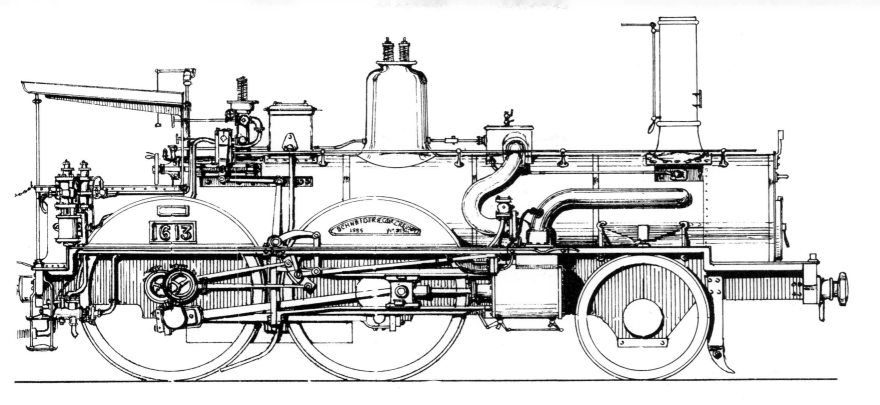

Locomotives of the Bulldog Class, South Eastern Railway

MAIN DIMENSIONS

Driving Wheels 4′ 6″
Cylinders 16″ × 24″
Wheelbase 12′ 4″
Water Capacity 200 gallons
Coke Capacity 4 cwt
Weight 26 tons

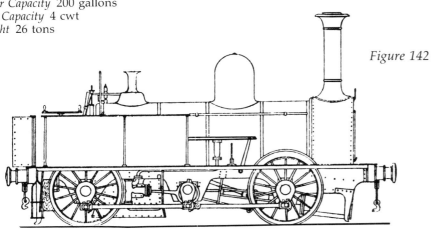

Figure 142

This class, consisting of five locomotives, was built in 1851 by R. Stephenson and Co. for the South Eastern Railway and numbered by the railway Nos. 152 to 156. There were several locomotives of this type used on many railways in Britain and the Continent and, although they tended to be called 'Cramptons', did in some cases pre-date the Crampton patents. They were mostly tank locomotives though the Shrewsbury and Chester Railway had one tender locomotive, as did the South Eastern Railway, which worked goods trains out of Bricklayers Arms in the 1850s.

The Bulldogs worked the Folkstone harbour branch, and some of their interesting features can be seen from the 4mm scale sketch (*figure 142*). The heavily angled cylinders with their slide bars passing under the leading axle, the water feed pump driven from the centre axle by an eccentric, and wooden brake blocks on the rear wheels only. Three of the class were eventually converted to six coupled engines with another pair of wheels added, the whole 'set' being up-tyred to 4′ 9¾″.

123

Locomotives of the London, Chatham and Dover Railway, Tiger Class

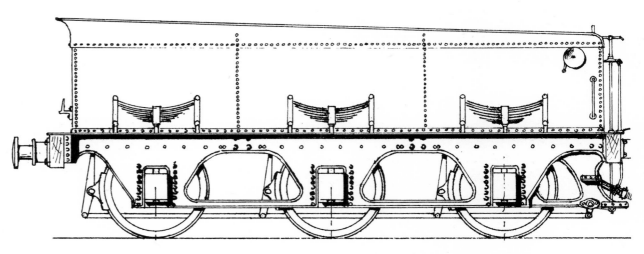

MAIN DIMENSIONS
Driving Wheels 5' 6"
Carrying Wheels 3' 6"
Tender Wheels 3' 9"
Wheelbase 4' 0" + 5' 6" + 5' 6"
Cylinders 16" × 22"
Adhesive Weight 21 tons
Total Weight 33 tons
Boiler Pressure 120 psi

The Dover line had a sad legacy of Crampton brain-children to live down in its infant years, due to the powerful Crampton-Cubitt mafiosa which ruled motive power affairs until the appointment of William Martley in 1860. The dummy-crankshaft *Flirt/Flora/Echo/Coquette/Sylph* quintumvirate have already been referred to. Contemporaneous with them was the Tiger class, a batch of twenty-one locomotives of the 4-4-0 type with inside frames, outside motion, and drive to the rear axle. The cylinders were located well behind the bogie, and supplied from the dome (via steam pipes) which emerged from the boiler housing just above its mid level. Gooch fixed link valve gear was employed. The bogie had only a simple central pin, with no provision for lateral movement or control. The twenty-one locomotives were built by three contractors as detailed below, and were delivered in 1861 and 1862.

Brassey and Co. No. 3 *Falcon*, No. 4 *Vulture*, No. 5 *Heron*, No. 6 *Stork*, No. 7 *Swift*, No. 8 *Dottrel*, No. 9 *Swallow*, No. 10 *Ostrich*, No. 11 *Petrel*, No. 12 *Pelican*.

Slaughter, Gruning and Co. No. 13 *Lynx*, No. 14 *Gorilla*, No. 16 *Tiger*, No. 18 *Leopard*, No. 19 *Jackall*, No. 21 *Panther*.

R and W. Hawthorn No. 15 *Cerberus*, No. 17 *Gorgon*, No. 20 *Harpy*, No. 22 *Pegasus*, No. 23 *Satyr*, No. 24 *Sphynx*, No. 25 *Siren*, No. 26 *Xanthus*.

The drawing (*figure 143*) depicts No. 21 *Panther* of the Slaughter Gruning batch; the Brassey engines were identical. The Hawthorn engines differed in having a much deeper valance which was broken at the cylinders, allowing the valve chest to project. These differences are visible in the model of *Xanthus* on *page 139*. The tender shown with the drawing is an early standard Martley tender such as many of the Tiger class hauled. Their career in 'as built' state was short. Total adhesion was not much greater than in a single Crampton, and in addition they caused damage to the track. Between 1863 and 1865 Martley rebuilt them all as 2-4-0s, with outside frames and inside cylinders, in which form they became good reliable engines. The last of them, *Leopard*, (ex No. 18) was broken up in 1907 with well over a million miles on the clock. By then she had become South Eastern and Chatham Railway locomotive No. 477.

All the Tigers were delivered in Martley's time, and originally bore his mid-green livery with black bands and borders, fine red and white lining, and brown underframes. Domes, safety valve covers and (sometimes) chimney caps were polished.

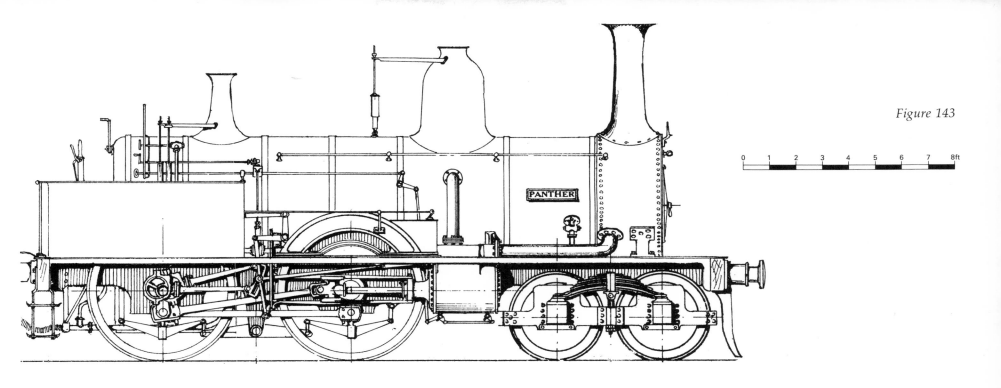

Figure 143

PANTHER

0 1 2 3 4 5 6 7 8ft

Ambergate, Nottingham, Boston and Eastern Junction Railway, Series 1–3 (G.N.R. 218–220)

MAIN DIMENSIONS
Driving Wheels 5′ 0″
Wheelbase 10′ 11″
Cylinders 11″ × 18″

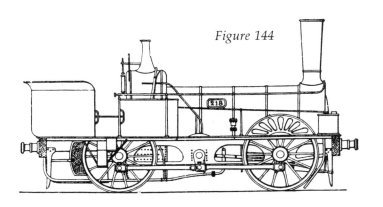

Figure 144

This is another locomotive similar to the Bulldog class but rather prettier, she was of a type built by E. B. Wilson and Co. of Leeds, over a four year period, for several different railways. The Ambergate, Nottingham, Boston and Eastern Junction Railway 7 mm scale drawing is on *page 126* (*figure 145*), and a further drawing (*figure 146*) is of No. 273 of the York and North Midland Railway, later to be merged into the North Eastern.

She looked rather a 'leggy' engine with only 14 spokes in her five foot driving wheels when 15 or 16 would have been more normal, and her low slung boiler which was some 9′ 3″ long with only a slender 3′ diameter, built to operate at a pressure of 100 psi, and a total heating surface of 576 sq ft. The copper firebox was pitched very high, with the ornately shaped bunker overhanging the rear buffers rather like a Victorian pram chassis! The bunker held one ton of fuel, I'm not sure if it was coal or coke, and the water capacity was 225 gallons.

125

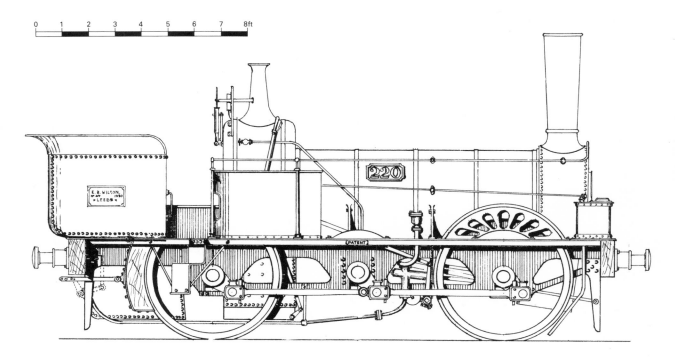

Other features of interest are the box splashers over the rear wheels which must have been a nuisance to climb over and would make the cab floor very hard to sweep and hose down. The locomotive has sanding gear and enormous wooden brake blocks on the rear wheels only. No. 273 was replaced in 1878 by one of Mr. Fletcher's bogie tank engines.

Figure 145

Locomotive No. 273 of the York and North Midland Railway

Figure 146

MAIN DIMENSIONS

Driving Wheels 5' 6"
Carrying Wheels 3' 3"
Wheelbase 3' 9" + 7' 0" + 6' 9"
Cylinders 15" × 20"

Class Names
Sondes, Crampton, Lake, Faversham, Sittingbourne, Chatham

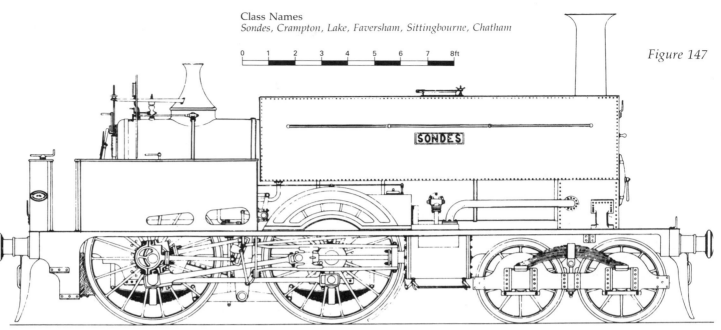

Figure 147

Other than the drawing of *Sondes* (*figure 147*) there is little information about these locomotives. They were built by Hawthorns in 1858 and are more or less a Tiger class saddle tank. They were not successful and were broken up very quickly, the boilers and wheels being used on new locomotives.

Plate 43

I am afraid little is known about this locomotive, the photograph (*plate 43*) was among the last batch of material to arrive from Dennis before his death so I do not know where he obtained it although it is clearly marked Eastern Railway of France No. 318. She was built in 1867 and also the photograph was dated 1867. The technical features compare with the English drawings on the last page, with the addition of the style of fittings which give it the French hallmark. The eccentrics driving the valve gear have been fitted to the centre jack shaft axle, the 'open plan' buffer casings, the cab roof on lovely ornate pillars, and the ugly squared off sand box and dome casing which, from the pipes plumbed into it, could be one of the double skinned feedwater pre-heater type as mentioned earlier.

127

The Woolwich Arsenal 2–2–2–2 Crampton Locomotive

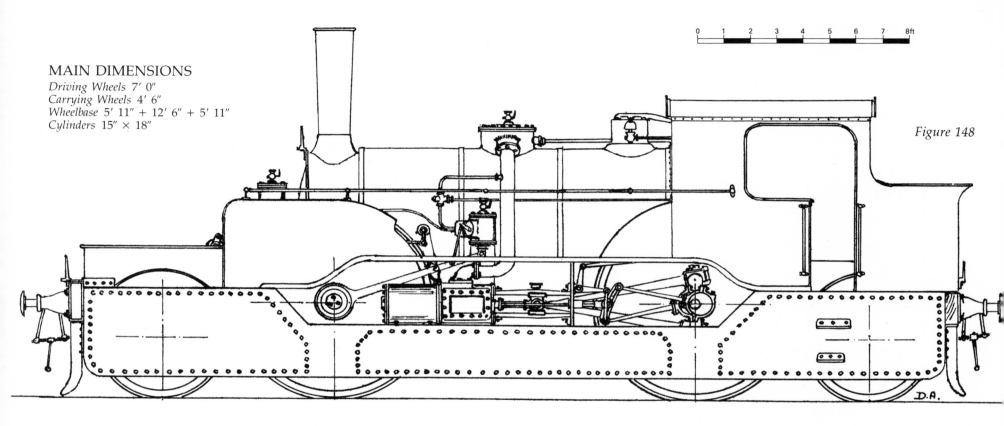

MAIN DIMENSIONS
Driving Wheels 7' 0"
Carrying Wheels 4' 6"
Wheelbase 5' 11" + 12' 6" + 5' 11"
Cylinders 15" × 18"

Figure 148

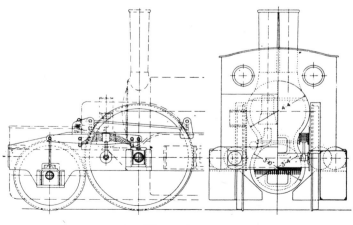

Figure 149

This locomotive is included because it is Crampton's last patent, taken out some 36 years after the original batch, and is *nothing* like the 'Classic Crampton' we have come to expect. This beast has, as usual, an uncertain pedigree! It is not known for sure whether the locomotive (as built) was exactly like the drawings (*figures 148, 149* and *150*), only that one very like it certainly was built and was running at Woolwich in the late 1880s. Who built it, and when, is still 'open market', though the claim that it was built at Woolwich Arsenal appeals greatly to me. It could not look *much* more like an armoured train—a four-pounder over the leading wheel platform, a maxim or two on brackets behind the cab. Paint the whole thing khaki, and off to war we go!

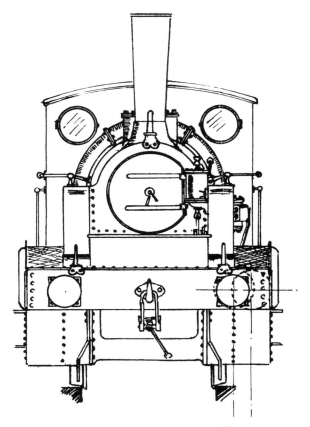

width of the loading gauge. There were no balance weights required, as all the reciprocating and rotating masses *did* balance out as intended, and despite the chapter heading, were *not* coupled! (I did not know *what* chapter to put it in.) With this 180 degree crank design, in theory, one could end up with all four cranks dead in line and mechanically locked, though in practice I would have thought *most* unlikely—imagine trying to do it deliberately! However, just in case it should happen, the long arm to a cylinder from the leading driving wheel centre on the 7mm left hand side drawing is a starting device, which will rotate the wheel just enough for the main drive to operate again and was apparently quite common on marine engines of the period—perhaps I should have equated it with the Navy and not the

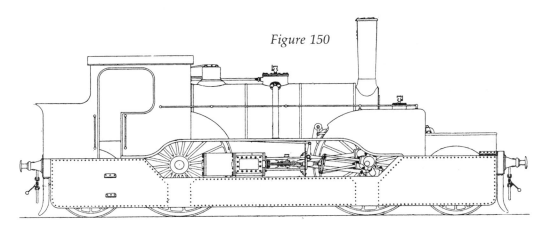

Figure 150

However, to be serious, and Thomas certainly was in his long battle to produce the 'ultimate' in a balanced engine, this was a culmination of many years practical experience. In this design we have a four cylinder engine which could be compounded, but in the drawings it is shown as a simple, and comprises two separate drive units built onto the same rigid frame. So, with no articulation, it could not claim to be in the Fairlie or Garrett ancestry.

The four cylinders are mounted in pairs, one unit each side and driving one wheel only by two cranks at 180 degrees. The slide valves are operated by Stephenson type gear driven by eccentrics, the valve chests being on the outside of the cylinders, making the whole assembly rather cramped and very near the maximum

Army—as the patent also suggests a simple marine boiler could be used, cutting costs and, due to the extensive frame support, reduce maintenance.

The suspension is interesting in that it is rigged by beams to allow the leading and trailing wheels to exert a loading on the driving wheels, the leading and trailing wheels only being actually sprung indirectly.

Finally, some working capacities. The wrap-around tanks contained 2000 gallons of water, though how it was pumped up to the boiler is not shown. The fuel capacity was 3 tons, and the working weight around 48-50 tons. For its day, a quite large machine!

Plate 44 Just a final reminder that the principles embodied in these four-coupled Cramptons were still being applied many years later. The final photograph in this chapter shows a locomotive in active use in 1965 that could well have been designed by Thomas Russell. It is a locomotive of the private Chemin de fer de Marle a Montcornet, in north east France, and was built by the Société de la Meuse in Belgium. There were several well-tanks of this design on the private lines around St. Quentin, and the type was popular as a prototype with 'O' gauge scratch-builders in France. The lines and the locomotives are gone now, of course, but you can still build models!

Chapter Eight

Modelling the CRAMPTON in 4m/m Scale

In this chapter I have not described just one model only. It seemed a better idea to give a 'blow by blow' account of how all the various components are made, with detailed drawings and, in the case of the chassis, actual gear layouts that have been used and tested.

I will not go into a thesis on the whole 'step by step' construction of a model as, if the builder has progressed from 'Ready to run' models through to kit building, he should by now be able to solder and already own the basic tools, plus having developed his own ideas on general construction anyway. I will, however, state my preferences for certain methods and give the reasons for them.

You will note that several of the drawings show items being produced on a lathe which, of course, not everyone owns! However, there really is no other way of doing justice to some of this detail and, having developed the desire to build a Crampton, I must assume you will gain access to a lathe by methods 'fair or foul'!

Starting with the chassis (*figures 151* to *156*), these are drawn in 4mm scale so that, having chosen your prototype, you can lay your available motors and gears over the drawings to see what will or, more likely, will not fit! Now here I must state a definite preference. Having built many models over the years using the time honoured method of slabs of 1/16" brass side frames joined by spacers, I have gradually evolved a method much easier to use. Side frames are now made from .015" to .020" nickel silver sheet,

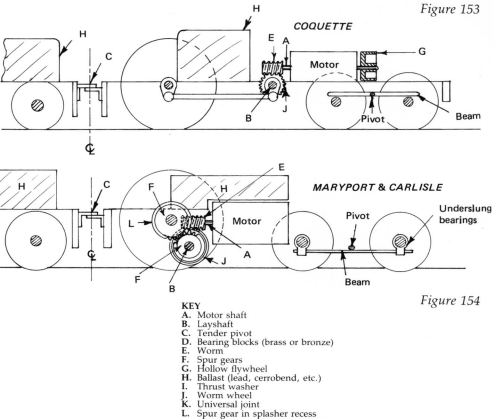

Figure 153

Figure 154

KEY
A. Motor shaft
B. Layshaft
C. Tender pivot
D. Bearing blocks (brass or bronze)
E. Worm
F. Spur gears
G. Hollow flywheel
H. Ballast (lead, cerrobend, etc.)
I. Thrust washer
J. Worm wheel
K. Universal joint
L. Spur gear in splasher recess

and bushes are used for the bearing surfaces in the thinner material. This gives so many advantages that one wonders why it was not advocated years ago. It is much easier to solder two thin sides together for drilling and filing to shape and, more to the point, easier to file and separate afterwards. There is much more room left between the frames for gears and motors etc., and frame spacers made from scrap thin material (*figure 157*) can easily be soldered and unsoldered while the builder lines up motor mounting plates and meshes gears. I am not keen on using turned brass spacers with threaded ends, as they are difficult to locate in thin material and can, in fact, come loose in service.

Now a few more points as general rules. Where at all possible design your model in the early stages so that it has as many sub-assemblies as possible, which either screw or peg together. This gives a very wide freedom of movement when it comes to soldering small parts together, and painting and lining them afterwards. A boiler painted *before* the saddle and dome are fitted looks 100% neater than trying to paint round things. With

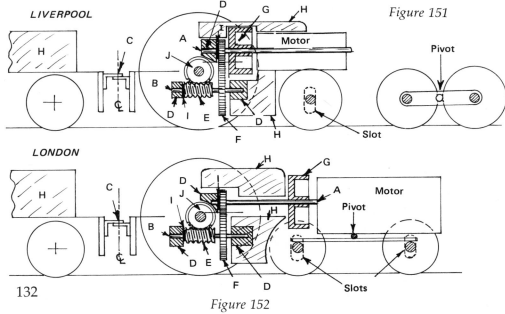

Figure 151

Figure 152

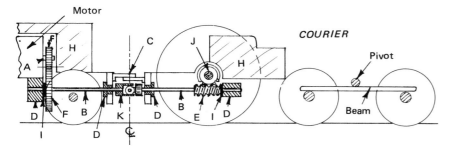

Figure 155

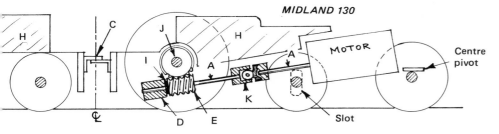

Figure 156

Figure 157

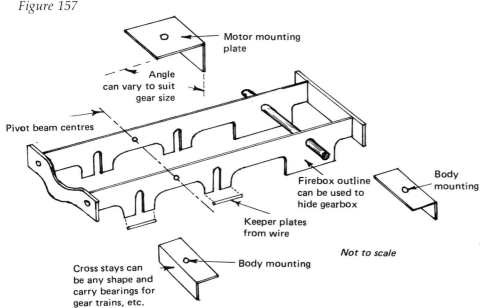

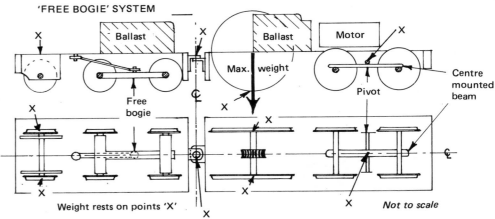

Figure 158

reference to wheels—a great number of today's wheels have nylon centres and, if you are using these, do try and arrange your axles and bearings so that they can be dropped in and out of the chassis easily, as nylon wheels, gears, and some motor bearings do not take kindly to heat, which will transfer through metal to where you do *not* want it much quicker than you would think possible! Keeper plates are simple to make as *figure 157* shows.

You will see from the drawings that reference is made to slots for axles, and beams to rest on them. The point of this is to get away from the rigid chassis with only a couple of wheels picking up current from the track at any one time, and move to the point where any vehicle is resting effectively on three points, like the old 'milking stool'. The drawing *figure 158* of the free bogie system shows this. The majority of the weight is channelled towards the driving wheels, the points of weight distribution being the two drivers and the centre of the pivot beam on the locomotive bogie, and the tender pivot and tow point resting on the loco draw bar and the two rear tender wheels. This arrangement makes the model Cramptons far out-perform their prototypes of long ago.

Now to details of some machined parts. The main prototype drawings are in 7mm scale which is the largest we could get them for the book to be economic. I prefer a drawing to be as large as possible as long as it has a scale in feet attached, because it is then a simple matter to use your dividers, transfer the size from the drawing, and multiply by the scale, be it 2mm, 3mm or whatever. This is more accurate, in the long run, than trying to build to a drawing in your chosen scale.

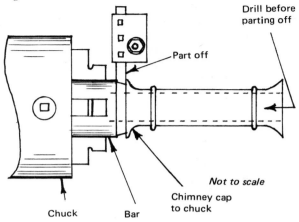

Figure 159

Drill before
parting off

Part off

Not to scale

Chuck   Bar   Chimney cap
to chuck

Where the chimney has a copper cap, these are turned from phosphor bronze rod, the reasons being two-fold. Phosphor bronze rod is easier to get and cheaper than copper and, secondly, much easier to turn on the lathe than copper. The sequence of events is to mount the rod in the chuck and drill down the centre to the inside diameter required, and then turn the profile, making sure that the cap end is towards the chuck. Then bore out the base to an even curvature, *figure 159*, so that, when parted-off, the chimney can be placed in a vice and the base contour formed over a round bar the same size as the smokebox diameter, *figure 160*.

The safety valves, water pumps etc., are all normal turning operations and do not really require further explanation. The pipe unions are simply lengths of bar drilled to the same diameter as the pipe, the flange shaping, etc., turned on, and the unions parted off. Remember to fit the unions on the pipes *before* bending as they will not slide round the bends afterwards. The pipes themselves are made from all sorts of sizes of copper wire as reclaimed from electrical fittings and cables, etc. Never throw away even two inches—it could be useful! Hexagonal unions can be made by drilling out small brass nuts and soldering them into place.

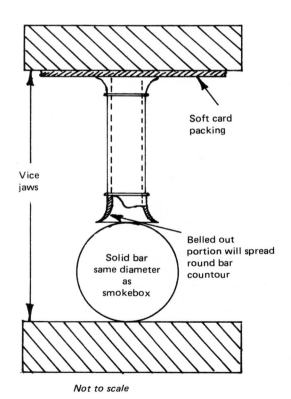

Soft card
packing

Vice
jaws

Solid bar
same diameter
as
smokebox

Belled out
portion will spread
round bar
countour

Not to scale

Figure 160

Figure 161

BATCH PRODUCTION BUFFERS

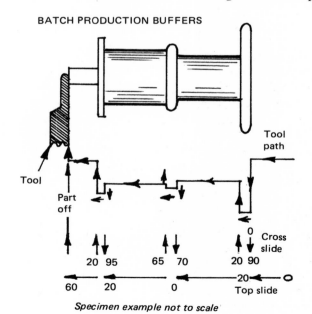

Tool
path

Tool

Part
off

0   Cross
slide

20 95   65 70   20 90

60   20   0   20   0
Top slide

Specimen example not to scale

134

The buffers are made by setting both the top and cross slides on your lathe to zero and then shaping the first buffer from the drawing (*figure 161*) taking a note of the figures from the micrometer scales at each stage. Then, when adjusted to your satisfaction, using the figures you can mass, produce as many components as you require. I usually run off at least two sets for the time when I build another engine by the same builders. *Figure 161* shows a typical set of figures which are not to scale, but merely serve to illustrate the system. Both the locomotive and tender dumb buffers are completed in the same way as are 'Salter' type safety valves, if a pair are required.

Figure 162

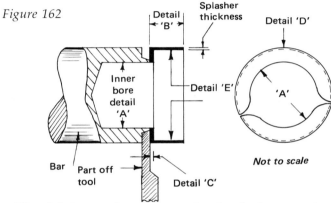

The driving and carrying wheel splashers are both turned in the same way and, although it is expensive in material, they are turned from solid. I have found that, although one can make these from strip and solder them up, it is difficult to make them hug the wheels without the possibility of shorts, especially as wheel bearings wear with age. Whereas the turned ones can be made to fit the wheels with an even clearance all round, and even better, any beading can be turned on with highly beneficial results to the completed appearance. The splashers are turned as follows from brass bar. First centre drill as large as possible and drill and bore out until the smaller diameter of the splasher is reached *Figure 162* (*detail A*). Then bore to the depth required for the splasher width (*detail B*) and to the diameter required to give sufficient clearance for the wheel to avoid electrical shorts (*detail E*), or, in some cases, to allow for the compensation of the wheels. Then part-off the first ring taking care to leave sufficient material, say 1/64", for the outer face of the splasher (*detail C*). If you then

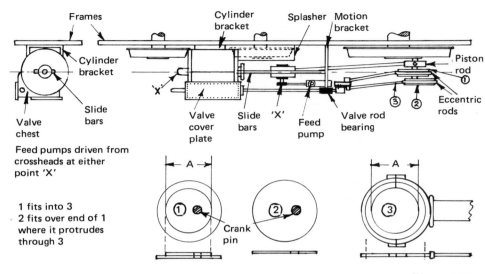

Figure 163

mark the ring to the size required, you can cut the number of splashers required, in this case we can halve the rings to give two splashers (*detail D*).

The eccentrics, *figure 163*, are formed by mounting a section of rod in the far jaw chuck, off centre, and then drilling it the correct size to fit over the crank pin. Now remove the rod and replace it in the self centering chuck and turn the eccentrics as shown in *figure 103*. In most cases there are four units, so we need four flanged parts and four end discs. Next solder four pieces of approx. .015" nickel silver sheet together in a four-tier sandwich, big enough to cut your valve rods from, and mark out the centres. *With great care* drill and file to shape. I stress **care**, as we are getting down to some pretty flimsy items by now. When satisfied, hold the iron to the parts and separate. Clean off the solder, polish the faces, and check that the large hole is a fine running-fit over the spiggot of the flanged eccentric. When the wheels are finally fitted and running true on the chassis, the eccentrics are fitted over the return cranks (flanged part first), then the rod, and lastly the disc. These can be soldered, but with nylon wheels I *strongly* recommend Araldite, used sparingly after careful degreasing. Beware the 'Instant' range of adhesives as some of them have capillary action, and will nip round the entire assembly and gum it up rock solid!

135

Now we come to one of the finest parts of the Tulk and Ley Cramptons, the ornate domes and saddles (*figure 164*). These are turned from a brass bar with the delicate contours hand finished with a small scraper, 'ground up' from a broken needle file. When the turning is complete do not part-off straight away as the final polishing and painting can still be completed in the lathe. With the chuck rotating, give the dome a good polish, then wipe clean with lighter fluid and, using a fine brush, add the fine paint lines which pick out the detail by holding the brush lightly against the rotating component. Now, *still* without parting-off, remove the complete bar from the chuck and place it in a dust-free corner to dry. To attempt to part-off with the paint still wet will result in a porcupine effect of metal particles sticking to the paint. How do I know? I tried it, of course! When dry, replace in the chuck and part-off leaving a peg at the base to fit into the saddle. In the case of a fluted dome it is best completed in separate parts as shown in *figure 164*.

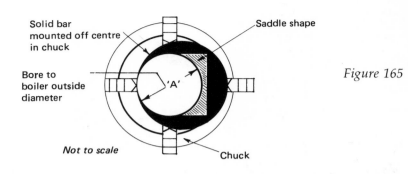

Figure 165

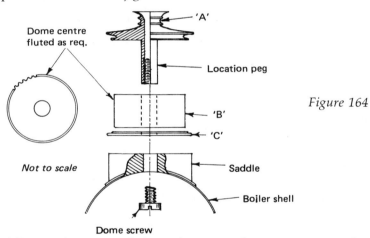

Figure 164

The saddle is also turned from brass and, contrary to what some people think, square parts *can* be turned on a rotating lathe! The job is best tackled by doing the curved under-surface first (*figure 165*). This must be bored out until it is a snug fit on the boiler barrel. Then, by very gentle handling in the chuck jaws, square-off the other faces. The edge beading can be either added afterwards or filed on by hand. Now, before the final polishing, drill a hole to receive the dome base peg when the final assembly stage is reached. These parts will be either glued or screwed to the boiler after painting as per the drawing (*figure 164*).

The following series of plates is a small sample of scale model locomotives of Crampton design.

Plate 45

Plate 48

Plate 49

Plate 46

Plate 47

Plate 50   *Plate 51*   *Plate 52*

Plate 53

Plate 54

139

Plate 55

Plate 57

Plate 56

Plate 58

Chapter Nine

Modelling the CRAMPTON in 7m/m Scale

Plate 59 A fine model of a PLM 604 in 7mm scale, built by D. Allenden.

This chapter first appeared as an article by Dennis in **Model Railways** *of February 1972.*

The long low lean locomotives of Thomas Russell Crampton could be found on several of the railways of Britain, of Germany, of Belgium, of the Austro-Hungarian empire, of the United States even (though it has to be admitted that there they were conceived with a disregard of aesthetics amounting almost to genius). But the real Crampton country started in what later became the Place de Verdun, and fanned out over Marne and Aisne, Champagne and Ardennes. In 1852 Crampton No. 80, the much-lauded *Le Continent* of the Compagnie de l'Est, hauled the first Strasbourg express out of Paris and put the name Crampton firmly into the lexicon.

But for all that the great Crampton hour of glory was evanescent as the snow on the dusty face of old Khayyam's desert. Train tonnage spiralled beyond the capabilities of the light-footed speedsters, and on line after line they were usurped by coupled wheels and side rods. The Est alone, with boundless blind confidence, remained faithful, striving to meet heavier traffic demands by improvement and modernisation of their Crampton fleet. That was how they came to drag No. 604 into Epernay works for a Flaman-boiler face life which earned her the unlovely nickname of the Camel. The year being 1889, la six-cents-quatre had to while away the summer at the Paris Exposition, after which she went down the P.L.M. for a series of trials in which the L.B.S.C.'s *Edward Blount* and S.E.C.R.'s *Onward* were also involved. There with 157 tons in tow she clocked up an all-time Crampton record of a shade under 90 mph.

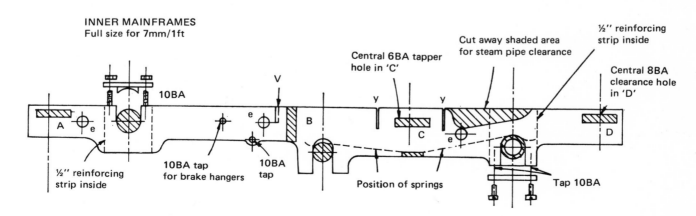

INNER MAINFRAMES
Full size for 7mm/1ft

Central 6BA tapper hole in 'C'

Cut away shaded area for steam pipe clearance

½'' reinforcing strip inside

Central 8BA clearance hole in 'D'

10BA

V

A   e

B

C   e

y   y

D

½'' reinforcing strip inside

10BA tap for brake hangers

10BA tap

Position of springs

Tap 10BA

Figure 166

It wasn't enough, of course. The Cramptons died just the same. Even so, 604 was the precursor of a fleet of high wheeled 4-4-0s that hawked their Flaman cookers around the Est for the next half century. And she went on to survive World War 1, becoming just about the last Crampton in service anywhere. The Est chose to preserve No. 80; I chose to reincarnate No. 604. One forty-third full size. Seven millimetres to the foot, twenty-three and a half to the metre. Messieurs, a la chasse!

. . . or, more specifically, au chassis. Like many Cramptons, No. 604 was double framed. In a model the outside frame is most conveniently made as a non-functional dummy, integral with the superstructure. The inner frame, the real one, is virtually invisible from any angle, and hence can be very simple. It is shown in *figure 166*. The sides are cut from 1/16" by 3/4" brass strip, reinforced on the insides by vertical strips of 1/16" by 1/2" brass at the front and rear bearings. Cut and drill the two sides together drill the axle centres with a small pilot drill, follow through with the axle size (1/4" for the driving axle, 3/16" for the others), then separate the frames, add the bearing strips, continue the drilling through them, then finally extend the bearing holes into slots. Although the driving wheels of 604 are not as large as was customary on Cramptons, there is nevertheless a considerable difference in level between driving and carrying axles. Had the driving axle been slotted downwards in the usual manner the frame would have had to be made from much wider strip; by slotting them upwards, not only is the frame construction simplified, but the motor and drive unit can be more easily dropped into place. There is prototypical precedent—some of the Cramptons did actually have inverted hornblocks on the driving axle. Note that the centre bearing slots are not reinforced; this is because the centre axle is carried in spring, floating bearings.

Chassis cross members are of 3/8" by 1/8" brass strip, 3/4" long and carefully sized and squared. They are

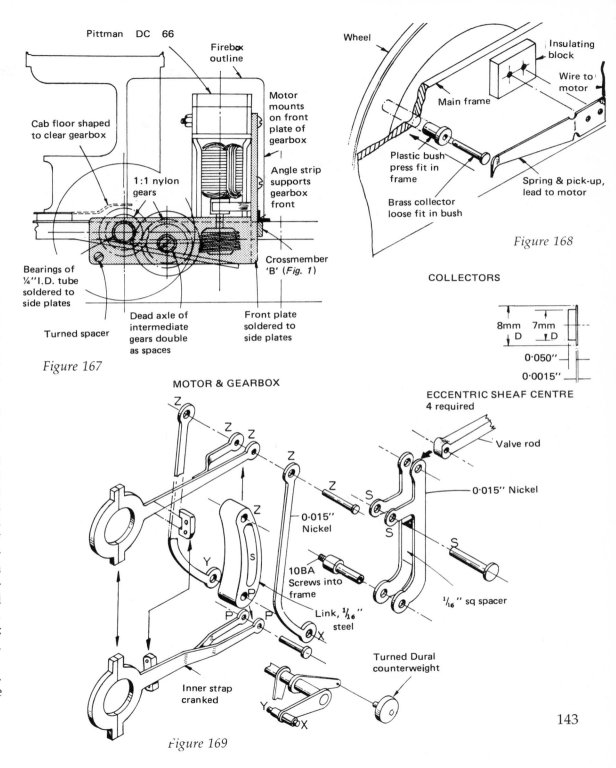

Figure 167

Figure 168

Figure 169

143

placed between the side frames and the assembly temporarily clamped together with long six BA screws through the predrilled holes *e*. The cross members are coaxed into their positions at *a, b, c, d*; the frame is then squared up on a surface plate and the whole soldered together with a large, clean iron. After soldering the joints are reinforced by 10 BA studs inserted into tapped holes and filed flush. The driving wheels are LMC, turned down to NMRA flange profile; their centres are bored out a little under ¼" and pressed on to an axle of ¼" tufnol rod. The cranks need be quartered with no more than eyeball accuracy, since there are no coupling rods. The tufnol axle provides insulation both sides and also avoids body contacts of a non social nature. Crankpin holes are insulated by tufnol bushes, tapped 10 BA. Positive location of the return crank is assured by crankpin locknuts behind the wheels.

Figure 167 shows how the drive is arranged. The motor is a Pittman DC66, small but adequately powerful. It sits vertically in the firebox, mounted in a gearbox frame of ⅟₁₆" brass, and drives the axle through a 50 : 1 worm and a pair of unity-ratio spur pinions. The configuration avoids a large gear wheel on the axle itself (difficult to hide with the axle behind the firebox and passing through the cab) and also gets the motor far enough forward that it doesn't have to push through the backhead. Remember the drive in a model is the one part that's absolutely unprototypical, and it's always worth taking trouble to conceal it. The gearbox rides on the rear axle, being carried on wide bearings of ¼" i.d. tube soldered into the gearbox sideframe. The front of the gearbox carries a small angle bracket which rests on the frame spacer *b*. The whole drive unit drops into the frames from above, and is retained by 10 BA screws. The driving axle can be allowed no side play at all; insulating washers between the wheels and mainframe are selected to have just the right thickness.

The front carrying wheels are CCW plastic centred tender wheels with—again—some doctoring of treads and flanges. They are mounted on a ³⁄₁₆" axle, and retained in the bearing slots by small keeper strips (*figure 166*). The intermediate wheels are LMC tender wheels bushed with tufnol and refitted to the original ³⁄₁₆" axle. This axle is carried in turned bearings which slide in the frame slots and are sprung, very lightly, with phosphor bronze strips. This axle is allowed considerable vertical play both up and down from its mean position.

Current pickups are located behind the tyres of leading and driving wheels; they consist of spring plungers riding in tufnol bushes, as shown in *figure 168*. These collectors are efficient and completely invisible. The ends of both carrying axles are extended some ⅜" outside the wheel faces to further the illusion that these wheels have bearings in the outside frame.

The cylinders of the prototype are slung between inner and outer frames. In the model they are carried completely on the inner chassis, and thus their construction and fitting can be very similar to that used on a conventional model. The block is built up of sheet brass front and back plates which drop into slots *y* in the mainframe. A horizontal centre separator of ⅟₁₆" brass carries a single 6 BA clearance hole through which the whole block is fixed to the cross member *c*. The outer surface of the block is a thin sheet wrapper. Turned cylinder ends screw into the front and rear faces of the block, the rear one being drilled for the ³⁄₃₂" piston rods and the ⅟₁₆" square crosshead guides, the latter being simply forced into their holes. The guides simply spring into locating notches in the motion plate at their rear ends; the motion plate itself, of nickel, drops into slot *v*. The crossheads are filed from brass, and can be considerably simplified because they're not visible. The connecting rods are of ⅟₁₆" steel, with all the big end detail (brasses, cotter, lubricator) reproduced. This is another aspect of a model which is too often neglected. In O gauge it's completely practical to make a con-rod end look like a con-rod end.

The outside link motion is far easier than its looks, and there

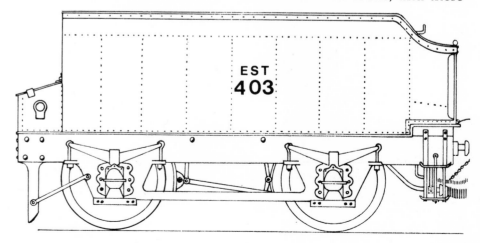

Plate 60 Shows chassis with outer side frames mounted.

two of them were countersunk, and the sheaves mounted in pairs on the return cranks with countersunk 10 BA screws. After setting to the correct relative locations, No. 71 holes were drilled from the back of the cranks through the two sheaves, and locking pins of 22 gauge wire forced in and filed flush. The anathematic exposed head of the fixing screw (scaling about four inches across) is mercifully hidden by the outer frame members. Which is just as well, because there just isn't clearance for a projecting head. The eccentric straps are of 18 gauge nickel or nickel silver; the large centre hole is first drilled under-size, filed out to fit the sheave, then the strap cut out round the hole. Forked ends, as per full size practice, are a necessity if the gear is not to flop about in a most unprototypical manner. Note that the inboard strap is cranked outwards by an amount equal to the thickness of the metal so that the fork ends, and hence the link, are truly vertical. The final touch on the straps is provided by the little soldered on strap flanges. Most of this is shown in *figures 169* and *170*.

are a number of attractive English prototypes which I suspect would have been modelled were it not for their outside eccentrics. I made the latter by turning a piece of ⅜″ dural rod in the three-jaw, with a ¹⁄₁₆″ packing piece under one jaw to off centre the work while a No. 51 hole was drilled about half an inch deep. Then the packing was removed, and four sheaves turned and parted off to the dimensions shown in *figure 169*. The holes in

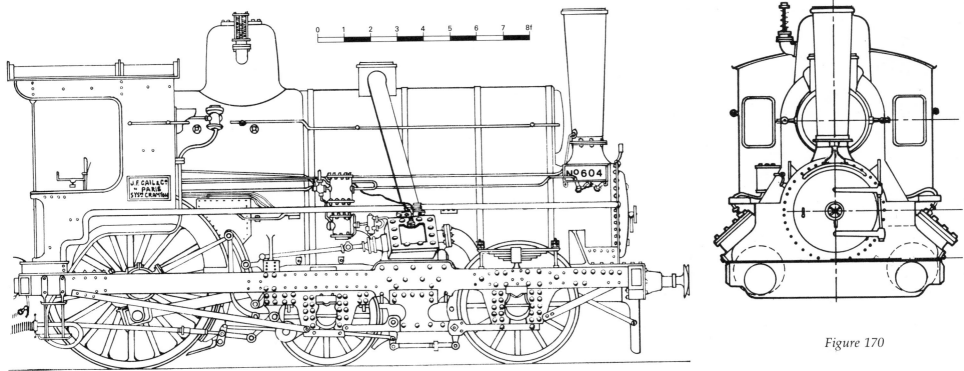

Figure 170

145

Reference to the drawing will show that the valve chests look as if they're ready to fall off. This comes about because of the compound angle at which they are mounted, about 15 degrees from the horizontal in the fore and aft direction, and about 40 degrees transversally. If the chests were mounted squarely on the blocks the valve rod would have, not only the desired vertical inclination, but would also be directed inwards towards the frames; skewing the chests eliminates the latter component. The chests themselves are made of blocks of ½" by ½" brass with turned brass valve glands, and each is attached to the cylinder block by a single countersunk 8 BA screw. To line up the chests a length of ¹⁄₁₆" brass rod is inserted in the valve bore and is used as a handle and a guide. In the correct position the rod, viewed from directly above, is parallel with the frame; the screw is tightened in this position and the chest then soldered to the block; the screw head is soldered over and filed flush. The recessed cover plate with its prominent bolt heads of ¹⁄₁₆" wire is made from two layers of ¹⁄₃₂" brass; the tiny turned lubricator doubles as fixing screw; positive location is ensured by allowed one of the wire 'bolts' to enter a mating hole in the valve chest.

Final detailing of the chassis included the brake gear, guard irons and dummy lower firebox and ashpan. The brake gear is prominent, with shoes on all wheels; shoes themselves are of styrene, riveted to thin metal hangers which are themselves carried on tubular spacers through which pass long 12 BA screws tapped into the inner frames. When the outer frames are in place these screws pass also through them, and the spacers do double duty as distance pieces. The dummy firebox is made of thin sheet metal, and is retained by clips which spring over the frame members and simulate the firebox expansion quides.

146

Plate 61 Completed inner chassis, showing full valve gear and part of brake rigging. Note detailing of big ends. Slot-headed screws holding eccentrics and con-rod small end are completely hidden by outer frames. Balance weights are added to driving wheels—unlike English ones, nearly all French Cramptons were balanced.

Plate 62

Plate 63 Outer side frame assembly and with it the dropped left hand side. Valve gear incomplete in this view.

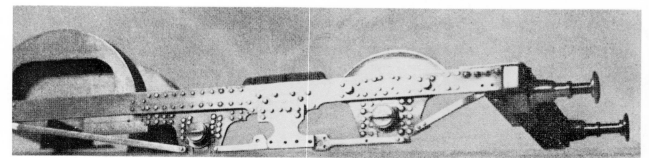

The upperworks, like the County of York, is in three parts. Right on top of the chassis goes a running plate, which carries the outside framing. Above that goes a two-unit boiler-firebox-cab structure. I am a great believer in multi unit assemblies—they make cleaning, painting and subsequent repairs very easy.

One of the features of early outside-framed engines is the variety and profusion of rivet and bolt heads which add so much to the character of the model when done properly, detract so much from it when done badly, and eliminate it completely when not done at all. On relatively thick metal such as will be used here punched rivet impressions look like embryonic acne, hence are OUT. This kind of riveting is done by drilling holes, forcing in brass wire, soldering over the back, and filing the front down nearly flush. On No. 604 three sizes of wire are used (22, 18, and 16 swg) which roughly correspond to bolt or rivet diameters of 20, 25, and 30 mm. (Sorry, but No. 604 had metric bolts anyway!) The frames are made of overlapped pieces of 20 swg brass, corresponding to about 22.5 mm plate. Cut out the separate parts and drill all the rivet holes. In each case choose a drill about 2-thou' smaller than the wire diameter, e.g. for the small 22 swg rivets I drilled No. 71 (0.026 in). This makes the wire a firm press fit in the hole—you may have to push it in with pliers—so that when you run solder over the back none of it seeps through to the front to mar the crispness of the impressions.

After cutting out, tin the backs of the pieces, clamp them together in correct location and tack them together with solder. Then choose two rivet holes of each overlap, and continue the drilled holes of the front piece through the back piece, force in rivet wire, and the pieces are now pegged in alignment. Then push the rivet wire in all the other holes, flux the back, and flow solder over the whole back surface before filing down the front. *Figure 171* shows the actual breakdown of frame parts. With two side

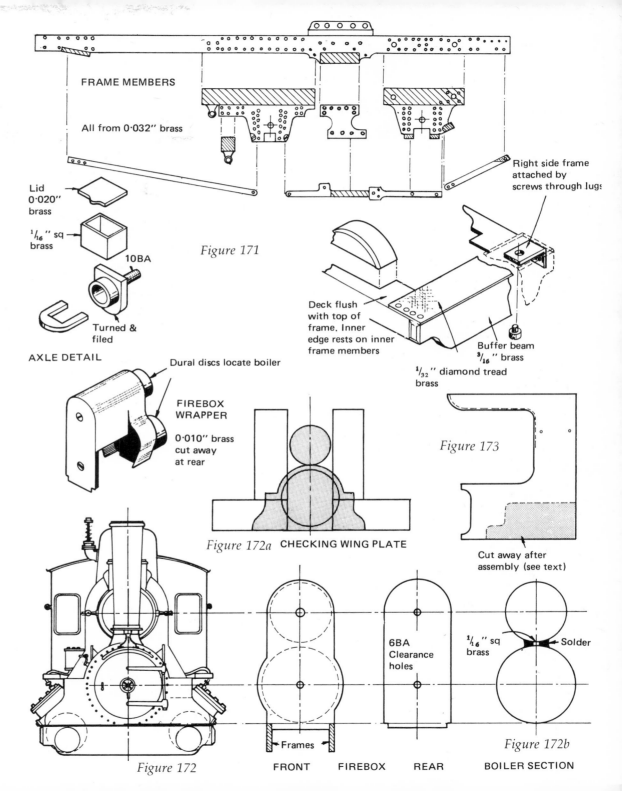

frames complete, cut the front and rear platforms, drill them, add the ³⁄₃₂″ square upper valance to the rear one, and screw the units to the chassis; then using the assembly as a jig, solder one side frame in place between the platforms. The other side frame is fitted with two soldered brackets by which it is screwed to the front and rear platforms; this is necessary to be able to disengage this unit without removing the cylinder block. (See *plate 63*.) The two rear splashers are made as part of the running plate. These must be made with care, because they clear the wheels front and back by the barest of margins; they are made of thin sheet brass, and are fitted to the main inner frames with temporary 14 BA screws. When they are in place the rear platform is dropped over them, and the splashers soldered to it. The screws are now superfluous and can come out. Check that the driving wheels rotate freely without contacting the splashers at any point. If you're worried, line the latter with black plastic insulating tape, but this should not really be necessary if your bearings are good and properly aligned. At the front end, the footplating over the front wheels is fitted, carrying splashers of turned brass and dummy leaf springs. It's desirable to make the latter removable so that the brass beading of the splashers can be polished; accordingly, the springs are held down by their own hanger bolts, 14 BA with heads under the footplating. Locate and solder in place the little lug, with its five bolt heads, that projects from the top of the outer frame and ostensibly supports the cylinder block. Making this lug as a separate piece greatly simplifies frame construction, since without the lug the frame is both flat and flat-topped, hence easy to assemble squarely. Furthermore, an integral lug would be difficult to bend cleanly.

The rear traction plate is of ⅛″ brass, soldered to the underside of the rear platform. In carrying out this operation, it is important to apply the heat to the heavy plate, not the light platform. Note the decorative chamfered ends. The buffer beam is of ³⁄₁₆″ brass. The prototype has a flitched timber beam, and this is represented in the model by a thin overlay plate, retained by the screw-in buffer sockets and safety chain eyes. This is not a case of art for art's sake—the separate flitch plate is far easier to paint and letter.
The beam proper is soldered to the front platform after all the holes are drilled and the beam has been shaped. Buffers have turned brass sockets and dural shanks and heads. True to prototype the right hand buffer head is flat, the left hand one convex.

Now fit the whole running plate to the chassis, and check for clearances. The eccentrics should clear the outside frame by what

Plate 64

Mike Sharman would define as 0.00000002 in fine weather—but clear they should. Mine didn't, and a little thinning of spacing washers was necessary before I could leave the whole lot running round the track while I made the boiler.

The real Flaman boiler had a conventional lower drum; the upper drum contained only water up to its mid-section, and was connected to the lower drum by pipes at several points along its length. It was mainly an attempt to increase both evaporative surface and steam collection volume. In the model the two drums are of brass tubing, 20 mm and 26 mm respectively; they are turned between centres to produce the boiler bands, care being taken to line up the bands on the two drums. It is important that the ends of the drums be square and this is best checked by standing them on end on a flat surface and checking all round with a square. To assemble the drums the firebox front plate is used as a jig, so it, and the back plate, are cut out from 20 swg brass at this stage. *Figure 172* shows these pieces.

Discs of ¹⁄₁₆″ dural are turned to be snug fits inside the drums, and are attached to the firebox front plate by 6 BA nuts and bolts. A piece of aluminium foil is sandwiched between the plate and the discs. When the drums are pushed over the discs, they should be true, parallel and about ¹⁄₁₆″ apart. Mark an axial line along the lower drum and solder along it a piece of ¹⁄₁₆″ square brass, so that

Plate 65

when the drums are replaced on the firebox front plate the gap between them is more or less filled. Tack solder the drums together at the front—if you can do this with silver solder so much the better, since there will then be no danger of it melting under the heat of the following operation.

Now for the joining operation proper, the object of which is to lay a smooth, liberal fillet of solder in the valley between the drums, giving a section like in *figure 172b*. Lay the drums on their sides and lay a length of thick wire solder (about ³⁄₁₆″ thick) between them. Flux well and apply a large hot iron TO THE SOLDER at the firebox end. Hold steady until the solder melts and transmits heat to the drums, at which point it will of its own volition flow smoothly between them. Slowly advance the iron towards the front, and the solder profile will follow right along. Don't go too fast, and don't jerk or you'll produce waves of unevenness. If this happens, back to square one and do it again. Add more solder if necessary. When one side is done, turn the drums over and do it again; the brass strip stops the solder dropping through. You should be able to remove the connected drums from the firebox plate and have a twin drum boiler with a smooth transition between drums and virtually no cleaning up to do.

Cut the smokebox wing plate from 22 gauge brass, cutting out the door opening and drilling the circle of No. 71 holes for the rivets of 22 gauge wire. Borrow the dural disc from the firebox front and bolt it to the wing plate as an aid to location of the main drum. Stand the drums and plate on a level surface and rotate the drums until the upper one is truly centred over the lower one. Two squares come in handy for checking this (*figure 172c*). Solder the wing plate to the lower drum. Object of the exercise here should be to get a good strong fillet of solder inside, but not outside where it will run into the rear ends of the wire rivets. The front of the upper drum is simply a push-fit turning. The smokebox door is of turned brass, hinged with nickel strips. The chimney is of turned brass, with a skirt formed from solder, and wire bolts forced into the median flange.

Meanwhile, back at the firebox . . . The front and rear plates are spaced by temporary spacers (note the rear plate doesn't bulge out) to the full diameter over the lower drum because there isn't clearance between the driving wheel splashers. A wrapper of 10-thou' brass is soldered around the plates; the rounded transition curves at the front can be made by depositing a liberal solder fillet inside the joint to allow for filing away—a better method is to solder a length of ¹⁄₁₆″ brass rod inside the seam, so that when you start filing there's good solid brass to bite into. Note that the wrapper, also is cut away ahead of the splashers, a simple right angle cut is permissible because the gap is hidden behind the sheet metal sandboxes (*figure 172* again).

Note the little notches which locate the firebox on the mainframe. When the firebox is assembled, remove the spacers, refit the dural discs on the front plate, push the boiler into position and check carefully for squareness and level when the unit sits on the chassis; make any minor adjustments by filing the locating notches. Set the boiler and firebox unit up in vee blocks and mark the top centre line and the lines of handrails, piping, and running boards, as well as the vertical line of the cab front.

Cut the cab front from 18 swg brass, and the sides from 24 swg. Impress the rivet detail of the latter before cutting them out to avoid deformation of the metal. The sides are initially cut to the shape shown in *figure 173*, and are profiled later to match the running boards. The latter are cut, initially as single full length strips, from 20 gauge brass. This is much heavier than prototype, but the thickness is hidden by the upturned edging of brass shim strip. The running plate is bent to form the rear steps, and adjusted for level by filing the bottom riser while checking with a height gauge. Tack the running board in position, and use it as a

149

guide for the location of the little brass angle brackets which support it ahead of and behind the cylinders. These brackets are soldered to the boiler and firebox sides, after which the running board is removed and separated into fore and aft lengths. The front part is soldered to its bracket, and to the wing plate. The rear one is screwed to its bracket by a single 14 BA screw. The right hand rear running plate unit carried the air pump (a Kemtron casting) and its associated piping. On both sides the water feed pipe is soldered into the running plate, so that removal of the latter also removes much of the boiler detail and makes for easier painting.

Once fitted, the running boards are used to mark the profile of the lower cab's sides, after which the cab is assembled and soldered to the firebox from the inside. Cabside and window beading is of fine wire. A cab floor is cut from 20 gauge brass and filed to a good push fit; *figure 167* shows how it is cranked up about ⅛" at the front end to cover the rear axle, so there is no sign at all of the drive inside the cab. The vertical roof stays are spring steel; the roof itself, of thin nickel, simply clips in place. Angles

Plate 66

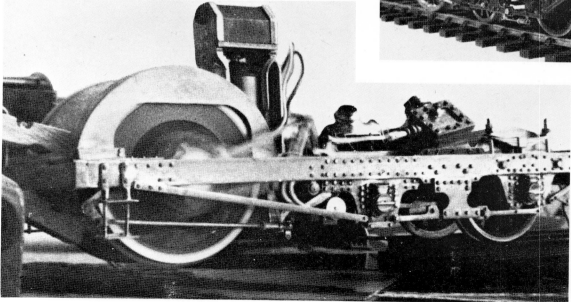

150

Plate 67

round cab edges and corners are rivet-impressed shim. The cab interior consists of a sheet brass backhead held in place by a single screw, on which the cab fittings and the prominent transverse axle spring are mounted. Cut off lever and brake standard are separate units secured by 12 BA screws through the cab floor.

The superdetail is mostly wire and brass turnings. Firebox washouts are Millholme, handrail supports are K's screwed into tapped brass strips inside the boiler—easier than fiddling with nuts, better than tapping the thin boiler wall. The right hand side of the engine carries the blower piping, the actuating rod for the variable orifice blast pipe, and the Lethuillier safety valve sprouting from the bolt-capped dome. Turned clacks are high up on the firebox side. Which leaves only the most fiddling job of all, the outside steam pipes to the cylinders. It's difficult to actually describe the fitting of these without lapsing into several kinds of profanity. The pipes are made of ¾″ o.d. copper tubing, filled with solder, and bent, filed, notched and several other things to shape. This was strictly a trial and error operation, the piece being frequently tested against the boiler. The two sides are held by screws to the brass header block, and at their lower ends just enter the turned unions on the cylinder block. And the best of luck!

The four-wheeled tender I won't inflict on you; it's like every other four-wheeled tender I've presented in the past. Which leaves only the decoration. Now, it has not escaped my notice at this stage almost everyone who writes a locomotive article engages low gear and proceeds with utmost caution. With vintage French there is the prima facie advantage that there are far fewer experts, both real and parenthetical; there is the balancing disadvantage that the whole subject is that much less well documented, so one's chances of being correct are reduced. However, No. 604 is finished in two coats of Floquil satin black (the clean stuff, not the grimy). Boiler bands, splasher beadings, smokebox hinges and a few minor bits of ferronerie d'art are polished metal. Lining out is in red dry-transfer. The front buffer beam is in red, lined white, and carries the road name and number in white sans serif symbols. On the cabside is the road name EST in white with red shading, produced by applying white dry transfer over, and slightly displaced from, the same letters in red. Engraved brass number plates below the stack, and works plates on the cabsides, are polished. The tender carries its number (which has nothing to do with the engine number) in letters of polished bronze on the tank side, with the word EST above in smaller letters. On the back of the tender, half way up the tank, appears the word EST and the *engine* number in white. The rear buffer beam is unrelieved black.

And last week the opening of a new section of the joint Nord-Est Great Outer Belt line allowed the first Est inter-regional train, hauled by Crampton No. 604, into Sainte Colline-des-Champs.

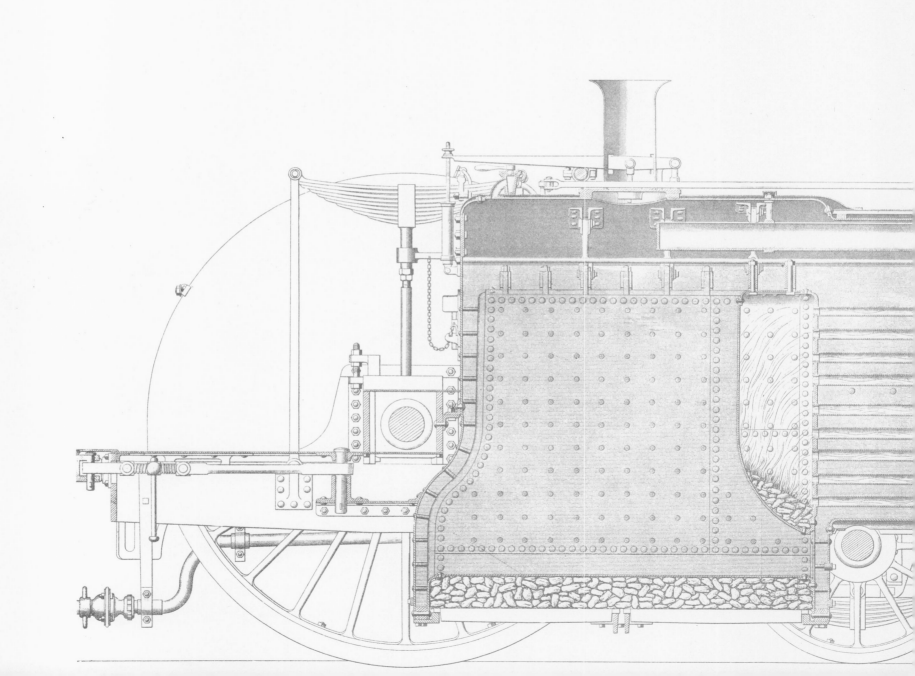